gilbert

LAW SUMMARIES

FUTURE INTERESTS AND PERPETUITIES

Fourth Edition

Jesse Dukeminier

Maxwell Professor of Law
University of California, Los Angeles

THE
barbri
GROUP

A COMPLETE PUBLICATIONS CATALOG IS
FEATURED AT THE BACK OF THIS BOOK.

HARCOURT BRACE LEGAL AND PROFESSIONAL PUBLICATIONS, INC.

EDITORIAL OFFICES: 176 W. Adams, Suite 2100, Chicago, IL 60603

gilbert
LAW SUMMARIES

REGIONAL OFFICES: New York, Chicago, Los Angeles, Washington, D.C.
Distributed by: **Harcourt Brace & Company** 6277 Sea Harbor Drive, Orlando, FL 32887 (800)787-8717

PROJECT EDITOR
Maureen A. Mitchell, B.A., J.D.
Attorney At Law

SERIES EDITOR
Elizabeth L. Snyder, B.A., J.D.
Attorney At Law

QUALITY CONTROL EDITOR
Blythe C. Smith, B.A.

gilbert
LAW SUMMARIES

Titles Available

Administrative Law
Agency & Partnership
Antitrust
Bankruptcy
Basic Accounting for Lawyers
Business Law
California Bar Performance
  Test Skills
Civil Procedure
Commercial Paper &
  Payment Law
Community Property
Conflict of Laws
Constitutional Law
Contracts
Corporations
Criminal Law
Criminal Procedure
Dictionary of Legal Terms
Estate & Gift Tax
Evidence

Family Law
Federal Courts
First Year Questions & Answers
Future Interests
Income Tax I (Individual)
Income Tax II (Corporate)
Labor Law
Legal Ethics (Prof. Responsibility)
Legal Research, Writing,
  & Analysis
Multistate Bar Exam
Personal Property
Property
Remedies
Sales & Lease of Goods
Securities Regulation
Secured Transactions
Torts
Trusts
Wills

Also Available:

First Year Program
Pocket Size Law Dictionary
The Eight Secrets Of Top Exam Performance In Law School

SUMMARY OF CONTENTS

Page

FUTURE INTERESTS AND PERPETUITIES CAPSULE SUMMARY I

TEXT CORRELATION CHART i

APPROACH TO EXAMS .... (i)

I. **CLASSIFICATION OF FUTURE INTERESTS** 1
   A. **Types of Estates** 1
   B. **Types of Future Interests** 3
   CHART: Possessory Estates 4
   C. **Reversion** 6
   D. **Possibility of Reverter** 7
   E. **Right of Entry** 9
   CHART: Future Interests in Grantor 12
   F. **Remainders** 15
   G. **Executory Interests** 22
   CHART: Future Interests in Grantee 25
   H. **Summary of Future Interests** 26

II. **(ALMOST) OBSOLETE RULES RESTRICTING REMAINDERS** 29
   A. **Destructibility of Contingent Remainders in Land** 29
   B. **The Rule in Shelley's Case** 33
   C. **The Doctrine of Worthier Title** 38
   CHART: Old Technical Rules of the Common Law 39

III. **RIGHTS AND LIABILITIES OF OWNERS OF FUTURE INTERESTS** 41
   A. **Disclaimer** 41
   B. **Transferability** 43
   C. **Taxation** 44
   D. **Future Interests in Personal Property** 46

IV. **CONSTRUCTION OF INSTRUMENTS** 49
   A. **Broad Rules of Construction** 49
   B. **Preference for Vested Interests** 50
   C. **Requirement of Survival** 51
   CHART: Requirement of Survival 54
   D. **Gifts Over on Death Without Issue** 55
   E. **Class Gifts** 57
   CHART: Class Gifts 63
   F. **Class-Closing Rules** 64
   CHART: Class-Closing Rule of Convenience 67
   G. **Implied Gifts** 68

V. **POWERS OF APPOINTMENT** 71
   A. **Classification of Powers** 71
   B. **The Theory that Donee Is Not Owner** 72
   C. **Release of Powers and Contracts to Appoint** 75

      CHART: General Powers of Appointment 76
      D.   Exercise of Powers 78
      E.   Invalid or Ineffective Appointments 81

VI.   THE RULE AGAINST PERPETUITIES 85
      A.   Introduction 85
      B.   Analysis of the Rule 87
      C.   Application to Defeasible Fees 91
      D.   The Classic Absurd Cases 92
      CHART: Application of Rule to Gifts to Individuals 93
      E.   Gifts to Classes 96
      CHART: Application of Rule to Gifts to Classes 100
      F.   Application to Powers of Appointment 101
      G.   Application to Commercial Transactions 104
      H.   Reforms of the Rule 105
      I.   Suspension of the Power of Alienation (New York Law) 111
      J.   Accumulation of Trust Income 113

REVIEW QUESTIONS AND ANSWERS 115

SAMPLE EXAM QUESTIONS AND ANSWERS 143

GLOSSARY OF TERMS 151

TABLE OF CASES 153

INDEX 157

gilbert

capsule summary

future interests and perpetuities

Text Section

I. CLASSIFICATION OF FUTURE INTERESTS

  A. TYPES OF ESTATES

    1. **Meaning of Estate:** An estate is an interest in property measured by some period of time. Estates may be created in possession (possessory estate) or as a future interest (estate which may become possessory in the future) ...... [1]

    2. **Fee Simple:** This estate has an infinite duration and is the largest estate. There are four types: fee simple *absolute* (cannot be divested); fee simple *determinable* (automatically ends when some specified event happens); fee simple *subject to a condition subsequent* (grantor, upon the happening of a condition, may elect to reenter and retake); fee simple *subject to an executory limitation* (upon happening of an event, property is divested in favor of a third person) .... [5]

    3. **Fee Tail:** This estate can be created only in land and can be inherited only by descendants of the original fee tail tenant. It has been abolished in all but a handful of states .... [10]

    4. **Life Estate:** A life estate is an estate that endures for a human life. A life estate may be made defeasible. Today, equitable life estates (in trust) are more common than legal life estates .... [12]

    5. **Term of Years:** This estate lasts for some fixed time period or for a period computable by the calendar or the clock. It may be made defeasible .... [15]

    6. **Hierarchy of Estates:** Possessory estates are ranked according to their potential duration .... [18]

  B. TYPES OF FUTURE INTERESTS

    1. **Categories Limited:** There are only five future interests permitted. Classification can be crucial. Each interest is classified in sequence .... [20]

    2. **Future Interests in Grantor:** The following future interests may be retained by the *grantor* (if by deed) or by the *testator's heirs* (if by will): *reversion, possibility of reverter, right of entry* .... [21]

      a. **Reversion:** A reversion is a future interest left in the grantor after the grantor conveys a vested estate of a lesser quantum than she has ...... [22]

      b. **Possibility of reverter:** This interest arises when a grantor carves out of her estate a determinable estate of the same quantum. It usually follows a determinable fee .... [23]

      c. **Right of entry:** This interest arises when the grantor creates an estate subject to condition subsequent and retains the power to cut short the estate .... [24]

      d. **Correlative possessory estates:** The following correlations exist between possessory estates and future interests: (i) life estate—reversion; (ii) fee simple determinable—possibility of reverter; (iii) fee simple subject to condition subsequent—right of entry .... [25]

    3. **Future Interests in Grantees:** The following future interests may be created in grantees, but never in a grantor or testator's heirs: .... [26]

      a. **Remainder:** This future interest in a grantee has the capacity of becoming possessory upon the natural termination of the prior estates. It cannot divest the prior estates .... [27]

b. **Executory interest:** This is a future interest in a grantee that, in order to become possessory, must divest the prior estate or spring out of the grantor at a future date .... [28]

4. **Transfer After Creation:** The name of a future interest is not changed after its creation by its transfer from the grantor to a grantee, or vice versa .... [31]

C. **REVERSION**
1. **Creation:** If not expressly created, a reversion arises by operation of law where no other disposition is made of the lesser estate .... [32]
2. **Rule of Reversions:** The owner of a fee simple will not have a reversion in fee simple if she transfers a possessory fee simple or a vested remainder in fee simple, but in all other cases she will have a reversion .... [33]
3. **Reversions Retained by Will:** Where a reversion results from a devise in a will, the reversion is left in the testator's heirs .... [34]
4. **Vested Interests:** All reversions are vested interests. However, they may be vested subject to divestment .... [35]
5. **Transferability:** A reversion is fully transferable inter vivos and by way of testate or intestate succession .... [36]

D. **POSSIBILITY OF REVERTER**
1. **Distinguished from Reversion:** A reversion arises when the grantor creates a vested estate that is *not of the same quantum* as she has. A possibility of reverter arises when the grantor conveys a *determinable* estate of the *same* quantum as the grantor has .... [38]
2. **Creation**
a. **Words creating possibility of reverter:** "So long as," "until," and "during" all connote a fee simple determinable, which precedes a possibility of reverter. Language expressly creating a possibility of reverter is not necessary .... [41]
b. **Can be retained only by grantor or her heirs:** A possibility of reverter is a retained interest; it cannot be created in a grantee. .... [43]
(1) **Possibility of reverter retained by will:** Where a possibility of reverter results from a devise of a determinable estate by will, the possibility of reverter is left in the testator's heirs .... [44]
3. **Becomes Possessory Automatically:** A possibility of reverter becomes possessory automatically upon the termination of the prior determinable estate ... [45]
4. **Vested Interest:** A possibility of reverter is a vested interest under the Rule Against Perpetuities .... [46]
5. **Transferability:** In most states, a possibility of reverter is assignable inter vivos, and it is descendible and devisable as well .... [47]

E. **RIGHT OF ENTRY**
1. **Distinguished from Possibility of Reverter:** A right of entry does *not automatically* become possessory; it may be exercised at the election of the grantor . . [49]
2. **Creation:** Appropriate language for the creation of a fee simple subject to a condition subsequent retaining a right of entry for a condition broken includes "but if," "on condition that," and "provided however" .... [50]
a. **Ambiguous language:** When language is ambiguous, a fee simple subject to a condition subsequent is preferred over a determinable fee ...... [51]
b. **Statement of purposes compared:** If the instrument states the purpose of the conveyance but does not use words appropriate for creation of a fee simple determinable or subject to condition subsequent, a court may construe it as a fee simple absolute .... [52]
3. **Cannot Be Created in a Grantee:** A right of entry cannot be created in a grantee .... [53]

II—Future Interests and Perpetuities

4. **Vested Interest:** A right of entry is vested under the Rule Against Perpetuities . . . . [54]

5. **Transferability**
   a. **Assignability:** Contrary to the common law rule, a large number of states hold that a right of entry is assignable . . . . [55]
   b. **Descendibility and devisability:** A right of entry is descendible and devisable in the same manner as a possibility of reverter . . . . [58]

6. **Right of Entry and Possibility of Reverter Compared:** Although the owner of a right of entry has legal rights similar to those of the owner of a possibility of reverter, there may be differences regarding: (i) assignability, (ii) running of the statute of limitations in adverse possession cases, (iii) application of the Rule Against Perpetuities, and (iv) state action in racial discrimination cases . . . . . . [59]

7. **Termination of Possibilities of Reverter and Rights of Entry:** Several states, by statute, limit the duration of possibilities of reverter and rights of entry to a fixed period of years (*e.g.*, 30 years) . . . . [64]

8. **Condemnation of Possibilities of Reverter and Rights of Entry:** Where title to land is taken by eminent domain, the majority holds that the owner of a determinable fee or a fee simple subject to a condition subsequent takes the entire condemnation award. A minority gives the owner of the defeasible fee only the value of the land as restricted . . . . [65]

F. **REMAINDERS**
   1. **Essential Characteristics**
      a. **Preceding estate:** A remainder can be created only by express words in the same instrument in which the preceding possessory estate is created. The prior estate can be a fee tail, life estate, or a term of years, but not a fee simple . . . . [70]
      b. **Capable of becoming possessory on expiration of preceding estate:** A remainder *must* have the capability (not certainty) of becoming *immediately* possessory upon the expiration of the preceding estate . . . . [72]
      c. **Must not be capable of divesting preceding estate:** A remainder cannot divest a preceding estate prior to its normal expiration. A remainder *can* divest a reversion in the grantor but can never divest a grantee . . . . . [73]
      d. **Estates in remainder:** An estate in remainder may be a fee simple, life estate, term of years, or in some jurisdictions, fee tail . . . . [76]
   2. **Classification of Remainders:** Remainders are classified either as "vested" or "contingent" . . . . [77]
      a. **Vested remainders:** A remainder is vested when it is created in an *ascertained person* and *not subject to a condition precedent*. There are three types of vested remainders: . . . . [78]
         (1) **Indefeasibly vested remainder:** The holder of this remainder is certain to acquire a possessory estate in the future, and is also certain to be entitled to retain permanently the possessory estate so acquired . . . . [81]
         (2) **Vested remainder subject to open:** This remainder is vested in a class of persons that may increase, but a class member's interest is not divested if he dies before the remainder becomes possessory . . [82]
         (3) **Vested remainder subject to divestment:** This remainder is vested subject to being divested by operation of a condition subsequent . . . [84]
            (a) **Note:** A remainder can be both vested subject to open and to complete divestment . . . . [85]
      b. **Contingent remainders:** A remainder is contingent if it is either given to an *unascertained person* or *subject to a condition precedent* . . . . [86]
         (1) **Unascertained persons:** An "unascertained" person is one who is not yet born or cannot be determined until the happening of an event . . . . [87]

    (2) **Condition precedent:** A condition precedent is an express condition (other than the termination of the preceding estate) that must occur before the remainder becomes possessory . . . . [90]

    (3) **Condition subsequent distinguished:** A condition precedent is incorporated into the gift of the remainder, whereas a condition subsequent divests a preceding vested estate . . . . [92]

    (4) **Consequences of classification:** At common law, there are four principal differences between vested and contingent remainders: A vested remainder (i) is *assignable*; (ii) *accelerates* into possession whenever and however the preceding estates end; (iii) cannot be *destroyed* if it does not vest before or at the termination of the preceding estate; and (iv) is not subject to the *Rule Against Perpetuities*. A contingent remainder has none of these qualities at common law . . . . [95]

G. EXECUTORY INTERESTS

An executory interest is a future interest in a grantee that *divests* the estate of another grantee (shifting) or *springs* out of the grantor at a future time (springing) . [101]

  1. **Historical Development:** Springing and shifting interests were void at law before 1536. The Statute of Uses made them valid . . . . [102]

  2. **Can Divest Possessory Estate or Remainder:** An executory interest can divest either a possessory estate or a preceding vested remainder . . . . [108]

  3. **Exception—Determinable Fee:** An interest in a grantee following a determinable fee is an executory interest, even though it neither springs nor shifts . . . . [109]

  4. **Vesting of Executory Interests:** Under the Rule Against Perpetuities, an executory interest following a fee simple determinable or divesting a fee simple cannot vest in interest before it becomes a possessory estate . . . . [110]

  5. **Functional Equivalence with Remainders:** The common law differences between remainders and executory interests have largely disappeared. Almost all executory interests are treated like contingent remainders . . . . [114]

II. (ALMOST) OBSOLETE RULES RESTRICTING REMAINDERS

A. DESTRUCTIBILITY OF CONTINGENT REMAINDERS

The common law could not tolerate a gap in seisin (a period of time when no freehold grantee was entitled to possession), hence the rule that a legal contingent remainder in land is destroyed if it does not vest at or before the termination of the preceding freehold estate. A modern justification for the rule is that it makes land alienable sooner . . . . [122]

  1. **Elements of the Rule**

    a. **Preceding freehold:** The preceding freehold estate in possession can be a fee tail or a life estate. The rule is inapplicable if the preceding estate is a leasehold . . . . [125]

    b. **Termination of life estate:** The life estate can terminate at or before the death of the life tenant . . . . [126]

      (1) **Natural or artificial:** A contingent remainder that does not vest upon the natural *or* artificial termination of the life estate is destroyed . . . . [127]

  2. **Interests Not Affected by Rule:** The rule is not applicable to vested remainders, executory interests, personal property, or interests in trust . . . . [134]

  3. **Avoidance of Rule:** Two common ways of avoiding the rule are to create a term of years rather than a life estate, and to create trustees to preserve contingent remainders . . . . [140]

  4. **Abolition:** The rule has been abolished in a majority of states. Where destructibility is abolished, a contingent remainder takes effect if the contingency occurs either before or after the termination of the life estate . . . . [143]

B. **RULE IN SHELLEY'S CASE**
   1. **Statement of Rule:** If one instrument creates a freehold in A and purports to create a remainder in A's heirs (or in the heirs of his body), and the estates are both legal or both equitable, the remainder becomes a remainder in fee simple (or fee tail) in A . . . . [145]
      a. **Merger:** Under the merger doctrine, a life estate in A and a remainder in A will merge unless: (i) there is an intervening estate, or (ii) the remainder is subject to a condition precedent to which A's life estate is not subject. Merger may or may not apply after the Rule in Shelley's Case has operated on the instrument . . . . [146]
   2. **Reasons for Rule:** The Rule in Shelley's Case probably arose to prevent feudal tax evasion. The Rule also makes land alienable one generation earlier. The Rule does not apply to personal property (minority view contra) . . . . [147]
   3. **Operation of the Rule**
      a. **"If one instrument creates a freehold estate in A":** All American cases applying the Rule have involved a life estate as the freehold. The life estate can be determinable or subject to a condition subsequent; it can be in possession or in remainder. The Rule does not apply if the life estate in A is subject to a condition precedent that is not also applicable to the remainder to A's heirs. If the intended life tenant dies before the testator, the life estate lapses (is never created), and the Rule does not apply . . . . [150]
      b. **"And purports to create a remainder":** The Rule applies to a remainder to the life tenant's heirs. The remainder may be contingent. The Rule does not apply to executory interests . . . . [157]
      c. **"In A's heirs (or the heirs of A's body)":** The Rule applies when a remainder is given to heirs or heirs of the body in an indefinite line of succession rather than a specific class. Some American courts have rejected this distinction . . . . [161]
      d. **"And the estates are both legal or both equitable":** The Rule applies only if the life estate and remainder are both legal or both equitable . . . . . [167]
   4. **The Rule Is a Rule of Law:** The Rule cannot be avoided by expressions of intent . . . . [168]
   5. **Avoidance:** The Rule can be avoided by creating a leasehold in A rather than a life estate . . . . [169]
   6. **Modern Status:** The Rule is fully in force in only a few states. However, because of its recent abolition in some states, the old law remains applicable to conveyances made before abolition . . . . [170]

C. **DOCTRINE OF WORTHIER TITLE**
   1. **Statement of Doctrine**
      a. **Inter vivos branch:** Where an inter vivos conveyance purports to create a future interest in the grantor's heirs, the future interest is void and the grantor has a reversion . . . . [172]
      b. **Testamentary branch:** A devise to the testator's heirs is a nullity if the interest limited in their favor is identical to that which they would have taken by intestate succession. The testamentary branch does not appear to exist in the United States . . . . [173]
   2. **Modern Rule:** The modern Doctrine applies to personal property as well as land. It is a *rule of construction* . . . . [174]
   3. **Operation of the Doctrine**
      a. **Limitation to heirs:** A future interest must be given to grantor's "heirs" or "next of kin" . . . . [176]
      b. **Type of future interest immaterial:** The Doctrine applies to a remainder or an executory interest limited to the grantor's heirs. The future interest may be legal or equitable . . . . [177]

			Text Section

    c. **Preceding estate:** The character of the estate preceding the future interest in grantor's heirs is immaterial . . . . [178]

    d. **Applications:** The Doctrine can affect revocation of trusts, creditors' rights, and subsequent transfers by the grantor . . . . [179]

    e. **Abolition of Doctrine:** Though abolished in many jurisdictions, the Doctrine is still applied in some . . . . [182]

III. RIGHTS AND LIABILITIES OF OWNERS OF FUTURE INTERESTS

A. DISCLAIMER

    1. **Disclaimer Permitted:** Any person given or devised a possessory estate or future interest has the right to accept or reject the interest . . . . [184]

    2. **Uniform Disclaimer Acts:** Under the uniform disclaimer acts, where a possessory interest is disclaimed, the disclaimed interest is treated as if the disclaimant had predeceased the testator . . . . [186]

    3. **Effect on Future Interest:** A disclaimer of a life estate may cause the acceleration of future interests, because the intended life tenant is treated as dead . [190]

B. TRANSFERABILITY

    1. **Assignment During Life**

        a. **Vested future interests:** At common law and under modern law, vested remainders and reversions are assignable by inter vivos conveyance . . . . [196]

        b. **Contingent remainders and executory interests:** At common law, these were considered "mere possibilities," and thus nothing to assign. *Exceptions:* (i) they could be released; (ii) if assigned and later vested, the owner was estopped by deed; and (iii) if transferred for valuable consideration, equity would give specific performance. Modern law holds both assignable by inter vivos conveyance, though a few states follow common law view . . . . [197]

    2. **Transfer at Death:** Reversions, remainders, and executory interests are descendible and devisable in the same manner as possessory interests, unless contingent upon surviving to the time of possession . . . . [204]

    3. **Creditors' Rights**

        a. **General principle:** Creditors can reach whatever interests in property a person can voluntarily alienate . . . . [205]

        b. **Vested interests:** Vested interests in most states are transferable and thus can be reached by judgment creditors . . . . [206]

        c. **Contingent interests:** Contingent interests in states following the common law have limitations on their alienation and thus **cannot** be reached by creditors . . . . [207]

        d. **Bankruptcy:** Under the Federal Bankruptcy Act, creditors can reach all legal and equitable interests of the debtor in property. Thus, the bankrupt's estate includes all vested and contingent future interests, regardless of their alienability under local law . . . . [208]

C. TAXATION

    1. **Federal Estate Taxation:** This tax is imposed on a decedent who dies owning a sufficiently large taxable estate. The gross estate includes all property the decedent can transmit at death . . . . [209]

        a. **Transmissibility controls taxation:** The value of any future interest transmissible by the owner is included in the gross estate. Transmissibility is the key to taxation, not whether the interest is vested or contingent. This is the reason for the estate planning precept that one should never create a future interest transmissible at death . . . . [210]

        b. **Valuation of future interests:** Future interests can be valued by determining the present value of a sum of money to be received on the life tenant's death if the life tenant dies as predicted by a mortality table . . . . [212]

2. **Federal Gift Taxation:** Where the owner of a future interest makes a gift of it, such gift is subject to federal gift taxation . . . . [214]

D. **FUTURE INTERESTS IN PERSONAL PROPERTY**
1. **Consumables:** A future interest in consumable personal property is void unless the life tenant has the power of sale . . . . [215]
2. **Remnant Gift Over:** If a grantor makes an absolute gift to A of personal property, such as the contents of a bank account, and then makes a gift to B of the amount left in the account at A's death, the gift to B is void. The gift over is repugnant to the fee simple given A . . . . [218]
3. **Security:** When a legal future interest is created in personal property, a court may require the life tenant to put up security . . . . [220]

IV. **CONSTRUCTION OF INSTRUMENTS**

A. **BROAD RULES OF CONSTRUCTION**
1. **In General:** Certain rules of construction exist for construing ambiguous instruments in order to carry out a person's intent and promote alienability. They are to be compared with rules of law, which apply regardless of intent . . . . [225]
2. **Preferences**
   a. **Against partial intestacy:** Courts prefer to construe a will so as to avoid partial intestacy . . . . [226]
   b. **For maximum validity:** When presented with a choice, a court should choose a valid construction over an invalid one . . . . [228]
   c. **For blood relatives:** Blood relatives are preferred to strangers. Equal distribution among all similarly related persons is also preferred . . . . [229]
   d. **For legislative scheme:** The legislative scheme for intestate succession is preferred when distribution is to members of a class . . . . [230]
   e. **For technical meaning:** When a lawyer draws an instrument, it is presumed that the words are used in their technical sense . . . . [231]
   f. **For general plan:** Courts may interpret words so as to carry out a testator's general plan for distribution . . . . [232]

B. **PREFERENCE FOR VESTED INTERESTS**
1. **Common Law:** If an interest might be considered vested or contingent, the common law preferred to classify it as vested. This gave rise to classification techniques designed to effectuate the preference . . . . [233]
2. **Surplusage Technique:** To vest a gift, a court may strike out language in the instrument deemed mere surplusage. For example, if an age condition on a gift to an individual is stated both as a condition precedent and a condition subsequent, the statement of condition precedent is surplusage and is struck out . . . [235]
3. **Power of Appointment:** A remainder limited in default of exercise of a power of appointment is not contingent upon nonexercise of the power. Exercise of the power is deemed a divesting event . . . . [238]

C. **REQUIREMENT OF SURVIVAL**
1. **Basic Rule:** If there are no express words requiring a remainderman to survive to the time of possession, none are implied . . . . [239]
2. **Class Gifts:** If the gift is to "children," no survivorship to possession is required. For gifts to "issue," survivorship to possession is required. A person must survive the ancestor to be an "heir" . . . . [242]
3. **Divesting Language Read Strictly:** When language divests a person in one stated event, it does not divest in other events . . . . [246]
4. **Alternative Devisee:** A gift to "A *or* her children" implies a requirement that A survive to possession . . . . [247]

5. **Apt Language:** When the testator requires survival elsewhere in the will, but does not expressly require survival for the gift at hand, survivorship is not required . . . . [249]

6. **Age Conditions**
   a. **Gift "at" a designated age:** Here, there is an implied condition of survivorship to the age . . . . [251]
   b. **Gift "payable at" a designated age:** Here, there is no implied condition of survivorship . . . . [252]
   c. **Gift of income vests the principal:** If income from property is to be paid in the meantime, with possession of the principal postponed, survivorship to the designated age is not required to take the property . . . . [253]

7. **Uniform Probate Code:** The UPC makes all remainders contingent upon survival, unless there is a contrary intent . . . . [256]

D. **GIFTS OVER ON DEATH WITHOUT ISSUE**
   1. **Indefinite or Definite Failure of Issue:** If there is a gift to A, with a subsequent gift to B if A dies without issue, virtually all states prefer a "definite failure" construction. Thus, if A dies leaving issue at his death, B never takes. If A dies without issue at his death, B takes . . . . [261]
   2. **Successive or Substitutional:** Assume T devises property "to A for life, remainder to B, but if B dies without issue, to C." Under a successive construction, B and then C, in succession, take the property if B dies (before or after A dies) without issue. Under a substitutional construction, at A's death, C takes the property only if B is then dead without issue. States are split as to which construction to follow . . . . [265]

E. **CLASS GIFTS**
   1. **What Is a Class?** When a gift is to beneficiaries *as an entity*, not individually, a class gift is created. Use of individual names ordinarily presumes individual gifts, as does specification of exact shares . . . . [268]
   2. **Gifts to "Children":** "Children" includes the immediate legitimate offspring of the person indicated as parent . . . . [273]
      a. **Adopted children:** In addition to the immediate legitimate offspring, modern law presumptively includes adopted children in a gift to "children" of another person . . . . [275]
      b. **Nonmarital children:** At common law, children born out of wedlock were not included in a class gift. Modern law is moving toward including these children, but presumption against inclusion may still apply in many states . [278]
      c. **Stepchildren:** Stepchildren are not included unless evidence shows an intent to include them . . . . [279]
   3. **Gift to "Grandchildren":** A gift to a person's "grandchildren" does not include great-grandchildren . . . . [281]
   4. **Gift to "Issue" or "Descendants":** "Issue" or "descendants" means all lineal descendants. Distribution is ordinarily per stirpes. The meaning of per stirpes varies from state to state . . . . [282]
      a. **Classic per stirpes:** In a classic or English per stirpes distribution, the property is divided into as many shares as the designated ancestor has children alive or deceased children with issue alive. Within each share, live issue represent dead parents . . . . [284]
      b. **Modern per stirpes:** In a modern per stirpes distribution, the property is divided initially into shares at the level the designated ancestor has issue alive . . . . [287]
   5. **Gifts to "A and Her Children" (Rule in *Wild's Case*)**
      a. **First resolution of *Wild's Case*:** If there is a devise of land "to A and her children" and A has no children at testator's death, A takes a fee tail. If the fee tail is abolished, A takes whatever estate is substituted by statute for

the fee tail. This rule is not followed in most states. The majority give A a life estate with remainder to A's children . . . . [292]

    b.   **Second resolution:** If there is a devise of land "to A and her children" and A has children at testator's death, A and her children share equally as co-tenants. This rule is followed in a majority of states . . . . [293]

6.   **Gifts "to A and the Children of B":** If A and the children of B are equally related to the testator, this is usually treated as one class with each member taking an equal share. If they are of differing degrees of relationship, presumably the gift is one-half to A and one-half to be divided among B's children . . . [296]

7.   **Gifts to "Heirs":** Heirs are ascertained at the time of the ancestor's death, unless this would result in an incongruity. In the latter case, and always under some statutes, heirs of the ancestor are determined at the time the remainder becomes possessory . . . . [301]

F.   CLASS CLOSING RULES
A closed class is one where it is not legally possible for others to **enter** the class, though some may drop out. Persons not in a class when it closes cannot share in the gift. A class of relatives closes physiologically when the parent of the class dies . . . [307]

1.   **Rule of Convenience:** This rule provides that the class will close whenever any member of the class can **demand** possession of her share, unless the transferor **expresses** otherwise. Thus, if a gift is **postponed** until termination of the prior estate or a specified condition occurs (*e.g.*, prior life estate, age contingency), the class will close when any member can demand her share . . . . [310]

G.   IMPLIED GIFTS
1.   **General Rule:** Generally, a court will not imply a gift that is not expressly made . . . . [326]

2.   **Implied Gift to Issue:** If property is devised "to A for life, then to B if A dies without issue," a remainder to A's issue is implied . . . . [327]

3.   **Cross-Remainders:** If a donor makes gift to a class for life (*e.g.*, "to X's children, A, B, and C for their lives, then to D"), it is not clear who takes A's share when A dies. Possibilities: (i) A's share **reverts** to O until B and C die; (ii) A's share passes to D (**fractional vesting** of remainder); (iii) A's share passes to A's estate until the death of B and C **(life estate pur autre vie)**; or (iv) A's share is divided between B and C (the surviving life tenants) until the death of the last survivor under the theory of **implied cross-remainders** for life, which is the most common solution . . . . [328]

V.   POWERS OF APPOINTMENT

A.   CLASSIFICATION OF POWERS
1.   **Testamentary or Inter Vivos:** A power of appointment may be created so that it is exercisable only by a certain type of instrument . . . . [335]

    a.   **Testamentary power:** This is a power that may be exercised by **will alone**. It may not be exercised during life . . . . [336]

    b.   **Inter vivos power:** This is a power that may be exercised either by a **deed alone** or by a **deed or will** . . . . [337]

2.   **General and Special Powers**

    a.   **General:** A general power is exercisable in favor of the donee, her estate, her creditors, or the creditors of her estate . . . . [339]

    b.   **Special:** A special power cannot be exercised to benefit the donee . . . . . [340]

B.   THE THEORY THAT DONEE IS NOT OWNER
1.   **Relation-Back Doctrine:** When a donee exercises a power, the donee is often viewed as filling in spaces in the donor's will. The theory is that the appointees take from the donor . . . . [342]

    2. **Taxation:** Federal estate and gift taxation does not follow the relation-back theory if the donee has a general power. A general power is treated as ownership by the donee . . . .   [344]

    3. **Creditors:** Creditors of the donee of a general power cannot reach the property unless the donee exercises the power . . . .   [349]

    4. **Choice of Law:** The law of the donor's domicile governs a trust of personal property. The relation-back theory is applied . . . .   [358]

C. RELEASE OF POWERS AND CONTRACTS TO APPOINT

    1. **Release of Power:** The donee may release the power, making indefeasible the interest of the taker in default if the interest is subject to no other condition. Release is not the same as disclaimer, which occurs *before* acceptance . . . . .   [360]

        a. **General power presently exercisable:** A general power presently exercisable can be released. If released *in part*, it turns into special power . . .   [362]

        b. **Special power:** A special power may be released in whole or in part . . .   [364]

        c. **Testamentary power:** A testamentary power may be released inter vivos . . . .   [366]

    2. **Contracts to Appoint**

        a. **General power:** The donee of a *general power* presently exercisable may make a present appointment; therefore, he may contract to appoint . . . . .   [367]

        b. **Special power:** A contract to exercise a *special power* to benefit a *non-object* is void; a contract to benefit an object is enforceable . . . .   [368]

        c. **Testamentary power:** A contract to exercise a *testamentary power* is void, but it is sometimes given effect as a release . . . .   [369]

D. EXERCISE OF POWERS

    1. **Formalities:** If the instrument specifies certain requirements, the power can be exercised only in compliance. A power is exercised by a specific reference to the power or a reference in a will to the property that is the subject of the power . . . .   [375]

        a. **Exercise by residuary clause:** There is a presumption that a residuary clause or a similar will clause does *not* exercise the power, absent evidence of contrary intent . . . .   [378]

    2. **Limits on Exercise of General Power:** The donee must exercise power within limits prescribed by the donor. Unless the donor specifies otherwise, a general power can be exercised by appointing a limited interest in the property to another. The donee can also create new powers of appointment in others or appoint in further trust . . . .   [381]

    3. **Limits on Exercise of Special Power:** A special power must be exercised in accordance with the instrument creating it. Unless the donor expresses contrary intent, the donee can appoint limited interests to objects of the power, create a new power in an object of power, or appoint in further trust . . . .   [383]

        a. **Exclusive power:** Special powers are either exclusive (donee may exclude some objects) or nonexclusive, with a presumption that donor intends exclusivity . . . .   [387]

E. INVALID OR INEFFECTIVE APPOINTMENTS

    1. **Appointment to Non-Object:** An appointment to a non-object of a special power is void. An appointment to an object in consideration of the object's giving money to a non-object is also void . . . .   [391]

    2. **Failure to Exercise Special Power:** If there is no gift in default of exercise of a special power, a court will imply a remainder to the objects if they are a defined limited class . . . .   [394]

    3. **Appointment to Deceased Persons:** If the donee of a general power appoints to a deceased person, the anti-lapse statute applies. It may also apply if the donee holds a special power . . . .   [398]

X—Future Interests and Perpetuities

4. **Allocation of Assets:** If the donee of a power blends her own property with appointive property and exercises the power invalidly, all of the property is allocated to the various takers to give maximum effect to the donee's intent . . . . [402]

5. **Capture by Donee:** If the donee of a *general power* makes an ineffective exercise but manifests intent to assume control of appointive property, the property is captured in the donee's estate. It does not go in default of appointment . . . . [406]

VI. THE RULE AGAINST PERPETUITIES

A. INTRODUCTION

1. **Statement of Rule:** No interest is good unless it must vest, if at all, not later than 21 years after some life in being at the creation of the interest . . . . [412]
   a. **Meaning of "if at all":** To be valid, the interest must vest *or fail* within the period . . . . [415]
   b. **Test is what might happen:** An attack on the interest will be successful if it is proven that there is a possibility that the interest *might* vest too remotely . . . . [416]
      (1) **Wait-and-see:** A majority of states now apply the wait-and-see doctrine to any interest violating the Rule . . . . [418]
2. **Interests Subject to the Rule:** The Rule applies to contingent remainders and executory interests. It does not apply to vested remainders or future interests in the grantor, which are treated as part of the grantor's estate and vested from the beginning . . . . [419]
3. **When Period Begins to Run:** The perpetuities period begins to run whenever the grantor or testator makes an irrevocable transfer . . . . [422]

B. ANALYSIS OF THE RULE

1. **Meaning of "Vest":** A remainder or executory interest is vested when it either vests in possession or turns into a remainder vested in interest . . . . [427]
   a. **Vest in possession:** An interest is vested in possession when it becomes possessory . . . . [428]
   b. **Vest in interest:** A remainder is vested in interest when it is owned by an ascertained person and is not subject to a condition precedent . . . . [429]
   c. **Exception—class gift:** A gift to a class is not vested under the Rule until the class has closed and all conditions precedent have been satisfied for every member of the class . . . . [432]
   d. **Vested with possession postponed:** A provision postponing payment until the beneficiary reaches a designated age does not create a condition precedent. The gift is vested with possession postponed . . . . [433]
2. **Validating Lives:** A validating life is a person alive whom you can use to demonstrate the validity of a contingent interest under the Rule. The only person you can use is a person who enables you to prove that the interest will vest or fail within 21 years after that person dies . . . . [434]
   a. **Not mentioned in instrument:** The validating lives need not be mentioned in the instrument . . . . [437]
   b. **Artificial validating lives:** A specified validating life is "artificial" if it otherwise has no interest in the property nor connection with the beneficiaries . . . . [438]
   c. **Other rules:** The validating lives must be reasonable in number. Only human beings can be used as validating lives. For purposes of the Rule, a person is treated as in being from the time of conception . . . . [441]
3. **Twenty-One Year Period:** If there are no validating lives, an interest must vest or fail within 21 years to be valid. The 21-year period cannot precede the validating lives . . . . [444]

4.   **Consequences of Violating Rule:** Any interest violating the Rule is stricken from the instrument. The valid part remains standing . . . . [445]

    a.   **Effect on defeasible interests:** If a divesting gift is stricken, the preceding gift is left and becomes indefeasible . . . . [446]

    b.   **Infectious Invalidity:** If an invalid interest is such an integral part of the transferor's scheme that, if it is invalid, the transferor would have preferred a valid interest also to fail, the valid interest will fail . . . . [447]

C.   **APPLICATION TO DEFEASIBLE FEES**

1.   **Determinable Fee:** A void executory interest following a determinable fee is struck out, leaving a possibility of reverter in the grantor . . . . [449]

2.   **Fee Subject to Executory Limitation:** A void executory interest divesting a fee simple is struck out, leaving a fee simple absolute in the grantee . . . . [451]

D.   **THE CLASSIC ABSURD CASES**

1.   **What-Might-Happen Test:** The what-might-happen test has given rise to absurd cases resulting from far-fetched assumptions . . . . [452]

    a.   **Fertile octogenarian:** It is assumed that a person can have a child at any age. The possibility of birth to an old person voids many gifts . . . . [453]

    b.   **Unborn widow:** It is assumed that a man's widow will not necessarily be a woman now alive . . . . [458]

    c.   **Slothful executor:** It is assumed that an estate may not be closed within lives in being plus 21 years . . . . [459]

2.   **Alternative Contingencies:** If the grantor makes a gift upon either of two contingencies, one of which must occur, if at all, within the perpetuities period, and the other which may not, the gift is valid if the first contingency actually occurs and void if the second contingency occurs. The instrument is treated as making two gifts . . . . [465]

3.   **Saving Clauses:** Saving clauses are widely used to prevent falling into one of the classic traps . . . . [469]

E.   **GIFTS TO CLASSES**

1.   **Class Must Be Closed:** A remainder in a class vested subject to open is not vested under the Rule. The class must be closed for the gift to be treated as vested . . . . [471]

2   **All-or-Nothing Rule:** A class gift must be valid for all, or it is valid for none. It is not vested until the class has closed and all conditions precedent for every member of the class are met . . . . [472]

3.   **Workable Test for Class Gifts:** Determine when the class will close. If it will close within the perpetuities period, determine when all contingencies will be resolved . . . . [475]

4.   **Rule of Convenience:** The rule is: A class closes whenever any member of the class can demand possession of her share. This rule may save a class gift . . . . [480]

5.   **Gifts to Subclasses:** Each gift to a separate subclass may be tested separately under the Rule. The key to a gift to subclasses is finding that separate gifts vest at different times . . . . [481]

6.   **Per Capita Gifts:** A separate gift of a fixed sum to each member of a class is not subject to the all-or-nothing rule. Each gift is tested separately . . . . [484]

7.   **Vested with Possession Postponed:** If a class gift is vested with possession postponed (*i.e.,* there is no condition precedent), the gift is valid if the class will close within the perpetuities period . . . . [485]

F.   **APPLICATION TO POWERS OF APPOINTMENT**

1.   **Introduction:** To apply the Rule to powers of appointment, ask three questions:

(i) is the power valid? (ii) is exercise of the power valid? (iii) is the gift in default of appointment valid? . . . . [487]

2. **General Powers Presently Exercisable:** A general power presently exercisable is treated the same as if the donee owned a fee simple. A general inter vivos power is valid if there is a certainty that the power will become exercisable, or fail, within the perpetuities period . . . . [488]

3. **Testamentary Powers and Special Powers:** A testamentary or special power is treated as if the donee is the donor's agent. The power is valid if it may not be exercised beyond the perpetuities period, which begins at the creation of the power. The power is void ab initio if it may be exercised beyond the perpetuities period . . . . [493]

   a. **Second look doctrine:** Although exercise of the power is read back into the donor's instrument, who is regarded as making the appointment, facts and circumstances existing at the date of exercise are taken into account in determining the validity of interests created by exercise . . . . [497]

4. **Effect of Invalid Appointment:** Generally property passes to the taker in default if the donee makes an invalid appointment. If there is no gift in default, the property reverts back to the donor's estate. The general rule is subject to the doctrine of *capture* (applicable only to a general power) . . . . [501]

G. APPLICATION TO COMMERCIAL TRANSACTIONS

1. **Options:** An option is subject to the Rule in many jurisdictions. If it can be exercised beyond the period, it is void . . . . [506]

2. **On-Completion Leases:** These are leases that are to begin upon completion of the building. Most courts hold them valid . . . . [511]

H. REFORMS OF THE RULE

1. **Cy Pres:** Under this doctrine, applicable in a few states, an invalid interest is reformed by a court to give effect to the grantor's intent as nearly as possible, within the limits of the Rule . . . . [514]

   a. **Limited cy pres:** New York and Illinois have limited correctives avoiding the absurd classic cases . . . . [519]

2. **Wait-and-See for Common Law Period:** Some states wait-and-see whether an invalid interest will actually vest within the period allowed by the common law Rule. The measuring lives for the waiting period are those persons who can affect vesting . . . . [520]

3. **Wait-and-See for 90 Years:** The Uniform Statutory Rule Against Perpetuities ("USRAP"), adopted in half the states, waits for 90 years before declaring an interest invalid. If an invalid interest has not vested within 90 years, it is then reformed to carry out the grantor's intent . . . . [535]

   a. **Longer period:** Seeking the longer of lives in being plus 21 years *or* 90 years to govern trust duration is prohibited under USRAP . . . . [540]

   b. **Commercial transactions:** USRAP exempts all commercial transactions from the Rule . . . . [544]

4. **Abolition of Rule:** The Rule has been abolished in four states, which permit trusts of personal property to endure forever . . . . [546]

I. SUSPENSION OF POWER OF ALIENATION
New York has a statute that provides for voiding any interest that suspends absolute power of alienation beyond the perpetuities period. The statute prevents spendthrift trusts from enduring longer than lives in being plus 21 years . . . . [552]

J. ACCUMULATION OF TRUST INCOME
Under the common law, income in a trust may be accumulated for the perpetuities period. A direction to accumulate income in excess of the perpetuities period is wholly void . . . . [554]

TEXT CORRELATION CHART

Gilbert Law Summary Future Interests and Perpetuities	Cribbet, Johnson, Findley, Smith Property 1996 (7th ed.)	Dukeminier, Johanson Wills, Trusts & Estates 1995 (5th ed.)	Dukeminier, Krier Property 1993 (3d ed.)	Nelson, Stoebuck, Whitman Contemporary Property 1996	Ritchie, Alford, Effland, Dobris Decedents' Estates and Trusts 1993 (8th ed.)	Waggoner, Wellman, Alexander, Fellows Family Property Law 1991
I. CLASSIFICATION OF FUTURE INTERESTS						
A. Types of Estates	200-264	747-758	191-262	222-245		840-845
B. Types of Future Interests	239-259, 265-315	749-750	263-264	245-246	876-891	845-846
C. Reversion	265	750-751	264-265	246-248	882, 884	846
D. Possibility of Reverter	239-259	750-751	266	248	883-884	847
E. Right of Entry	239-259, 295-297, 308-315, 1349-1359		266	248-249	884	847-848
F. Remainders	265-273	751-754	266-274	249-263	884-886	848-861
G. Executory Interests	284-315	754-758	274-282	263-266	886-891	848-849, 886-889
II. (ALMOST) OBSOLETE RULES RESTRICTING REMAINDERS						
A. Destructibility of Contingent Remainders in Land	270-273	757-758	295-299	251, 254-259	888-889	863-869
B. Rule in Shelley's Case	274-278	811-812	291-293	266-268	895-898	869-873
C. Doctrine of Worthier Title	278-284	811	294-295	268	898-906	957-968
III. RIGHTS AND LIABILITIES OF OWNERS OF FUTURE INTERESTS						
A. Disclaimer	265-270	761-770	273-274	247-249, 258, 263	908-909, 1104-1112	877-886
B. Transferability		759			906-909	873-876
C. Taxation		760-761			647-649	
D. Future Interests in Personal Property		713-719		268-269	892-895	
IV. CONSTRUCTION OF INSTRUMENTS						
A. Broad Rules of Construction		759		262		
B. Preference for Vested Interests			272			856-862
C. Requirement of Survival		770-790	271		1032-1042	892-929
D. Gifts Over on Death Without Issue		781	316		1083-1097	929-932
E. Class Gifts	274-284	792-817		213-215	1050-1082	942-957
F. Class Closing Rules		817-825		262-263	1042-1050	932-941
G. Implied Gifts		812-817			1097-1104	969-981
V. POWERS OF APPOINTMENT						
A. Classification of Powers	294	701-703			911-919	797-804
B. The Theory That Donee Is Not Owner		703-712			957-964	804-814
C. Release of Powers and Contracts to Appoint		719-725			950-957	836-837
D. Exercise of Powers		725-736			920-950	814-824
E. Invalid or Ineffective Appointments		736-745			965-974	825-835
VI. THE RULE AGAINST PERPETUITIES						
A. Introduction	295-297	827-832	299-301	269	1113-1116	983-986, 1004-1015
B. Analysis of the Rule		833-837		269-273	1116-1122	986-1003

TEXT CORRELATION CHART—continued

Gilbert Law Summary Future Interests and Perpetuities	Cribbet, Johnson, Findley, Smith Property 1996 (7th ed.)	Dukeminier, Johanson Wills, Trusts & Estates 1995 (5th ed.)	Dukeminier, Krier Property 1993 (3d ed.)	Nelson, Stoebuck, Whitman Contemporary Property 1996	Ritchie, Alford, Effland, Dobris Decedents' Estates and Trusts 1993 (8th ed.)	Waggoner, Wellman, Alexander, Fellows Family Property Law 1991
C. Application to Defeasible Fees	308-315	837-851	302-308	270	1187	1091
D. The Classic Absurd Cases		852-863	312-319	271-273	1122-1125	1003-1004, 1015-1037
E. Gifts to Classes		863-874	317	270	1138-1147	1060-1068
F. Application to Powers of Appointment					1147-1167	1068-1079
G. Application to Commercial Transactions			308-311	270		1080-1091
H. Reforms of the Rule		876-901	318-324	273	1125-1138	1037-1059
I. Suspension of the Power of Alienation (New York Law)		901-903			1167-1170	1092-1094
J. Accumulation of Trust Income					1170-1181	1094-1097

approach to exams

Future Interests, and particularly the Rule Against Perpetuities, has a reputation for difficulty. Perhaps this is deserved. Future Interests requires you to think and analyze in an unfamiliar way. You must look carefully at the *exact words* used in a deed or will, and *classify* these words as creating one of several future interests. Paying attention to each precise word of an instrument is something you are probably not accustomed to doing, but it is a practice that will stand you in good stead on your exams, as well as in reading all kinds of documents.

Once you carefully read a deed or will and determine what kind of future interest, if any, is created, you must determine what rules are applicable to that particular future interest. There are six types of future interests—reversion, possibility of reverter, right of entry, vested remainder, contingent remainder, and executory interest—and each type has a separate set of rules applicable to it.

The great heyday of Future Interests was the eighteenth century, when this fine artificial system was thought to provide an effective and rational way of curtailing the "dead hand," of preventing fathers from controlling too long the property passing to their descendants. But the world has changed enormously since the eighteenth century and so has the law of Future Interests. It has been simplified and justified by modern reasoning in most states. Nonetheless, many contemporary rules can best be understood by a page of their history. Generally, this Summary presents only so much history as is helpful in understanding modern law, always keeping central that it is the contemporary law of Future Interests that students need to learn. However, since some law professors prefer to paint the entire historical picture, Chapter II deals with rules that are obsolete in most jurisdictions, but are covered in many Future Interests courses. If your teacher does not cover one or more of these rules in class, you can skip them.

Because each chapter of this Summary is a building block for the next, you should master one chapter at a time before proceeding. To help you do this, there are short-answer questions (with answers) for each chapter at the end of the Summary. These test your understanding of each chapter. You would be wise to try to answer the questions on one chapter before turning to the next chapter.

Also, at the end of the Summary is a Glossary of Terms, which may be useful when you desire quick illumination.

The aim of this Summary is to teach you how to classify Future Interests correctly and how to apply the applicable rules, including the Rule Against Perpetuities. We emphasize the fundamental ideas, which are essentially simple and can be expressed in language comprehensible to any student. These should not be hard to grasp once you catch on to what we are doing: looking closely at the words of an instrument, making future interests out of these words, and applying rules governing the future interests. Once you catch on, you may find the subject expands your mind in all kinds of challenging ways. Like mathematics, Future Interests has a strong appeal to people who like to do puzzles.

One important way in which a Future Interests problem differs from a puzzle, however, is its starting point. Most puzzles can be started from any point, but a Future Interests problem must be attacked in order, with each step building on the one preceding it. Therefore, when confronted with an exam question with possible Future Interests aspects, you should take the following steps to solve the puzzle:

1. Look closely at the *language* of the instrument. What kind of an estate does it create?

2. Does the possessory estate created have a *correlative future interest*? If so, is the future interest in the grantor or is it in another grantee? For example, if the instrument creates a life estate, is it followed by a reversion in the grantor or a remainder in a grantee?

3. *Classify the interests created in order.* The classification of an interest may depend on the name given to the preceding interest.

4. If your instructor has spent time on the old technical *rules restricting remainders* (the doctrine of destructibility of contingent remainders, the Rule in Shelley's Case, the Doctrine of Worthier Title) consider whether a discussion of these rules would be appropriate given the facts contained in the exam question. Did an interest fail to vest before the end of the preceding estate? Was a remainder created in the grantee's or grantor's heirs?

5. Finally, apply the common law *Rule Against Perpetuities* to any contingent future interest in a grantee (contingent remainder or executory interest) to test its validity. The interest must vest or fail within a life in being plus 21 years. If you find the interest is invalid, discuss the effects of the invalidity on the remaining interests in the instrument, as well as whether the result might change under any of the perpetuities reform statutes—cy pres, wait-and-see, and the Uniform Statutory Rule Against Perpetuities (alternate 90-year vesting period).

I. CLASSIFICATION OF FUTURE INTERESTS

A. TYPES OF ESTATES

1. **Meaning of Estate:** [§1]   The English feudal system developed a system of estates in land, which is central to our law, both in theory and in practice. An estate is an interest in land (and, today, in personal property as well) *measured by a period of time*. All estates have a specified duration. The estates recognized by our law are a fee simple, a fee tail (now virtually obsolete), a life estate, a term of years, and other leasehold estates. Each of these estates has subcategories.

    a. **Possessory estates and future interests:** [§2]   Each estate may be created *in possession*, in which case it is a possessory estate, or *as a future interest*, in which case the estate may become possessory in the future. Thus, suppose that O (the owner) conveys Blackacre "to A for life, then to B and her heirs." A has a *possessory life estate*, and B has a *remainder in fee simple*. This description of B's interest means that when B's remainder becomes possessory B will have a fee simple. (For a detailed treatment of possessory estates, *see* the Property Summary.)

    b. **Grants and devises:** [§3]   Each of these estates may be created by an inter vivos grant or by a will. In this Summary, the word *grantor* refers both to persons who make lifetime transfers and to testators.

    c. **Freehold estates:** [§4]   The fee simple, the fee tail, and the life estate are freehold estates. A term of years is a leasehold estate. At common law, the holder of a freehold estate had *seisin*, whereas a leaseholder had only possession. In feudal times, the holders of seisin (freehold tenants) were responsible for the payment of taxes and other obligations, responsibilities not visited upon mere possessors. The differences between seisin and possession have disappeared in modern law.

2. **Fee Simple:** [§5]   A fee simple, the longest estate known to law, has an *infinite duration*. At common law, a fee simple was created by a conveyance of Blackacre "to A and his heirs." The words "and his heirs" are words of inheritance indicating A's estate is a fee simple inheritable by A's heirs if A does not convey or devise Blackacre to others. A's heirs are given no interest in Blackacre by those words, only the hope of inheritance. At common law, words of inheritance were necessary to create a fee simple by deed, but today a fee simple can be created by any language indicating a fee simple is intended. If the instrument does not indicate what estate is conveyed, it is *presumed that the grantor is conveying as large an estate as the grantor has*. Hence if the grantor has a fee simple, it is presumed that the grantor grants a fee simple. In line with modern authority, words of inheritance are not generally used in this Summary in hypotheticals creating a fee simple. There are four types of fees simple, briefly noted below.

    a. **Fee simple absolute:** [§6]   A fee simple absolute is a fee simple that cannot be divested and will not end if any event happens in the future. If A has a fee simple absolute in Blackacre, *no person has a future interest* in Blackacre.

        (1) **Example:** O (the owner of Blackacre) conveys Blackacre to "A and her heirs" or, in modern times, "to A." A has a fee simple absolute.

b. **Fee simple determinable:** [§7]   A fee simple determinable is a fee simple so limited that it will **end automatically** when a stated event happens. A fee simple determinable is created by language indicating that the fee simple is to endure only until an event happens. After almost every fee simple determinable there is a **possibility of reverter** in the grantor or her heirs.

(1) **Example:** O conveys Blackacre "to School Board so long as it is used for school purposes." The School Board has a fee simple determinable. O has a possibility of reverter. (This estate is discussed further *infra* at §§37-47, 59-67.)

c. **Fee simple subject to condition subsequent:** [§8]   A fee simple subject to a condition subsequent is a fee simple so limited that it **may be cut short** or divested by the **grantor** or her heirs exercising an **optional right of entry** when a stated event happens.

(1) **Example:** O conveys Blackacre "to School Board, but if the Board ceases to use Blackacre for school purposes, O may reenter and retake the premises." The School Board has a fee simple subject to condition subsequent. O has a future interest known as a right of entry for condition broken. (This estate is discussed further *infra* at §§48-67.)

d. **Fee simple subject to executory limitation:** [§9]   A fee simple subject to an executory limitation is a fee simple so limited that, upon the happening of a stated event, it is **automatically** divested by an executory interest in a **grantee**.

(1) **Example:** O conveys Blackacre "to School Board, but if the premises are not used for school purposes during the next 20 years, to A." The School Board has a fee simple subject to executory limitation. A, a grantee, has a future interest known as an **executory interest**. This estate differs from a fee simple determinable and a fee simple subject to a right of entry in that a **grantee**, rather than the grantor, has the right to enforce forfeiture. (This estate is discussed further *infra* at §108.)

3. **Fee Tail:** [§10]   A fee tail is an estate in land that endures so long as the original fee tail tenant is alive or has descendants alive. It can be inherited only by the descendants of the original fee tail tenant. For example, O conveys Blackacre "to A and the heirs of his body." A has a fee tail. It can be inherited only by A's descendants, in successive generations. The fee tail, developed in England to maintain a landed aristocracy, has been abolished in all but a handful of American states. It can be created in only a few states. In states still recognizing the fee tail, a fee tail tenant can disentail by conveying a fee simple absolute to another person, thereby converting the fee tail into a fee simple. Hence, in no American state can land be tied up permanently in a fee tail to descend to successive generations.

a. **Fee tail language becomes fee simple:** [§11]   In most states, language that would create a fee tail at common law creates a fee simple. Thus, where a grantor conveys land "to A and the heirs of her body," this creates a fee simple in A. In a few states, A takes a life estate, and A's issue take the remainder.

4. **Life Estate:** [§12] A life estate is an estate that endures for a human life; *e.g.,* O conveys Blackacre "to A for life." A life estate can be a *legal* estate. For example, a husband may devise the family farm "to my wife for life, and on her death to our children." A has a legal life estate. Or a life estate may be in property held in trust and called an *equitable* life estate. For example, a testator might devise property "to First National Bank in trust to pay the income to A for life, and on A's death to distribute the trust assets to B." A has an equitable life estate.

   a. **Equitable life estate:** [§13] Except for legal life estates given to surviving spouses in land, almost all life estates today are in trust. In a trust, the trustee owns the legal fee simple in the trust assets and can sell them. The life tenant, holding an equitable life estate, is entitled to all the income from the trust assets.

   b. **Defeasible life estates:** [§14] A life estate may be created so as to be defeasible in the same manner as a fee simple is defeasible. Thus, a grantor may create a life estate determinable ("to A for life so long as she remains unmarried"), a life estate subject to condition subsequent ("to A for life, but if A does not keep up the fences, O retains a right to reenter and retake possession"), or a life estate subject to an executory limitation ("to A for life, but if B gets sick to B").

5. **Terms of Years:** [§15] A term of years is an estate that lasts for some fixed period of time computable by the calendar or the clock; *e.g.,* O conveys Blackacre "to A for 20 years." Unless limited by statute, a term of years can be created to last any period of years, even a thousand years.

   a. **Defeasible terms:** [§16] A term of years may be created so as to be defeasible in the same manner as a fee simple is defeasible. Thus, a grantor may convey a term of years determinable ("to A for 100 years if A so long lives"), or a term of years subject to a condition subsequent, or a term of years subject to an executory limitation.

   b. **Other leasehold estates:** [§17] In addition to the term of years, other leasehold estates include the periodic tenancy and the tenancy at will. These estates are mainstays of landlord-tenant law and are not treated in this Summary.

6. **Hierarchy of Estates:** [§18] Possessory estates are ranked as "greater" or "lesser" according to their potential duration. A *fee simple* is potentially longer in duration than a fee tail (and therefore of a greater quantum). A *fee tail* is potentially longer in duration than a life estate (and therefore of a greater quantum). A *life estate* measured by the life of the life tenant is potentially longer than a life estate measured by the life of another (a life estate pur autre vie). Because of considerations of feudal dignity, all freehold estates are deemed to be greater (and therefore longer) than nonfreehold estates.

B. TYPES OF FUTURE INTERESTS

1. **Meaning of Future Interest:** [§19] A future interest is an interest in property that is not now, but in the future may become, possessory. A future interest is a *presently existing interest*. The owner of the future interest may transfer it to another, and as a valuable interest, it may be subject to inheritance or estate taxation if the owner dies before it becomes possessory.

POSSESSORY ESTATES

Estate	How Created	Duration	Future Interest in Grantor	Future Interest in Grantee
Fee Simple Absolute	"to A and her heirs"	Forever	None	None
Fee Simple Determinable	"to A and her heirs so long as" or "while" a condition is met	So long as condition is met, then reverts automatically to grantor	Possibility of Reverter	(*See* Fee Simple Subject to Executory Limitation, below)
Fee Simple Subject to Condition Subsequent	"to A and her heirs, but if" condition broken, grantor has right to reenter	Until condition broken *and* grantor exercises right to reenter	Right of Entry	(*See* Fee Simple Subject to Executory Limitation, below)
Fee Simple Subject to Executory Limitation	(1) "to A and her heirs so long as condition performed, then to B" *or* (2) "to A and her heirs, but if the condition is broken, to B"	Until condition broken, then title passes automatically to B	None	Executory Interest in B
Fee Tail	"to A and the heirs of his body"	Until A and his descendants are all dead	Reversion	None (but a remainder could be created)
Life Estate (*may be made defeasible*)	(1) "to A for life"	A's life	Reversion	None (*but see* (2) below)
	(2) "to A for life, then to B"	A's life	None	Remainder in B
Term of Years (*may be made defeasible*)	(1) "to A for 20 years"	20 years	Reversion	None (*but see* (2) below)
	(2) "to A for 20 years, then to B"	20 years	None	Remainder in B

a. **Example:** O conveys property "to A for life, remainder to B." B has a presently existing interest. If B dies during A's life, B's remainder passes to B's heirs or devisees. It may be subject to inheritance taxes, and B's creditors may be able to reach it and sell it to pay B's debts.

2. **Categories Limited:** [§20] There are five, and only five, future interests permitted: *reversion, possibility of reverter, right of entry, remainder*, and *executory interest*. (Remainders can be further divided into vested remainders and contingent remainders.) The first three of these are interests *retained by the grantor*. The last two are future interests *created in a grantee*. It is important to give the correct name to the future interest involved, because in many cases different rules apply to different future interests. Classification thus can be crucial.

3. **Future Interests in Grantor:** [§21] Future interests can be divided into two groups, those retained by a grantor and those created in a grantee. If the future interest is retained by the *grantor*, the future interest must be called either a *reversion, possibility of reverter*, or *right of entry*. A remainder or an executory interest can never be retained by the grantor, nor may a reversion, possibility of reverter, or right of entry be created in a grantee. Each future interest in the transferor is briefly described below and discussed in detail later. Future interests retained by the grantor are collectively called reversionary interests.

   a. **Reversion:** [§22] A reversion stands for the general idea that the property may return to the grantor in the future because the grantor has not specified who will take it when the possessory estates expire. But a reversion has a more technical definition. A reversion is a future interest left in the grantor after the grantor conveys a vested estate of a lesser quantum than the grantor has. (*See infra*, §§32-36, for detailed analysis.)

      (1) **Example:** O conveys Blackacre "to A for life." Since O conveyed only a life estate to A, and did not dispose of the fee simple on A's death, O has a reversion. When A dies, Blackacre will revert to O.

   b. **Possibility of reverter:** [§23] A possibility of reverter arises when a grantor carves out of his estate a *determinable* estate of the same quantum. In almost all cases it follows a *determinable* fee. (*See infra*, §§37-47, for detailed analysis.)

      (1) **Example:** O conveys Blackacre "to the Town Library so long as Blackacre is used for library purposes." The Library has a determinable fee. O has a possibility of reverter. O's interest is not a reversion because O, owning a fee simple, has conveyed a fee simple determinable to the library. All fees simple, whether absolute, determinable, or subject to condition subsequent or executory limitation, are of the same quantum.

   c. **Right of entry:** [§24] A right of entry is retained when the grantor creates an estate subject to *condition subsequent* and retains the power to cut short the estate. (*See infra*, §§48-67, for detailed analysis.)

      (1) **Example:** O conveys Blackacre "to the Town Library, but if the library ceases to use Blackacre for library purposes, O may reenter and retake possession." The Library has a fee simple subject to condition subsequent. O has a right of entry.

    d.   **Correlative possessory estates:** [§25]   From the above, it is easy to see that possessory estates have correlative future interests in the grantor, O:

      (1)   If A has a life estate, O has a reversion;

      (2)   If A has a fee simple determinable, O has a possibility of reverter; and

      (3)   If A has a fee simple subject to condition subsequent, O has a right of entry.

  4.   **Future Interests in Grantees:** [§26]   If a future interest is created in a grantee, it must be either a *remainder* or an *executory interest*. These interests may be created only in grantees, never in the grantor.

    a.   **Remainder:** [§27]   A remainder is a future interest in a grantee that has the capacity of becoming possessory upon the natural termination of the prior estates and cannot divest the prior estates. (*See infra*, §§68-100, for detailed analysis.)

      (1)   **Example:** O conveys Blackacre "to A for life, and on A's death to B." A has a possessory life estate; B has a remainder in fee simple. B's interest is a remainder because it can become possessory upon A's death, and it will not cut short A's life estate prior to A's death.

    b.   **Executory interest:** [§28]   An executory interest is a future interest in a grantee that, in order to become possessory, must *divest* or cut short the prior estate or *spring out* of the grantor at a future date. The basic difference between a remainder and an executory interest is that a remainder never divests the prior estate, whereas an executory interest can divest the preceding interest. (*See infra*, §§101-115, for detailed analysis.)

      (1)   **Shifting executory interest:** [§29]   Suppose O conveys Blackacre "to A, but if B marries, to B." A has a fee simple subject to an executory limitation. B has a shifting executory interest, which can become possessory only by divesting A of the fee simple.

      (2)   **Springing executory interest:** [§30]   Suppose O conveys Blackacre "to B upon B's marriage." O retains the fee simple and creates an executory interest in B to spring out of O in the future upon B's marriage.

  5.   **Transfer After Creation:** [§31]   The name of an interest is given when it is created. The name does not thereafter change if the interest is conveyed to another person. Thus, interests initially retained by the grantor do not undergo a name change if subsequently conveyed to a grantee. If O retains a reversion and subsequently conveys her interest to A, A has a reversion, not a remainder. Similarly, the name of a remainder does not change to a reversion if, after the remainder is created, it is transferred back to O. Therefore, it is important in classifying interests to determine whether the person in whom the interest was originally created was the grantor or a grantee.

C.   REVERSION

  1.   **Definition:** [§32]   A reversion is a future interest left in the grantor when the grantor transfers one or more vested estates of *lesser duration* than the grantor

originally had. If not expressly created, a reversion will arise by operation of law where no other disposition of the property is made after the expiration of the lesser estate. Thus if O conveys "to A for life," and says nothing about who is to take on A's death, O retains a reversion. A reversion means there is a possibility, or perhaps a certainty, that the property will return to the grantor some day.

   a. **Example:** A has a life estate. A conveys her life estate to B for B's life. A has carved out of her life estate an estate of lesser duration, an estate measured by B's life. If B dies before A, A will get the property back. Therefore A has a reversion. If A dies before B, the property will return to O. The hierarchy of estates (*supra*, §18) governs what is a lesser estate.

2. **Rule of Reversions:** [§33]   From the definition of a reversion a "rule of reversions" arises which tells when a grantor has a reversion. It is this: O, owner of a fee simple, will *not* have a reversion in fee simple *if O transfers a possessory fee simple or a vested remainder in fee simple.* In all other cases where O transfers a present possessory interest, O will have a reversion in fee simple. If O, owner of a fee simple, carves from her estate anything less than a vested fee simple, either in possession or remainder, it is possible for the property to return to O.

   a. **Example:** O conveys Blackacre "to A for life, then to B if B survives A." O has created a life estate in A, and a contingent remainder in fee simple in B. Under the rule of reversions, O has a reversion because O has not created a vested remainder in fee simple. It is possible for Blackacre to return to O.

3. **Reversions Retained by Will:** [§34]   If a reversion results from devises in a will, the reversion is left in the testator's *heirs*. It cannot be left in the testator, who is dead. The reversion is left in the testator's heirs, who are substituted for the testator by operation of law.

   a. **Example:** T devises the residue of her property "to A for life, then to B if B survives A." T's heirs have a reversion.

4. **Reversions Are Vested Interests:** [§35]   All reversions are vested interests. They are considered to be part of the grantor's old estate. They are interests retained by the grantor. All reversions are vested even though not all reversions will necessarily become possessory. Some reversions will certainly become possessory—*e.g.*, when O conveys "to A for life, reversion to O." Other reversions may or may not become possessory.

   a. **Example:** O conveys "to A for life, remainder to B if B reaches 21." At the time of the conveyance, B is age 15. O's reversion is vested, but it will be divested if B reaches 21.

5. **Transferability:** [§36]   A reversion has always been regarded as fully transferable both inter vivos and by way of testate or intestate succession. Creditors can ordinarily reach whatever property the debtor can voluntarily alienate. Hence, creditors of the reversioner can seize the reversion and sell it to pay their claims.

D. POSSIBILITY OF REVERTER

1. **Definition:** [§37]   A possibility of reverter is a future interest retained by the grantor when the grantor transfers a *determinable estate of the same quantum as*

the grantor originally had. A possibility of reverter almost always arises upon the creation of a determinable fee.

a. **Example:** O, owner of a fee simple, conveys Blackacre "to Town Library so long as used for library purposes." The Town Library has a fee simple determinable. O has a possibility of reverter.

b. **Distinguished from reversion:** [§38] Do not confuse a possibility of reverter with a reversion. Each is a distinct interest, with different characteristics. A reversion arises when the grantor does *not transfer a vested estate of the same quantum* as the grantor has. Thus, if O, owning a *fee simple*, conveys "to A for *life, contingent remainder in fee simple* to B if B survives A," O has a reversion. A possibility of reverter arises when the grantor transfers a *determinable estate of the same quantum* as the grantor has. Thus if O, owning a *fee simple*, conveys "to A *and her heirs* (a fee simple) so long as the fences are repaired," O has a possibility of reverter.

(1) **Example:** O conveys Blackacre "to A *and her heirs* so long as she remains unmarried." A has a fee simple determinable. O has a possibility of reverter. If O conveys Blackacre "to A *for life* so long as A remains unmarried," A has a life estate determinable, which is a lesser estate than O's fee simple. O's interest is a reversion because O has transferred an estate of a lesser quantum than O had. (Some say that in this latter example O has a reversion to take effect on A's death *and* a possibility of reverter to take effect on A's remarriage. If the possibility of reverter merges into the reversion, as some go on to say, the end result is as aforesaid.)

(2) **Possibility of reverter is a name:** [§39] The name of the interest being discussed is "possibility of reverter." The word "possibility" is part of the name and does not refer to the factual possibility that the grantor will be entitled to possession in the future. There is no such interest as a "possibility of reversion," a confusing phrase which refers both to the proper name of an interest ("reversion") and the factual possibility of the reversion becoming possessory. That phrase should never be used.

2. **Creation:** [§40] Problems involving creation of a possibility of reverter are usually one of two kinds. What words create a possibility of reverter? In whom can a possibility of reverter be created?

a. **Words creating possibility of reverter:** [§41] In almost all cases a possibility of reverter follows a fee simple determinable, and hence to know when a possibility of reverter is created, it is necessary to know first when a determinable fee is created. A determinable fee is created by conveying an estate in fee simple that is to last only until a specified event happens and is to automatically terminate upon that event. Examples of words creating a fee simple determinable include a transfer by O "to Trinity Church *so long as* used as a church," "to A and her heirs *until* Gloversville is incorporated as a village," and "to B and her heirs *during* widowhood." *Note:* The words "so long as," "until," and "during" all have durational connotations. [Mahrenholz v. County Board, 417 N.E.2d 138 (Ill. 1981); Mayor & City Council of Ocean City v. Taber, 367 A.2d 1233 (Md. 1977)]

(1) **Implied by law:** [§42] Language expressly creating a possibility of reverter is not necessary. A possibility of reverter arises by operation of law when a determinable fee is created because the grantor has not conveyed the entire fee simple. [Donehue v. Nilges, 66 S.W.2d 553 (Mo. 1954)]

b. **Can be retained only by grantor or his heirs:** [§43] A possibility of reverter is a *retained* interest, a part of the grantor's old estate left in the grantor. It cannot be created in a grantee. A comparable interest created in a grantee is an executory interest.

   (1) **Example:** O conveys Blackacre "to Memorial Hospital so long as used for hospital purposes, and when it shall cease to use Blackacre for hospital purposes, to Town Library." Town Library does not have a possibility of reverter. It has an executory interest (*see infra,* §109).

   (2) **Possibility of reverter retained by will:** [§44] If a possibility of reverter results from a devise of a determinable estate by will, the possibility of reverter is left in the testator's *heirs*. It cannot be left in the testator, who is dead. Neither can a possibility of reverter be left in a residuary devisee, who is a transferee. (*Remember:* A possibility of reverter cannot be created in a transferee.) The possibility of reverter is left in the testator's heirs, who are substituted by law for the testator.

      (a) **Example:** T devises Blackacre "to the Baptist Church so long as it is used for church purposes." T devises the rest and residue of her property to A. T's heirs, and not A, have a possibility of reverter in Blackacre. [*In re* Pruner's Estate, 162 A.2d 626 (Pa. 1960); *but see* Brown v. Independent Baptist Church of Woburn, 91 N.E.2d 922 (Mass. 1950)—contra: A has a possibility of reverter]

3. **Becomes Possessory Automatically:** [§45] A possibility of reverter becomes possessory *automatically* upon the termination of the prior determinable estate. No action by the owner of the possibility of reverter is required. Upon termination of the preceding estate, title passes back automatically to the owner of the possibility of reverter. (In this way a possibility of reverter differs from a right of entry, which restores title to the owner only upon exercise of the right; *see infra,* §61.)

4. **Vested Interest:** [§46] A possibility of reverter is a vested interest under the Rule Against Perpetuities.

5. **Transferability:** [§47] In most states, the owner of a possibility of reverter can assign it during life, though a few states follow the common law rule that possibilities of reverter are not assignable. In all states, possibilities of reverter are inheritable and, in most states, possibilities of reverter are devisable as well.

E. RIGHT OF ENTRY

1. **Definition:** [§48] A right of entry is a future interest retained by the grantor when the grantor transfers an estate *subject to a condition subsequent*. This interest is sometimes called a *power of termination*. A right of entry is usually retained for breach of a condition imposed by the grantor on a fee simple, but a life estate may also be made subject to a right of entry. In the discussion below, it will be assumed that a fee simple subject to condition subsequent is involved.

a. **Example:** O, owner of a fee simple, conveys Blackacre "to Town Library, but if Blackacre is not used for library purposes, O has a right to reenter and retake Blackacre."

b. **Distinguished from possibility of reverter:** [§49]   A right of entry may be exercised at the election of the grantor; it does *not automatically* become possessory as does a possibility of reverter. Unless and until entry is made, the possessory fee simple continues in the party who has it. This is the essential difference between a right of entry and a possibility of reverter.

2. **Creation:** [§50]   Whether a grantor has created a fee simple subject to condition subsequent, retaining a right of entry for a condition broken, depends upon the words used in the instrument. A fee simple subject to a condition subsequent is created by a conveyance of a fee simple ("to A and her heirs"), followed by language providing that the fee simple may be divested by the grantor if a specified event happens. Appropriate language includes "to Town Library, *but* [or *on condition that* or *provided however*] if the land is not used for library purposes, O has a right to reenter and retake the premises." Any one of these variations in language indicates that Town Library's fee simple estate may be cut short at the grantor's election.

a. **Ambiguous language:** [§51]   Instruments sometimes are drafted in a manner indicating that the drafter had either a determinable fee or a fee simple subject to a condition subsequent in mind, but it is not clear which. Or perhaps the drafter did not understand the difference between these two estates.

(1) **Examples:** O conveys Blackacre "to Town Library *so long as* used as a library, and when it ceases to be used as a library O has a *right of entry*." Or O conveys Blackacre "to Town Library, *but if* Blackacre is not used for library purposes, Blackacre is to *revert* to O." In the first example, the drafter has coupled language pointing to a determinable fee ("so long as") with language retaining a right of entry. In the second example, the drafter has coupled language of condition subsequent ("but if") with an automatic reverter (which only a possibility of reverter can do). Under the law of estates, a determinable fee cannot be followed by a right of entry, and a fee simple subject to condition subsequent cannot be cut short by a possibility of reverter. If a determinable fee is created, O has a possibility of reverter. If Town Library has a fee simple subject to condition subsequent, O has a right of entry. A well-known rule of construction provides that when language is ambiguous, a fee simple subject to a condition subsequent with a right of entry in the grantor is preferred. An optional forfeiture (right of entry) is deemed less drastic a remedy for breach of the condition than an automatic forfeiture (possibility of reverter). [Storke v. Penn Mutual Life Insurance Co., 61 N.E.2d 552 (Ill. 1945); Oldfield v. Stoeco Homes, Inc., 139 A.2d 291 (N.J. 1958); Higbee Corp. v. Kennedy, 428 A.2d 592 (Pa. 1981)]

b. **Statement of purposes compared:** [§52]   If the language of the instrument states the purpose of the conveyance but does not use the standard words for creating a fee simple determinable or a fee simple subject to condition subsequent, a court may construe the instrument to create a fee simple absolute.

(1) **Example:** O conveys Blackacre "to Town Library to be used for library purposes." O has not used words indicating the estate will terminate upon cessation of library use. Nor has O retained a right to re-enter. The court may construe the deed as giving Town Library a fee simple absolute. A statement of purpose of the transfer does not ordinarily imply a right retained by the grantor to enforce the purpose. This construction enhances marketability. [Roberts v. Rhodes, 643 P.2d 116 (Kan. 1982); Wood v. Board of Commissioners, 759 P.2d 1250 (Wyo. 1988)—both cases holding a fee simple absolute; *but see* Forsgren v. Sollie, 659 P.2d 1068 (Utah 1983)—holding fee on condition subsequent]

3. **Cannot Be Created in a Grantee:** [§53]   Like a possibility of reverter, a right of entry cannot be created in a grantee. If O transfers Blackacre "to Town Library, but if Blackacre ceases to be used for library purposes, to the Red Cross," the Red Cross has an executory interest and not a right of entry.

4. **Vested Interest:** [§54]   A right of entry is a vested interest under the Rule Against Perpetuities.

5. **Transferability**

   a. **Assignability:** [§55]   At common law, the owner of a right of entry could not assign it during life. A right of entry was treated as a chose in action (a right to sue), and choses were not assignable on the theory that assignment of choses would stir up litigation. This common law prohibition against assignment still exists in some states.

      (1) **Variation on common law rule:** [§56]   In a few states, not only is a right of entry nonassignable, but the *mere attempt* to transfer a right of entry destroys it. [Rice v. Boston & Worcester Railroad, 94 Mass. 141 (1866)] This view is supported neither by history nor by logic. Forfeiture of the right is a harsh penalty for doing a forbidden act. On the other hand, this harsh approach does tend to eliminate rights of entry and make land marketable.

      (2) **Common law rejected:** [§57]   In most states, a right of entry is assignable. These states reason that since choses in action are now assignable, the reason for the common law rule has disappeared and rights of entry should be treated as any other property interest.

   b. **Descendibility and devisability:** [§58]   A right of entry is inheritable at its owner's death. In most states a right of entry can be devised.

6. **Right of Entry and Possibility of Reverter Compared:** [§59]   The owner of a right of entry has legal rights very similar to the owner of a possibility of reverter. These two interests may, however, differ in the following ways:

   a. **Assignability:** [§60]   In a particular state there may be different rules applicable to the assignability of these interests. In some states, neither a possibility of reverter nor a right of entry is assignable, but an attempt to assign a right of entry destroys it. In others, a possibility of reverter is assignable, whereas a right of entry is not. (*See supra*, §§47, 55-57.)

 **FUTURE INTERESTS IN GRANTOR**

Future Interest	Prior Possessory Estate	Becomes Possessory	Transferable?
Reversion	Fee tail *or* life estate *or* term of years, *but not* a fee simple of any type	Automatically upon expiration of prior estate	Yes
Possibility of Reverter	Fee simple determinable ("to School so long as used for a school")	Automatically when condition broken	In majority of states, yes; but in a few, no.
Right of Entry	Fee simple subject to condition subsequent ("to School, but if land is not used as school, the grantor has the right to reenter")	At the grantor's election when condition broken, *not* automatically	In majority of states, yes; in a few, no, and attempt to transfer right of entry may destroy it.

NOTE: None of these interests in the grantor is subject to the Rule Against Perpetuities.

b. **Adverse possession:** [§61]   Since a possibility of reverter becomes possessory automatically, whereas a right of entry is optional, there may be a difference in the application of the statute of limitations. Suppose that Town Library, holding a fee simple determinable upon nonlibrary use, moves out of the library and rents the building to Pizza Hut. Title to the land now reverts to O, and Town Library is an adverse possessor. If O does not bring an action in ejectment within the period allowed by the statute of limitations, Town Library will acquire title by adverse possession. If O had a right of entry rather than a possibility of reverter, in some states a similar result is reached. The statute of limitations starts running when the condition is breached. [Johnson v. City of Wheat Ridge, 532 P.2d 985 (Colo. 1975)] In other states, the statute of limitations does not begin to run until O elects to exercise the right of entry and is rebuffed by Town Library. Even in these states, however, the equitable doctrines of laches, waiver, and estoppel may apply to bar O from exercising a right of entry after a reasonable period of time has passed. [Martin v. Seattle, 765 P.2d 257 (Wash. 1988)]

c. **Rule Against Perpetuities:** [§62]   Neither possibilities of reverter nor rights of entry are subject to the Rule Against Perpetuities. If an executory interest following a determinable fee violates the Rule, however, a possibility of reverter in the grantor is implied, whereas a right of entry is not implied in a similar situation. This is best seen by an illustration comparing two examples.

(1) **Example:** O conveys Blackacre "to Town Library so long as it is used for library purposes, and if the land ceases to be so used, then to A." The purported executory interest in A violates the Rule Against Perpetuities (*see infra*, §449). All the language making the void gift to A, beginning with "and if," is struck out. This leaves a determinable fee in Town Library and, since O did not convey the whole fee simple, a possibility of reverter in O. [First Universalist Society of North Adams v. Boland, 29 N.E. 524 (Mass. 1892); Institution for Savings v. Roxbury Home for Aged Women, 139 N.E. 301 (Mass. 1923); City of Klamath Falls v. Bell, 490 P.2d 515 (Or. 1971)]

(2) **Example:** O conveys Whiteacre "to Town Library, but if Whiteacre is not used for library purposes, then to A." The purported executory interest in A violates the Rule Against Perpetuities (*see infra*, §451). All the language making the void gift to A, beginning with "but if," is struck out. This leaves a fee simple absolute in Town Library. [Proprietors of the Church in Brattle Square v. Grant, 69 Mass. 142 (1855)]

d. **Racial discrimination—state action:** [§63]   Any *action* by a *state* that discriminates against persons because of race violates the Fourteenth Amendment to the United States Constitution. Hence, a court cannot enforce a covenant restricting the use of land to white persons. Judicial enforcement is state action resulting in discriminatory treatment. Similarly, a court cannot enforce a right of entry retained to penalize use by nonwhite persons. [Capitol Federal Savings & Loan Association v. Smith, 316 P.2d 252 (Colo. 1957)] But a determinable fee may be different. Suppose that O conveys Blackacre "to Charlotte Park Commission so long as it is used as a park for white persons only, and if it ceases to be so used, to revert to O." It has been held that upon breach of the condition, title reverts to O automatically by operation of law and does not involve state action. [Charlotte Park & Recreation Commission v. Barringer, 88 S.E.2d 114 (N.C. 1955)] Thus, a determinable fee may be effectively used to impose a racial restriction on property when a fee simple subject to a condition subsequent may not be. [Evans v. Abney, 396 U.S. 435 (1970)]

7. **Termination of Possibilities of Reverter and Rights of Entry:** [§64]   These interests are not subject to the Rule Against Perpetuities, but are objectionable because they tie up the use of land, potentially forever, making the land unmarketable. In a number of states (but not a majority), statutes limit the duration of possibilities of reverter and rights of entry to a fixed period of years. A typical statute provides that after 30 years a possibility of reverter or right of entry becomes unenforceable, and the determinable fee or fee simple subject to a condition subsequent becomes an absolute fee simple. [*See, e.g.*, Mass. Gen. Laws Ann. ch. 184A, §7, which has been copied in several states]

8. **Condemnation of Possibilities of Reverter and Rights of Entry:** [§65]   Where title to land is taken by eminent domain, the majority view is that the owner of a determinable fee or a fee subject to a condition subsequent takes the entire condemnation award. The holder of a possibility of reverter or a right of entry takes nothing. The reason is that these reversionary interests are incapable of valuation. It is impossible to tell when or whether the condition will be breached. [Restatement of Property (hereafter "Rest.") §53, comment b]

   a. **Minority view:** [§66]   The majority view has been criticized on the grounds that it gives the owner of the defeasible fee more than the value of the defeasible fee, which is usually restricted to one particular use, and that it unfairly deprives the reversionary interest holder of a valuable right without any compensation. Responding to this criticism, some courts hold that the owner of the defeasible fee should receive the value of the land for use in the manner permitted (*e.g.*, for a park), and the owner of the reversionary interest should receive the value of the land for any use other than that permitted the defeasible fee owner. [Ink v. City of Canton, 212 N.E.2d 574 (Ohio 1965); Leeco Gas & Oil Co. v. County of Nueces, 736 S.W.2d 629 (Tex. 1987)] There are two problems with this view. First, it may be impossible to determine the market value for the determinable fee unless there is a market in properties with similar restrictions. Second, the remaining value should be discounted by the probability of the reversionary interest becoming possessory, which is hard to foretell. If it is not discounted, a possibility of reverter or right of entry is worth more upon condemnation than its preexisting value.

      (1) **Example:** O conveys Blackacre "to the City so long as used for a park." The state takes Blackacre by eminent domain. Under the minority view, the city receives the value of Blackacre for park use. O receives the difference between that value and the fair market value of an unrestricted fee simple.

   b. **Criticism:** [§67]   The majority rule seems unfair to the future interest owner, because it deprives the owner of any compensation. The minority rule seems unworkable where no comparable market for similarly restricted land exists. A sensible solution in cases where public or charitable facilities are condemned is to give the entire condemnation award to the defeasible fee owner, require that owner to buy replacement land, and transfer the reversionary interest to the replacement land. This would put both parties in the same position they were in before condemnation.

F. REMAINDERS

1. **Definition:** [§68]   A remainder is a future interest created in a grantee that is *capable of becoming a present possessory estate upon the expiration* of all prior possessory estates created in the same instrument. A remainder *never divests* or cuts short a preceding estate but always waits patiently for possession until the preceding estate expires.

   a. **Example:** O conveys Blackacre "to A for life, and on A's death to B." B has a remainder because B's interest is capable of becoming possessory upon termination of A's life estate and cannot cut short the life estate before it ends at A's death.

2. **Essential Characteristics:** [§69]   The essential characteristics of every remainder are:

   a. **Must have preceding estate:** [§70]   A remainder can be created only by *express words* in the *same instrument* in which the *preceding possessory estate* is created. Unlike a reversion, it cannot arise by operation of law. If no preceding possessory estate has been created in a grantee, the future interest is not a remainder. The old way of putting this was to say: "A remainder needs a preceding freehold to support it."

      (1) **Example:** O conveys "to A if A marries B." No preceding estate has been created by O in anyone; thus A does not have a remainder. A has instead a springing executory interest. (*See infra*, §101.)

      (2) **Preceding estate can be either a fee tail, life estate, or term of years:** [§71]   The estate preceding a remainder can be a fee tail, a life estate, or a term of years. A remainder can follow any of these estates. But a remainder cannot follow a fee simple. (*See infra*, §74.)

         (a) **Example—fee tail:** O conveys "to A and the heirs of his body, and if A dies without issue, to B." In states permitting a fee tail, which are very few, A has a fee tail, and B has a remainder in fee simple.

         (b) **Example—term of years:** O conveys "to A for ten years, then to B." A has a term of years, and B has a vested remainder in fee simple. At early common law, B's interest was not called a remainder. Why not? Before the Statute of Uses (1536), O could convey a freehold only by going on the land and performing the formalities required for livery of seisin. When O conveyed "to A for ten years, then to B and his heirs," A, a termor, could not take seisin because he did not have a freehold estate. In the eyes of the law, seisin moved immediately from O to B, the grantee of a freehold. Therefore, it was said that B held a fee simple subject to A's term of years. Since livery of seisin is not important today, it is common and correct in the above situation to say B has a remainder.

b. **Must be capable of becoming possessory on expiration of preceding estate:** [§72]   A remainder must have the capability, though not necessarily the certainty, of becoming possessory immediately upon the expiration of the preceding estates.

(1) **Example:** O conveys Blackacre "to A for life, then to B if B survives A." If B is living at A's death, B will be entitled to possession. Hence it is possible, though not certain, that B's interest will become possessory on A's death. B's interest is a remainder.

(2) **Example:** O conveys Whiteacre "to A for life, then to B if B gives A a proper funeral." Since some period of time must elapse between A's death and A's funeral, it is not possible for B to be entitled to possession immediately upon A's death. Hence B's interest is not a remainder (it is an executory interest).

c. **Must not be capable of divesting preceding estate:** [§73]   A remainder cannot divest a preceding estate prior to its normal expiration. If the future interest can divest a preceding estate, it is an *executory interest*, not a remainder.

(1) **Example:** O conveys "to A for life, but if B returns from Rome during the life of A, to B." B does not have a remainder. B has a shifting executory interest (*see infra*, §101).

(2) **No remainder after a fee simple:** [§74]   Since a remainder is an estate that becomes possessory on the natural termination of the preceding estate, *there can never be a remainder following a fee simple*, which has a potentially infinite duration. Any interest divesting a fee simple *must be an executory interest*, not a remainder.

(a) **Example:** O conveys "to A and his heirs, but if A dies without issue surviving him, to B." B has an executory interest, not a remainder.

(3) **Can divest a reversion:** [§75]   When and if a *contingent* remainder vests, it divests a reversion in the grantor. But this is not inconsistent with the principle that a remainder cannot divest a *preceding estate in a grantee*.

(a) **Example:** O conveys Blackacre "to A for life, then to B if B survives A." The state of the title is: A has a life estate, B has a contingent remainder in fee simple, O has a reversion in fee simple. If B survives A, B will divest O's reversion. But B can never divest A, who has the preceding estate.

d. **Estates in remainder:** [§76]   An estate in remainder may be a fee simple, a life estate, a term of years, or in those jurisdictions where such an estate is permitted, a fee tail.

(1) **Example:** O conveys "to A for life, then to B for ten years, then to C for life, then to D." B has a remainder for a term of years, C has a remainder for life, and D has a remainder in fee simple.

3. **Classification of Remainders:** [§77]   Remainders are classified either as *vested* or *contingent*. A *vested* remainder is a remainder that is *both* created in an ascertained person *and* is not subject to any condition precedent. A *contingent* remainder is a remainder that is *either created in an unascertained person or subject to a condition precedent*.

    a. **Vested remainders**

        (1) **Definition:** [§78]   The most common definition of a vested remainder is the one given above: A remainder created *in an ascertained person* and *not subject to a condition precedent*. Gray, *Rule Against Perpetuities* §101, defines it somewhat differently: "A remainder is vested in A, when, throughout its continuance, A, or A and his heirs, have the right to immediate possession, whenever and however the preceding freehold estates may determine." Gray's definition emphasizes that a vested remainder must follow hard on the heels of the preceding estates, however they end, but both definitions add up to the same thing—*i.e.*, a remainder in an unascertained person or subject to a condition precedent cannot follow hard on the heels of the preceding estates, however and whenever they expire, because it is not capable of doing so.

            (a) **Example:** O conveys "to A for life, then to B." B (an ascertained person) has a remainder not subject to a condition precedent. The word "then" following a life estate is a word of art meaning "on the expiration of the life estate." Whenever and however the life estate terminates, B (or her successor in interest) will be entitled to possession. B's remainder is vested.

            (b) **Condition precedent:** [§79]   A condition precedent is an *express condition* attached to the remainder, such as, "then to B if B reaches age 30" or "then to B if B survives A." The expiration of the preceding estate is *not* a condition precedent.

        (2) **Subclassification of vested remainders:** [§80]   There are three different types of vested remainders—indefeasibly vested, vested subject to open, and vested subject to divestment. These differences are explained *infra*. Generally speaking, however, the crucial distinction is between vested remainders on the one hand and contingent remainders on the other. For most purposes, all vested remainders have the same legal consequences (a principal exception is the treatment of remainders vested subject to open under the Rule Against Perpetuities; *see infra*, §471). It is important to master these distinctions primarily because of the light they shed on how vested remainders are distinguished from contingent remainders.

            (a) **Indefeasibly vested remainder:** [§81]   When a remainder is indefeasibly vested, the holder of the remainder is *certain to acquire* a possessory estate at some time in the future, and is also certain to be entitled to *retain permanently* thereafter the possessory estate so acquired.

                1) **Example:** O conveys "to A for life, then to B." B (or her successor in interest) is certain to take possession on A's death. If

B dies before A, B's heirs or devisees are entitled to possession. Thus, B's remainder is indefeasibly vested.

(b) **Vested remainder subject to open:** [§82]   When a remainder is vested subject to open, it is vested in a *class of persons*, at least one of whom is qualified to take possession, but the shares of the members of the class are not yet fixed because more persons can subsequently qualify as members.

   1) **Example:** O conveys "to A for life, then to A's children." If A has no children, the remainder is contingent, because no child is yet born. If A has a child, B, the remainder vests in B subject to "open up" and let in other children. B's remainder is sometimes called *"vested subject to partial divestment,"* which means the same thing as "vested subject to open." The remainder is ultimately divided into as many shares as A has children. [Kost v. Foster, 94 N.E.2d 302 (Ill. 1950)]

   2) **Transmissible at death:** [§83]   If a person takes a vested remainder subject to open, his interest is not divested if he dies before the remainder becomes possessory. In the preceding example, if B were to die before A, B's share would go to B's heirs or devisees.

(c) **Vested remainder subject to divestment:** [§84]   When a remainder is vested subject to divestment, it can be divested by the operation of a *condition subsequent*.

   1) **Example:** O conveys "to A for life, then to B, but if B does not survive A, to C." The vested remainder in B is vested because it is not subject to a condition precedent. It is subject to a condition subsequent, and will be divested by C if B dies leaving A surviving.

   2) **Vested subject to open and to complete divestment:** [§85]   A remainder can be both vested subject to open and to complete divestment. For example, O conveys "to A for life, then to the children of A, but if no child survives A, to B." A, who is living, has a child, C. C has a vested remainder subject to open up and let in her brothers and sisters. It is also subject to complete divestment if A leaves no child surviving him (*i.e.*, if C and all other children of A die before A).

b. **Contingent remainders**

(1) **Definition:** [§86]   A remainder is contingent if it either is given to an *unascertained person* or is subject to a *condition precedent*.

(2) **Remainders in unascertained persons:** [§87]   A remainder limited to an "unascertained" person means the person is not yet born or cannot be determined until the happening of an event. Such a remainder is contingent.

(a) **Example—unborn children:** O conveys "to A for life, then to A's children." A has no children. The remainder is contingent because the takers are not ascertained at the time of the conveyance. If a child is born, the remainder vests in that child subject to open and to let in other children born later.

(b) **Example—heirs:** O conveys "to A for life, then to B's heirs." B is alive. Since the heirs of B cannot be known until B dies, the takers of the remainder are not ascertained. Therefore, the remainder is contingent. If B dies during A's life, the remainder will vest in B's heirs at B's death.

    1) **Meaning of "heirs":** [§88] "Heirs" means those persons who survive B and succeed to B's property *if B dies intestate*. They are set forth in each state's statute of descent and distribution. Children and descendants are preferred everywhere over parents and more remote kin. To be an heir of B, a person must survive B. Dead persons do not inherit property. If, for example, B has a son, C, who dies before B, C is not an heir of B.

(c) **Example—ascertainment determined by first reaching an age:** O conveys "to A for life, then to A's first child to reach 21." A has two children, age 10 and 12. The remainder is contingent because the taker is not now ascertained. If a child reaches 21, the remainder will vest in that child.

(d) **Reversion:** [§89] In each of the above examples, there is a reversion in O. *Note: Whenever O creates a contingent remainder in fee simple, there is a reversion in O*. It is possible for the property to return to O. Whenever O creates a vested remainder in fee simple, there is never a reversion in fee simple in O.

(3) **Remainders subject to a condition precedent:** [§90] A remainder subject to a condition precedent is a contingent remainder. A condition precedent is a *condition expressly stated in the instrument* (other than the termination of the preceding estate) that must occur before the remainder becomes possessory.

(a) **Example:** O conveys "to A for life, then to B *if B marries C*." B has a remainder subject to an express condition precedent. The condition precedent is marrying C. If B marries C during A's life, the remainder vests indefeasibly in B.

(b) **Termination of the preceding estate is not a condition precedent:** [§91] O conveys "to A for life, then to B." B has a vested remainder. The termination of A's life estate is not a condition precedent to vesting. (It is a condition precedent to *possession*, but *not to vesting*). If O conveys "to A for life, and on A's death, to B," the words "on A's death" merely refer to the natural termination of the life estate and do not state a condition precedent. B's remainder is vested. [Kost v. Foster, *supra*, §82]

(4) **Conditions subsequent distinguished:** [§92]   Sometimes it is difficult to distinguish between a vested remainder subject to divestment (*i.e.*, subject to a condition subsequent) and a remainder subject to a condition precedent. Whether a condition is precedent or subsequent depends upon the words of the instrument. The words must be read in sequence, and the interests classified in sequence. The test, according to Gray, *Rule Against Perpetuities* §108, is as follows: "Whether a remainder is vested or contingent depends upon the language employed. If the conditional element is incorporated into the description of, or into the gift to, the person taking the remainder, then the remainder is contingent; but if, after words giving a vested interest, a clause is added divesting it, the remainder is vested."

(a) **Example:** O conveys "to A for life, then to B, but if B does not survive A, to C." B has a vested remainder subject to divestment by C's executory interest. The words of condition ("but if B does not survive A") are not part of the gift to B, but state a condition precedent attached to C's gift.

(b) **Example:** O conveys "to A for life, then to B if B survives A, but if B does not survive A, to C." B and C have alternative contingent remainders. A condition precedent ("if B survives A") has been expressly attached to B's remainder, and a condition precedent ("but if B does not survive A") has been attached to C's remainder. O intended exactly the same thing as in the preceding example, but O's intention was phrased differently. Here, O stated the condition twice, once in connection with each remainder. [Quilliams v. Koonsman, 279 S.W.2d 579 (Tex. 1955)]

(c) **How to classify:** [§93]   The easiest way to classify remainders is as follows: Take each interest *in sequence* as it appears. Determine whether it is given to an ascertained person or is subject to a condition precedent. Classify it. Move on to the next interest and do the same thing. Classification of each interest *in sequence* is the key to correct classification. In the preceding example, take each interest in sequence. First, "to A for life." This gives A a life estate. Second, "then to B if B survives A." Stop at the comma, which ends B's interest, and classify it: B has a *contingent* remainder because it is subject to the express condition precedent, "if B survives A." Third, move on to the next interest, "and if B does not survive A, to B's children." Classify it: The interest is a *contingent* remainder because it is subject to the express condition precedent, "and if B does not survive A." If the words of an instrument are classified *in sequence*, as in this example, the classification of remainders is not too difficult a task.

(d) **Reversion in O with alternative contingent remainders:** [§94]   In the preceding example where alternative contingent remainders are created, there is a reversion in O. How is it possible for the property to revert to O? Inasmuch as B will take if B survives A, and if B does not survive A, C will take, it looks impossible for the property to revert to O on A's death. The answer is: *We must assume that the life estate can terminate before the death of the life* *tenant*. If this happened, neither B nor C would be ready to take on the termination of the life estate, and the property would revert to O. In feudal times, a life estate was forfeited (disappeared) in cases of breach of feudal obligations. Today, long after forfeiture of life estates was abolished, we still classify future interests as if forfeiture is a possibility.

(5) **Consequences of classification:** [§95] The common law drew—and still draws—a sharp distinction between vested and contingent remainders. At common law, there were four principal differences between vested and contingent remainders. These differences, briefly mentioned here, are discussed in detail later. In many states, most of these differences have disappeared, except for the application of the Rule Against Perpetuities. There, the distinction between vested and contingent remainders remains crucial.

  (a) **Transferability:** [§96] A vested remainder was assignable *inter vivos* at common law. A contingent remainder was not assignable *inter vivos*. (*See infra*, §197.) All remainders in fee simple, vested and contingent, are, however, *transferable to heirs or devisees* at the death of the remainderman unless a condition of survivorship is attached to the remainder.

    1) **Example:** T devises property "to A for life, then to B." B dies intestate. B's heirs take the remainder. The same result would follow if the remainder had been given "to B if A dies childless," for no condition of survivorship is attached to B's remainder. But if the remainder had been given "to B if B survives A," it would not pass to B's heirs if B died before A, because a condition of survivorship is attached to B's remainder.

  (b) **Acceleration:** [§97] A vested remainder accelerates into possession whenever and however the preceding estates end. A contingent remainder cannot become possessory until the contingencies are resolved.

    1) **Example:** T devises property "to A for life, then to B, but if C returns from Rome, to C." A dies. B's vested remainder will accelerate into possession, even though it can still be divested if C returns from Rome.

  (c) **Destructibility:** [§98] At common law, a contingent remainder in land was destroyed if it did not vest before or at the termination of the preceding estate. A vested remainder, being vested, could not be so destroyed. Destructibility of contingent remainders is discussed *infra*, §§121-144.

  (d) **Perpetuities:** [§99] A vested remainder is not subject to the Rule Against Perpetuities. A contingent remainder is subject to the Rule. The Rule Against Perpetuities is discussed *infra*, Chapter VI.

(6) **Preference for vested construction:** [§100]   If two constructions were possible, common law judges preferred to classify a remainder as vested. This preference gave rise to some important, and sometimes striking, rules of construction. (*See infra*, Chapter IV.)

G.   EXECUTORY INTERESTS

1. **Definition:** [§101]   An executory interest is a future interest in a grantee that must, in order to become possessory, (i) *divest* an interest in another grantee or (ii) *spring out* of the grantor at some future time. The first type is called a *shifting* executory interest, the second a *springing* executory interest.

2. **Historical Development**

   a. **Before Statute of Uses (1536):** [§102]   Executory interests grew out of the more or less accidental circumstance that England had separate courts of law and equity. The law courts were much concerned with the concept of seisin and keeping freehold tenants (responsible for feudal obligations) in uninterrupted possession. They laid down two rules prohibiting shifting and springing interests. Equity, moved by the chancellor's duty to treat persons equitably, refused to enforce these rules. To come within the chancellor's jurisdiction, a person had to raise a use (the forerunner of the modern trust) that the chancellor enforced. (*See* Property Summary.)

      (1) **No shifting interest:** [§103]   At law, a person could not create a future interest in a grantee that would cut short a freehold estate. Thus, if O conveyed "to A and his heirs, but if B returns from Rome, to B and his heirs," A took a fee simple absolute. B took nothing. The reasons for this rule were (i) O could not derogate from his grant to A, and (ii) O could not create a right of entry in a stranger, which a shifting interest resembled.

         (a) **In equity:** [§104]   The chancellor, sitting in equity, saw no harm in shifting interests, which permitted O to plan for contingent events. Therefore, if O would "enfeoff X and his heirs *to the use of* A and his heirs, but if B returns from Rome, to B and his heirs," thus raising a use and invoking chancery jurisdiction, the chancellor would enforce the use against X. The chancellor ordered X to stand seised to the use of (*i.e.*, to pay all the rents and profits to) A and, if B returned from Rome, B.

      (2) **No springing interest:** [§105]   At law, a person could not create a freehold estate to spring out in the future. Why not? Because O could not create a freehold estate without conveying seisin (handing over a clod of dirt in the ceremony of livery of seisin). O had to convey seisin now, not in the future. Thus if O conveyed "to my daughter A and her heirs upon her marriage," the conveyance was void at law because O did not thereby convey seisin to A. Seisin remained in O.

         (a) **In equity:** [§106]   The chancellor, favoring marriage and the highly commercial marriage arrangements of the times, saw nothing wrong with a springing interest. If O would "enfeoff X and his heirs to the use of O, and upon the marriage of A, to the use of A," the chancellor would enforce the use. X would be seised of the land, but O—and upon marriage A—would be entitled to all the income and profits.

b. **The Statute of Uses (1536):** [§107]   In 1536 Parliament enacted the Statute of Uses, with the purpose of abolishing uses. The Statute turned equitable interests into legal interests. Thus any interest that the chancellor enforced before 1536 became a legal interest. Shifting and springing interests, enforced by the chancellor, could be created as legal interests after 1536. If after 1536 O conveyed "to A and her heirs, but if B return from Rome, to B and her heirs," B had a legal shifting executory interest. As strange as it may seem, what we today call executory interests are interests that were void at law before 1536. (The Statute of Uses is explored in detail in the Property Summary.)

3. **Can Divest a Possessory Estate or a Remainder:** [§108]   An executory interest can divest either a possessory estate or a preceding vested remainder. But it will divest a preceding estate only if the specific divesting event happens. Judges construe instruments strictly against forfeiture. (*See infra*, §246.)

a. **Example—divesting a possessory fee simple:** O conveys Blackacre "to A, but if A dies childless, to B." A has a fee simple subject to divestment. B has a shifting executory interest. If A dies childless, B will divest A's heirs of the fee simple.

b. **Example—divesting a remainder:** O conveys Whiteacre "to A for life, then to B, but if B does not survive A, then to C." B has a vested remainder subject to divestment. C has a shifting executory interest. If B dies during A's lifetime, C divests B's vested remainder and takes a vested remainder himself. (*Note:* Any interest in a transferee after a vested remainder in fee must be an executory interest, for the only way for such an interest to become possessory is to divest the preceding vested remainder.)

4. **Exception—Determinable Fee:** [§109]   One exception to the definition of an executory interest as a divesting interest should be mentioned. An interest in a grantee following a determinable fee is an executory interest even though it does not divest the preceding estate.

a. **Example:** O conveys Blackacre "to Town Library so long as used for a library, then to the Red Cross." The future interest in the Red Cross takes effect upon the natural termination of the fee simple determinable. It does not divest it. Nonetheless, it is not a remainder but is an executory interest. Why? There was an old rule that a remainder cannot follow a fee simple, and to recognize the Red Cross's interest either that rule or the definition of an executory interest as shifting or springing had to give way. The definition gave way, so we have an odd executory interest that neither shifts nor springs.

5. **Vesting of Executory Interests:** [§110]   It is sometimes said that an executory interest, unlike a remainder, cannot vest in interest before it becomes possessory. This statement is misleading. In most contexts, executory interests are indistinguishable from remainders when the question is whether they can vest in interest.

a. **Can turn into vested remainder:** [§111] An executory interest following a life estate may have the capacity, as do many contingent remainders, of vesting in interest by turning into a vested remainder. There is no difference between contingent remainders and executory interests on this score.

(1) **Example:** O conveys Blackacre "to A for life, then to B, and if B does not survive A, to C." If B dies within the lifetime of A, C's executory interest will divest B and turn into a vested remainder.

b. **To become possessory on a day certain:** [§112] If O conveys "to A for 40 years, then to B," B has a vested remainder. An equivalent executory interest is treated as a vested remainder under the Rule Against Perpetuities and perhaps for other purposes as well. For example, a conveyance "to B 40 years from now" gives B a valid executory interest that is vested from the date of the deed. [Restatement (Second) of Property, Donative Transfers (hereafter "Rest. 2d"), §1.4, illus. 18 (1986)] The two conveyances in this paragraph cannot be distinguished in policy.

c. **Following possessory fee simple:** [§113] The only context in which the statement that an executory interest cannot vest in interest makes sense is where an executory interest follows a determinable fee or divests a possessory fee simple upon an uncertain event. Suppose, for example, that O conveys Blackacre "to the Town Library so long as it is used for a library, then to A and her heirs." This oddball executory interest (*see supra*, §§62, 109) has always been treated as contingent under the Rule Against Perpetuities until it becomes possessory (*see infra*, §451). A correct reformulation of the statement about the vesting of executory interests is as follows: Under the Rule Against Perpetuities, an executory interest following a fee simple determinable or divesting a fee simple cannot vest in interest before it becomes a possessory estate.

6. **Functional Equivalence with Remainders:** [§114] The historical categories of remainders and executory interests are part of the current vocabulary of judges and lawyers and are standard analytical tools of the law of future interests. However, today remainders and executory interests are in most states functional equivalents. The legal consequences attached to remainders and executory interests are in most states the same. Executory interests are inheritable and devisable in the same manner as remainders (*supra*, §96). Executory interests are treated differently from remainders only if the jurisdiction applies the common law doctrine of destructibility of contingent remainders or the Rule in Shelley's Case, both of which are abolished in almost all states.

a. **Statutory obliteration of executory interests:** [§115] Modern statutes often include executory interests in an all-inclusive definition of a remainder, abolishing executory interests as a separate category of future interests. New York Estates, Powers & Trusts Law section 6-4.3, for example, defines the term "remainder" as "a future estate created in favor of a person other than the creator." Thus all future interests in grantees are remainders, and the historical distinctions between remainders and executory interests are obliterated in New York.

 **FUTURE INTERESTS IN GRANTEES**

Future Interest	Example	Reversion in Grantor Following Future Interest?	Transferable?
Indefeasibly Vested Remainder	"To A for life, then to B."	No; remainder certain to become possessory	Yes; B's remainder transferable during life and at death
Vested Remainder Subject to Open	"To A for life, then to A's children." A has a child, B. B has a vested remainder subject to open.	No; A's children are certain of possession	Yes; B's remainder transferable during life and at death
Vested Remainder Subject to Divestment	"To A for life, then to B, but if B dies before A, to C." B has vested remainder subject to divestment by C.	No; no possibility of property reverting to grantor	B's remainder transferable during life but not transferable at B's death if B predeceases A
Contingent Remainder	(1) "To A for life, then to A's children." A has no child.	Yes	No; no child is alive
	(2) "To A for life, then to A's children who survive A." A has a child, B.	Yes	B's contingent remainder is transferable during life, but is not transferable at B's death if B predeceases A
	(3) "To A for life, then to B if B reaches 21." B is 17.	Yes	B's remainder is transferable during life, but remainder fails if B dies under 21
	(4) "To A for life, then to B's heirs." B is alive.	Yes	No; no one is heir of B until B dies
	(5) "To A for life, then to B if B survives A, and if B does not survive A, to C."	Yes	B's remainder transferable during life, but fails if B predeceases A; C's remainder transferable during life and at C's death if A is then alive
Executory Interest	(1) "To A, but if B returns from Rome, to B."	No	Yes
	(2) "To A for life, then to B, but if B does not survive A, to C."	No	C's executory interest is transferable during life and at C's death if A is alive
	(3) "To A upon her marriage."	No reversion, but grantor has possessory fee until A's marriage	Yes

NOTE: In a few states, contingent remainders and executory interests are not transferable during life except in certain circumstances. *See infra* §§197-203.

H. SUMMARY OF FUTURE INTERESTS

1. Future Interests in the Grantor

a. **Reversion:** [§116]   A reversion is an interest remaining in a grantor who transfers a vested estate of a lesser quantum than the grantor has. A reversion can follow any kind of possessory estate except a fee simple. If O, owner of a fee simple, makes a conveyance of a fee tail, a life estate, or a term of years and does not create a vested remainder in fee simple, O has a reversion.

   (1) **Example—fee tail:** O conveys "to A and the heirs of her body." O has a reversion because a fee tail is an estate of a shorter duration than a fee simple.

   (2) **Examples—life estate**

      (a)   O conveys "to A for life." O has a reversion. If A subsequently conveys "to B for B's life" or "to C for 90 years," A (as well as O) has a reversion. By the hierarchy of estates, a life estate pur autre vie and a term of years are estates of shorter duration than a life estate.

      (b)   O conveys "to A for life, remainder to B if B survives A." O has a reversion.

      (c)   O conveys "to A for life, remainder to B if B survives A, but if B does not survive A, to C." O has a reversion because O has not transferred a vested remainder in fee simple.

      (d)   O conveys "to A for life, remainder to B." O does not have a reversion.

   (3) **Examples—term of years**

      (a)   O conveys "to A for 99 years." O has a reversion.

      (b)   O conveys "to A for 99 years, and then to A's heirs." O has a reversion.

b. **Possibility of reverter:** [§117]   A possibility of reverter is a future interest remaining in the grantor when the grantor creates a determinable estate of the same quantum as the grantor had. Almost always a possibility of reverter follows a fee simple determinable. A possibility of reverter becomes possessory automatically.

   (1) **Example:** O conveys "to A and her heirs so long as liquor is not sold on the premises." O has a possibility of reverter, which arises by operation of law because only a determinable fee has been granted A.

c. **Right of entry:** [§118]   A right of entry is a future interest retained by the grantor giving the grantor power to terminate, at his election, the estate granted. Usually it is retained when granting a fee simple subject to condition subsequent.

(1) **Example:** O conveys "to A and her heirs, but if liquor is sold on the premises, O has a right to reenter." O has a right of entry, which O can exercise or not when the condition is breached.

2. Future Interests in Grantees

a. **Remainder:** [§119]   A remainder is a future interest in a grantee that is capable of becoming possessory upon the expiration of the preceding estate. A remainder never divests the preceding estate. A remainder cannot follow a fee simple, but can follow any other kind of possessory estate. Remainders are vested or contingent. A vested remainder is created in an ascertained person and is not subject to a condition precedent. A contingent remainder either is created in an unascertained person or is subject to a condition precedent.

(1) **Examples—fee tail**

(a) O conveys "to A and the heirs of her body, and if A dies without issue, to B." B has a vested remainder. The words "if A dies without issue" merely refer to the expiration of the fee tail and do not state a condition precedent.

(b) O conveys "to A and the heirs of her body, and if A dies without issue, to B if B is then alive." B has a contingent remainder, subject to the condition precedent of B surviving the expiration of the fee tail.

(2) **Examples—life estate**

(a) O conveys "to A for life, then to B." B has a vested remainder.

(b) O conveys "to A for life, then to B's heirs." B is alive. B's heirs have a contingent remainder because the takers are unascertained.

(c) O conveys "to A for life, then to B if B reaches 25." B is age 15. B has a contingent remainder because it is subject to a condition precedent.

(d) O conveys "to A for life, then to B if B survives A, and if B does not survive A, to C." B and C have alternative contingent remainders; each is subject to a condition precedent.

(e) O conveys "to A for life, then to B, and if B does not survive A, to C." B has a vested remainder subject to divestment by C's executory interest.

(f) O conveys "to A for life, then to A's children." If A has no child, the remainder is contingent because the taker is unascertained. If A has a child, B, the remainder is vested in B subject to open up and let in other children born to A. B's remainder is sometimes called a remainder vested subject to partial divestment.

(3) **Example—term of years:** O conveys "to A for ten years, then to B." B has a vested remainder.

b. **Executory interest:** [§120]   An executory interest is a future interest in a grantee that may divest another grantee (a shifting executory interest) or may spring out of the grantor at a future date (a springing executory interest). An executory interest can divest any type of possessory estate or future interest.

(1) **Examples—fee simple**

    (a) O conveys "to A, but if B return from Rome, to B." B has a shifting executory interest which will divest A's fee simple if the condition happens.

    (b) O conveys "to B if B marries A." B has a springing executory interest which will divest O's fee simple if B marries A.

    (c) *Exception to rule*: O conveys "to A so long as it is used for a library during the next 20 years, and if not so used, to B." B has an executory interest even though it will not divest the preceding fee simple determinable. It is an executory interest because of the rule that a remainder cannot follow a fee simple.

(2) **Example—fee tail:** O conveys "to A and the heirs of his body, but if A inherits the family manor, to B and his heirs." B has a shifting executory interest.

(3) **Examples—life estate**

    (a) O conveys "to A for life, but if B returns from Rome during A's life, to B." B has a shifting executory interest which may divest A's life estate.

    (b) O conveys "to A for life, then to B, but if B does not survive A, to C." C has a shifting executory interest which may divest B's vested remainder.

    (c) O conveys "to A for life, then one day after A's death to B." B has a springing executory interest which will divest O's fee simple one day after A's death.

(4) **Examples—term of years**

    (a) O conveys "to A for ten years, but if A does not keep up the fence, to B." B has a shifting executory interest which may divest the term of years.

    (b) *Exception to rule*: O conveys "to A for 100 years if A so long lives, then to A's heirs." A's heirs have an executory interest even though it will not divest the preceding term of years determinable. It is an executory interest because before the Statute of Uses one could not have a contingent remainder following a term of years. In modern times, the interest in A's heirs is sometimes called a contingent remainder.

NOTE: The law of Future Interests resembles building blocks; it builds on prior foundations. Therefore, it is useful to test your understanding of the material in one chapter before moving on to the next. To help you, questions and answers for each chapter are provided in the Review Questions of this Summary (*infra,* p. 115). If you understand the material in Chapter I., you are ready to proceed.

II. (ALMOST) OBSOLETE RULES RESTRICTING REMAINDERS

A. DESTRUCTIBILITY OF CONTINGENT REMAINDERS IN LAND

1. **Introduction:** [§121]   Although future interests have been permitted for hundreds of years, judges have always been jealous of them. When created in land, they make land less alienable. They also extend the power of the dead hand. Contingent future interests have been thought to be more objectionable than vested future interests, since they may be more difficult both to transfer and to value. Judges therefore laid down a number of rules to curb contingent future interests. Among these rules were the doctrine of destructibility of contingent remainders, the Rule in Shelley's Case, and the Doctrine of Worthier Title. The first two of these rules have been abolished in almost all states. Another restrictive rule is the Rule Against Perpetuities, discussed in Chapter VI.

2. **Statement of Destructibility Rule:** [§122]   A legal contingent remainder in *land* is *destroyed if it does not vest at or before the termination of the preceding freehold estate*. If the preceding freehold terminates before the remainder vests, the remainder is struck down and can never take effect.

   a. **Example:** O conveys Blackacre "to A for life, remainder to A's children who reach 21." At A's death, A's children are all under 21. The remainder is destroyed. Blackacre reverts to the reversioner, O, who owns it in fee simple absolute.

   b. **Reason for rule—gap in seisin:** [§123]   The common law abhorred an abeyance, or gap, in seisin. Feudal obligations (taxes) were imposed on the person seised of the land, and the location and continuity of seisin was important to the functioning of the feudal system. Thus the courts laid down this rule: If, upon termination of the preceding freehold, the holder of the remainder *is not able to take seisin* because his remainder is still contingent, the remainder is wiped out. (Of course, the judges could have said that seisin returned to the reversioner, O, and then sprung out of the reversioner to the holder of the remainder later when he qualified. But this would look like a springing interest, and springing interests were not permitted until 1536. *See supra*, §105).

   c. **Modern reason:** [§124]   Feudal services are irrelevant today, but a new reason can be advanced to support the destructibility rule. *The rule makes land alienable sooner*. To illustrate this, look at the example above: "To A for life, remainder to A's children who reach 21." At A's death, with children all under 21, O takes a fee simple title and the land is immediately alienable. It is not necessary to wait and see which, if any, of A's children reach 21.

3. **Elements of the Rule**

   a. **Preceding freehold:** [§125]   The preceding freehold estate in possession can be a fee tail or a life estate, both of which are estates having seisin. Since the fee tail is largely obsolete, this discussion will assume the freehold is a life estate. *The rule does not apply if the preceding estate is a leasehold*, because the termor does not have seisin.

(1) **Example:** O conveys "to A for 100 years if A so long live, then to A's children who reach 21." Subsequently A dies, leaving an eldest child of 19. The destructibility rule has no application because A did not have a freehold. When any child of A reaches 21, seisin will spring out to such child, who will take a vested fee simple subject to partial defeasance by other children reaching that age.

b. **Termination of life estate:** [§126] The life estate can terminate either upon the death of the life tenant *or before the life tenant's death*. It is this latter proposition that makes the rule more difficult than it appears.

(1) **Natural termination of life estate:** [§127] A contingent remainder that does not vest upon the *natural* termination of the life estate (*i.e.*, at the life tenant's death) is destroyed.

(a) **Example:** O conveys "to A for life, remainder to the heirs of B." B is alive. This conveyance creates a life estate in A, contingent remainder in the heirs of B, reversion in O. Subsequently A dies, survived by B. At A's death, B has no heirs, because no one can be an heir of the living. The contingent remainder in the heirs of B is destroyed, and O owns the land.

(2) **Artificial termination of life estate:** [§128] A contingent remainder that does not vest upon the *artificial termination* of the life estate is destroyed. "Artificial termination" refers to the following methods of termination:

(a) **Forfeiture:** [§129] At common law, a person forfeited his property if he made a tortious conveyance (*i.e.*, a conveyance by which a life tenant conveyed a fee simple). Such a conveyance was treated as breaching the feudal oath of loyalty to the lord, by repudiating and claiming a fee simple. The penalty for breach of the feudal oath was forfeiture of the life estate. Any contingent remainders dependent on the life estate failed.

1) **Example:** O conveys "to A for life, then to A's children who reach 21." A makes a tortious conveyance in fee simple to B while A's children are under 21. The life estate is forfeited and the remainder is destroyed. O owns Blackacre.

2) **Modern status:** [§130] Forfeiture for tortious conveyance is wholly obsolete in the United States. In the above example, B would receive merely a life estate pur autre vie. The remainder would not be affected.

(b) **Merger:** [§131] If the life estate and a vested remainder or reversion in fee simple come into the hands of the same person, any intermediate contingent remainders are destroyed. The lesser estate (life estate) is merged into the larger (fee simple) and ceases to exist as a separate estate. A life tenant and reversioner can thus conspire to destroy contingent remainders.

1) **Example:** O conveys "to A for life, remainder to B if B survives A." While B is alive, O conveys her reversion to A. The life estate merges into the reversion, and B's contingent remainder is destroyed. A has a fee simple absolute.

2) **Exception—fee tail:** [§132]   Life estates merge into a fee simple, but fee tails do not merge into a fee simple if merger would destroy an intervening contingent remainder. Thus, suppose a conveyance "to A and the heirs of his body, and if A dies without issue, to B and her heirs if B is then living." A conveys his fee tail to O, the reversioner. B's remainder is not destroyed. However, a fee tail tenant in possession may at any time destroy any remainders by a disentailing deed (conveying a fee simple to the grantee).

3) **Exception—simultaneous creation:** [§133]   If a life estate and the next vested estate are created simultaneously, they do not merge *at that time* to destroy intervening contingent remainders. Thus, suppose that T devises Blackacre "to A for life, remainder to A's children who survive A." A is also T's heir and inherits the reversion. The life estate and reversion do not merge at that time; otherwise the intent of T in creating the remainder would be frustrated. But if *A subsequently conveys the life estate and reversion to B*, the estates then merge, destroying the contingent remainder.

4. **Interests Not Affected by Destructibility Rule:** [§134]   The destructibility rule does not apply to the following interests in property.

a. **Vested remainders:** [§135]   Since vested remainders accelerate into possession whenever and however the preceding estate terminates, vested remaindermen are always ready to take seisin when it is offered to them.

   (1) **Example:** O conveys "to A for life, then to B for life, then to A's children who survive A." A conveys his life estate to O. The life estate cannot merge into the reversion because the vested remainder in B blocks it. O takes a life estate pur autre vie (for A's life).

b. **Executory interests:** [§136]   Executory interests are indestructible because no gap in seisin can ever precede these interests. In the case of a shifting executory interest, this interest shifts seisin away from a prior vested interest in a grantee prior to its termination. By definition, no gap in seisin occurs. The executory interest simply grabs seisin from the preceding holder. (*Example:* O conveys "to A and his heirs, but if B returns from Rome, to B and his heirs.") In the case of a springing executory interest, it always shifts seisin out of the grantor in the future. (*Example:* O conveys "to A and her heirs when she marries B.") [Pells v. Brown, 79 Eng. Rep. 504 (1620)]

   (1) **Example:** O conveys "to A, but if A dies leaving children, to A's children who survive A, and if A dies without children, title shall return to

O." A has a fee simple, subject to divestment by an executory interest in A's children who survive A, and subject also to a possibility of reverter in O. Later O conveys his interest to A, the fee simple owner. This cannot affect the executory interest in A's children. They take the land on A's death. [Stoller v. Doyle, 100 N.E. 959 (Ill. 1913)]

    (a) **The rule of *Purefoy v. Rogers*:** [§137] In *Purefoy v. Rogers*, 35 Eng. Rep. 1181 (1670), it was held that any limitation capable of taking effect as a remainder must be construed to be a remainder and could not take effect as an executory interest. This was simply another way of stating that the destructibility rule was still in effect.

c. **Personal property:** [§138] The destructibility rule has no application to personal property. There is no seisin in personal property, only in land.

d. **Interests in trust:** [§139] Interests in trust—that is, equitable estates—are not subject to the destructibility rule. The trustee, owning the legal fee simple, has seisin. Upon the expiration of the *equitable* life estate, seisin is not offered to the next estate—and therefore the destructibility rule, based on continuity of seisin, does not apply.

    (1) **Example:** O conveys Blackacre "to X and his heirs in trust to pay the income to A for life, then in trust to convey Blackacre to the children of A who reach 21." Subsequently A dies, and his eldest child is 19. The remainder is not destroyed. The trustee X has seisin. Such children as reach age 21 will take the land. [Abbiss v. Burney, 17 Ch. D. 211 (1881)]

5. **Avoidance of Rule:** [§140] The destructibility rule can be easily avoided by a competent lawyer. The two most common ways of avoiding the rule are as follows.

a. **Term of years:** [§141] If a drafter creates a term of years rather than a life estate, the destructibility rule can be avoided.

    (1) **Example:** O conveys "to A for 100 years if A so long lives, then to A's children who reach 21." Seisin remains in O. A has a term of years determinable. A's children have an executory interest and not a contingent remainder. If A dies leaving all children under 21, seisin stays in O, and the executory interest is not destroyed. It springs out of O when a child reaches 21.

b. **Trustees:** [§142] The destructibility rule can also be avoided by creating ***trustees to preserve contingent remainders***. The device works this way. O conveys "to A for life, then to X, Y, and Z as trustees for the life of A and to preserve contingent remainders, remainder to A's children who survive A." The trustees have a *vested* remainder following A's life estate. If the life estate terminates in any way, prior to A's death, the trustees step up and take seisin and hold it until A's death, paying the income to A. The purpose of this device was to *prevent artificial destruction* of contingent remainders by the termination of the life estate prior to the life tenant's death. If the life estate terminated before the death of A, the trustees took seisin, and blocked its passage on to the reversioner. Thus, A could not destroy the contingent remainders with the collusion of O.

6. **Abolition:** [§143]   The destructibility doctrine has been abolished by statute or judicial decision in almost all states. It is possible that the doctrine exists in Arkansas, Florida, North Carolina, Oregon, and Pennsylvania, but there have been no cases applying the doctrine for more than 50 years. In the only case raising the issue in modern times, the New Mexico court flatly rejected the destructibility doctrine as being obsolete and serving no good purpose. [Abo Petroleum Corp. v. Amstutz, 600 P.2d 278 (N.M. 1979)] The Restatement of Property declares that the doctrine does not exist in this country. [Rest. §240]

   a. **Effect of abolition:** [§144]   Where destructibility is abolished, a contingent remainder takes effect if the contingency occurs *either before or after the termination of the life estate*. Thus, if O conveys "to A for life, remainder to A's children who reach 21," and A dies leaving all children under 21, A's children take if and when they reach 21. Their interest takes effect in possession after A's death, and is called either an indestructible contingent remainder or an executory interest. In the meantime, before any child reaches 21, O, the reversioner, is entitled to possession.

B. THE RULE IN SHELLEY'S CASE

1. **Statement of Rule:** [§145]   If (i) one instrument (ii) creates a life estate in land in A, and (iii) purports to create a remainder in A's heirs (or in the heirs of A's body), and (iv) the estates are both legal or both equitable, then the remainder becomes a remainder in fee simple (or fee tail) in A. [Martin v. Knowles, 142 S.E. 313 (N.C. 1928); *and see* Rest. 2d §30.1]

   a. **Examples**

      (1) **Remainder to A's heirs:** O conveys "to A for life, then to A's heirs." The Rule in Shelley's Case converts the remainder limited to A's heirs into a remainder in fee simple in A. *Then* the doctrine of *merger* steps in, and A's life estate and vested remainder merge, giving A a fee simple in possession.

      (2) **Remainder to heirs of A's body:** O conveys "to A for life, then to the heirs of A's body." The Rule in Shelley's Case converts the remainder limited to "the heirs of A's body" into a remainder in fee tail in A. The fee tail is then changed into whatever estate is substituted for a fee tail under state law, probably a fee simple. Then the remainder in A merges with A's life estate.

   b. **Doctrine of merger:** [§146]   The doctrine of merger is an entirely separate doctrine from the Rule in Shelley's Case. Under the doctrine of merger, a life estate in A and a remainder in A (including a remainder created by the Rule in Shelley's case) will merge unless: (i) there is an intervening estate, *or* (ii) the remainder in A is subject to a condition precedent to which A's life estate is not subject. The doctrine of merger may or may not apply *after* the Rule in Shelley's Case has operated on the instrument (*see supra,* §§131-133).

2. **Reasons for Rule:** [§147]   The Rule in Shelley's Case prevented feudal tax evasion. Feudal inheritance taxes were due at A's death if land descended from A to A's heir, but not if A's heir took as a remainderman from O. The Rule in Shelley's

Case resulted in the land descending. In addition, the Rule makes land ***alienable*** one generation earlier. In the preceding example, a fee simple can be conveyed by A immediately after the conveyance from O. The land is not tied up during A's lifetime. On the other hand, the primary objection to the Rule in Shelley's Case is that it defeats the intent of the grantor.

a. **Not applicable to personal property:** [§148] At English law, the Rule in Shelley's Case did not apply to personal property, only to land. The reasons for its existence related only to taxation and marketability of land. Occasionally, however, an American court has slipped and applied the Rule to personal property. [Society National Bank v. Jacobson, 560 N.E.2d 217 (Ohio 1990)]

3. **Operation of the Rule:** [§149] The Rule is more readily understood if each element of the Rule is separately analyzed.

a. **"If one instrument creates a life estate in A":** [§150] The life estate and remainder must be created by the same instrument. If, for example, O conveys a life estate to A during O's life, and subsequently by will O devises the reversion to A's heirs, the Rule in Shelley's Case does not apply. If a remainder is given to A's heirs by the instrument creating the life estate, the Rule will apply if the life estate given A is measured by A's life or by the life of another.

(1) **Example:** O conveys "to A for the life of B, remainder to A's heirs." The Rule in Shelley's Case applies, the life estate and vested remainder merge, and A has a fee simple. This makes sense. Inasmuch as the remainder in A becomes possessory whenever and however the life estate ends, a life estate in A (even measured by B's life), and a vested remainder in A comprise the totality of interests in the land. *But compare:* If O had conveyed "to A for the life of B, remainder to B's heirs," the Rule in Shelley's Case would not apply. The life estate must be given to the ancestor of the heirs given the remainder.

(2) **Life estate determinable:** [§151] The life estate can be determinable or subject to a condition subsequent.

(a) **Example:** O devises a farm "to my wife W during widowhood, and upon W's death or remarriage, remainder to W's heirs." The Rule in Shelley's Case applies, giving W the remainder. The remainder merges with W's life estate, giving W a fee simple. [Lydick v. Tate, 44 N.E.2d 583 (Ill. 1942)]

(3) **Life estate is in remainder:** [§152] The life estate can be in possession or in remainder. The Rule in Shelley's Case applies to a conveyance "to A for life, then to B for life, remainder to B's heirs." B has a remainder in fee simple.

(a) **Subject to condition precedent:** [§153] If the life estate in A is subject to a condition precedent that is not also applicable to the remainder to A's heirs, the Rule in Shelley's Case does not apply until the condition is satisfied.

1) **Example:** O conveys "to A for life, then if B marries C, to B for life, remainder to the heirs of B (whether or not B marries

C).” The life estate is subject to a condition precedent that is not also applicable to the remainder. The Rule in Shelley's Case does not apply. If B marries C during A's life, the Rule in Shelley's Case *then* applies.

2) **Remainder subject to same condition precedent:** [§154] If the remainder is subject to the same condition precedent as the life estate, then the Rule in Shelley's Case applies. Thus if, in the preceding example, the language in parentheses had been omitted and the condition precedent of B marrying C were construed to be a condition precedent on the remainder as well as on B's life estate, the Rule in Shelley's Case would have applied. B would have taken a remainder in fee simple subject to the condition precedent of marrying C.

(4) **Lapse of life estate:** [§155] If O's will gives A a life estate, with remainder to A's heirs and *A predeceases O*, A's life estate lapses (or fails). The Rule in Shelley's Case does not apply because the life estate is never created.

(5) **Joint life estate:** [§156] Suppose that O conveys “to H and W as tenants in common for their lives, remainder to the heirs of W.” Does the Rule in Shelley's Case apply? The authorities are divided. Some say that W has the entire remainder in fee simple because W, as a tenant in common with H, was seised of a life estate in the whole, meaning W could enjoy the entire property for life (as of course could H). [Bails v. Davis, 89 N.E. 706 (Ill. 1909)] The Restatement of Property says W has a remainder in fee simple only as to an undivided half. The heirs of W take the other half as purchasers. [Rest. 2d §30.11, comment q]

b. **“And purports to create a remainder”:** [§157] The Rule applies to a remainder to the heirs of A, the life tenant, even though there is an intervening estate between the life estate and remainder. For example, the Rule applies to a conveyance “to A for life, then to B for life, then to A's heirs.” A has a remainder in fee simple by the operation of the Rule. A's remainder does not, however, merge with A's life estate; B's intervening remainder for life prevents merger.

(1) **Contingent remainder:** [§158] The remainder may be a remainder contingent upon the happening of some condition precedent. Thus, the Rule in Shelley's Case applies to a conveyance “to A for life, then to A's heirs if A survives B.” A has a life estate and a contingent remainder, contingent upon A's surviving B. The life estate and contingent remainder do not merge until the condition is satisfied.

(a) **Compare:** [§159] In §153, *supra*, it was noted that the Rule did *not* apply if the life estate were subject to a condition precedent not also applicable to the remainder. But the Rule *does* apply in the converse situation, where there is a condition precedent on the remainder but not on the life estate. [Rest. 2d §30.1, comment o]

(2) **Executory interest:** [§160] The Rule in Shelley's Case applies only where a remainder, not an executory interest, has been created.

    (a) **Example:** O conveys "to A for life, remainder to B, but if B predeceases A, to A's heirs." The interest given A's heirs is an executory interest, and therefore, the requirement of a remainder is not satisfied. But if B dies before A, the executory interest given A's heirs becomes a remainder by divesting B, and the Rule in Shelley's Case then applies.

c. **"In A's heirs (or the heirs of A's body)":** [§161]   The remainder must be given to A's heirs or heirs of the body in "an indefinite line of succession rather than a specific class of takers. The remainder must be to the heirs of the first taker *by the name of heirs* as meaning a class of persons to succeed to the estate from generation to generation. Where to the word *heirs* other words are added which so limit its meaning that it does not include the whole line of inheritable succession but only designates the individuals who are at the death of the life tenant to succeed to the estate . . . the Rule in Shelley's Case does not apply." [Arnold v. Baker, 185 N.E.2d 844 (Ill. 1962); Finley v. Finley, 318 S.W.2d 478 (Tex. 1958)]

    (1) **Indefinite line of succession:** [§162]   The distinction between the word "heirs" as referring to those persons who take on A's death and "heirs" as referring to an indefinite line of succession is hard to grasp. It is easier to understand in the English context of primogeniture, where the distinction originated. Under the doctrine of primogeniture, a person has only one heir, and therefore, the word "heirs" can easily be taken to describe an indefinite succession of heirs. After primogeniture was abolished, the distinction became pretty ephemeral, and some courts have not grasped it—or have ignored it.

    (2) **Words meaning indefinite line of succession:** [§163]   The Rule in Shelley's Case does not apply to a remainder limited to "A's children," because those words cannot be taken to mean heirs in an indefinite line of succession. The words "heirs" or "heirs of the body," however, are usually said to refer to heirs in an indefinite line of succession, unless the grantor shows he means something different.

        (a) **Example:** J. H. Sybert devises land "to Fred for life, and after his death to vest in fee simple in the heirs of his body." Fred dies intestate and childless, leaving his wife Eunice as his heir. The Rule in Shelley's Case applies, giving Fred a life estate and remainder in fee tail, which is converted by the fee tail statute into a remainder in fee simple, which merges with Fred's life estate, giving Fred a fee simple. Fred's fee simple passes to his wife on Fred's death. The words "heirs of the body" are traditional words bringing the devise within Shelley's Case, and the Rule applies. [Sybert v. Sybert, 254 S.W.2d 999 (Tex. 1953)]

        (b) **Remainder to issue:** [§164]   A remainder limited to the "issue" of a life tenant may meet the requirements of the Rule in Shelley's Case if a court construes "issue" to mean "heirs of the body." [*See* Rest. 2d §30.1, comment g, illus. 8—suggesting a court should so construe "issue"]

(3) **"Heirs" used, but contrary intent shown:** [§165] If the grantor indicates that he does not intend to use "heirs" in the technical sense, but is using the words with some other meaning, the Rule in Shelley's Case will not apply. [Ray v. Ray, 155 S.E.2d 185 (N.C. 1967)]

(4) **Distinction rejected:** [§166] The requirement that "heirs" refer to an indefinite line of succession has been ignored by some American courts, which have applied the Rule in Shelley's Case to the following: "to A for life, then to such persons as will inherit real property from A at his death." The Restatement (Second) of Property approves of this approach, but it widens the application of the Rule in Shelley's Case by applying it to instruments the English courts would not have applied it to. [Rest. 2d §30.1, comment g, illus. 7]

d. **"And the estates are both legal or both equitable":** [§167] The life estate and remainder must be either both legal or both equitable. If one is legal and the other is equitable the Rule in Shelley's Case does not apply.

(1) **Example:** O conveys Blackacre "to X in trust to pay A the income and profits, remainder to the heirs of A." If X has a legal life estate for A's life, A has an equitable life estate and A's heirs have a legal remainder in fee simple. Since A's life estate is equitable and the remainder to A's heirs is legal, the Rule in Shelley's Case does not apply. On the other hand, if the trustee has a legal fee simple (the usual result), then both the life estate and remainder are equitable, and the Rule in Shelley's Case applies. [City Bank & Trust Co. v. Morrissey, 454 N.E.2d 1195 (Ill. 1983); Seymour v. Heubaum, 211 N.E.2d 897 (Ill. 1965)]

4. **The Rule Is a Rule of Law:** [§168] The Rule in Shelley's Case is a *rule of law* (not a rule of construction) that applies regardless of O's intent. It cannot be avoided by expressions of intent, such as, "I intend that the Rule in Shelley's Case not apply." O's intent is irrelevant. If the conveyance by O comes within its terms, the Rule in Shelley's Case applies regardless of what O wants. [Perrin v. Blake, 1 W. Bl. 672 (1770)]

5. **Avoidance of Rule:** [§169] The Rule cannot be avoided by a direct expression of intent, but it can be avoided by failing to come within its requirements. A conveyance "to A for 100 years if A so long live, then to A's heirs" is the standard device used by skilled drafters to avoid the Rule. The Rule does not apply because A has a *leasehold*, not a life estate.

6. **Modern Status:** [§170] The Rule in Shelley's Case has been abolished by statute in almost all states. The Rule appears to be fully in force only in Arkansas, Delaware, and Indiana, and possibly in a few other states. In some states, the abolition of the Rule in Shelley's Case is fairly recent, so the old law, which remains applicable to conveyances made before abolition, will be of some concern for many years. These states include Illinois, North Carolina, and Texas.

a. **Effect where abolished:** [§171] If the Rule in Shelley's Case is abolished, a conveyance "to A for life, then to A's heirs" creates a life estate in A, and a contingent remainder in A's heirs.

C. THE DOCTRINE OF WORTHIER TITLE

1. Statement of the Doctrine

a. **Inter vivos branch:** [§172]   When an inter vivos conveyance purports to create a future interest in the *heirs of the grantor*, the future interest is *void* and the grantor has *a reversion*. This is sometimes known as a rule against a remainder in the grantor's heirs.

    (1) **Example:** O conveys "to A for life, then to O's heirs." The remainder to O's heirs is void, and O has a reversion.

b. **Testamentary branch:** [§173]   When T devises to his heirs the identical interest the heirs would take by descent, the devise is a nullity and the heirs take by descent. The Restatement states that the testamentary branch of the Doctrine does not exist in the United States [Rest. 2d §30.2(2); *and see* Estate of Kern, 274 N.W.2d 325 (Iowa 1979)] In the discussion below, "Doctrine of Worthier Title" will refer to the inter vivos branch of the rule.

2. Modern Rule: [§174]   The common law Doctrine of Worthier Title differs from the rule as applied today. At common law, the Doctrine of Worthier Title was a *rule of law* applicable to *land* only. The modern Doctrine of Worthier Title, as set forth by Cardozo, J., in *Doctor v. Hughes*, 225 N.Y. 305 (1919), applies to *personal* property as well as to land. It is a *rule of construction*, not a rule of law. It raises a presumption that no remainder has been created, but this presumption can be rebutted by evidence of a contrary intent of the grantor.

a. **Justification:** [§175]   The Doctrine of Worthier Title can be justified as a rule designed to carry out the grantor's intent. It is assumed that grantors seldom intend to create a remainder in their heirs that they cannot change, and therefore, the Doctrine gives the grantor the right to change her mind by voiding the remainder and creating a reversion in the grantor. Another justification for the modern rule is that it makes property alienable earlier. In the above example, A and O can together convey a fee simple. If the Doctrine did not apply, a fee simple could not be conveyed until O's death, when O's heirs are ascertained.

3. Operation of the Doctrine

a. **Limitation to heirs:** [§176]   For the Doctrine to apply, a future interest must be given to the grantor's "heirs" or the "next of kin," or some equivalent term must be used. The Doctrine does *not* apply to a future interest limited to "O's children" or "O's issue," or to "O's heirs ascertained at the death of the life tenant A." [Harris Trust & Savings Bank v. Beach, 513 N.E.2d 833 (Ill. 1987); Braswell v. Braswell, 81 S.E.2d 560 (Va. 1954)] This requirement of the Doctrine is rather similar to the requirement of the Rule in Shelley's Case that the technical word "heirs" be used. (*See supra*, §161.)

b. **Kind of future interest immaterial:** [§177]   The Doctrine applies to a *remainder* or an *executory interest* limited to O's heirs. The future interest may be *legal or equitable*, or subject to a condition precedent other than the ascertainment of heirs.

 **gilbert** LAW SUMMARIES

OLD TECHNICAL RULES OF THE COMMON LAW

	Rule	Example	Result	Modern Law
Destructibility of Contingent Remainders	A contingent remainder is destroyed if it does not vest upon the termination of preceding estate.	"To A for life, remainder to A's children who reach age 21." At A's death, no child of A has reached 21.	Contingent remainder in A's children destroyed. Title reverts to grantor.	Rule abolished in almost all states. A's children take if they reach 21.
Rule in Shelley's Case	A remainder given to heirs of life tenant becomes a remainder in the life tenant.	"To A for life, then to A's heirs."	A has remainder in fee simple, which merges with life estate, creating a fee simple in A.	Rule abolished in almost all states. A's heirs take a contingent remainder.
Doctrine of Worthier Title	A remainder created in grantor's heirs is void; grantor has reversion.	"To A for life, then to the grantor's heirs."	A has a life estate; the grantor has a reversion. The grantor's heirs have no interest.	Doctrine abolished in many states; in others it is a rule of construction, which can be overcome by contrary intent. If so, grantor's heirs have contingent remainder.

    c.   **Preceding estate:** [§178] The character of the estate preceding the future interest in O's heirs is immaterial. It may be a fee simple defeasible, fee tail, life estate, or term of years.

    d.   **Typical applications**

        (1) **Revocation of trust:** [§179] Suppose that O conveys property "to X in trust to pay the income to O for life, and on O's death to convey the trust assets to O's heirs." O retains no power to revoke. Subsequently O wants to revoke the trust and get the property back. Under trust law, a trust can be terminated if *all owners* of the equitable interests consent. Hence, if O's heirs do not have a remainder, but O has a reversion, O owns all the equitable interests in the trust and can terminate it. Under the Doctrine of Worthier Title, O is presumed to have a reversion and can terminate the trust. (Of course, contrary evidence can show that O intended to create a remainder in O's heirs, and there has been considerable litigation over what contrary evidence is sufficient to rebut the presumption of a reversion.) [Matter of Burchell, 299 N.Y. 351 (1949)]

        (2) **Creditors' rights:** [§180] Suppose that O conveys Blackacre "to A for life, then to O's heirs." O runs up bills and O's creditors attempt to reach his interest. If the Doctrine applies, the creditor of O can reach O's reversion.

        (3) **Devise by O:** [§181] Suppose that O conveys Blackacre "to A for life, then to O's heirs." Subsequently O dies, devising all his property to B. O's heir is C. Under the Doctrine, O is presumed to have a reversion (and his heirs nothing). Therefore, O devises his reversion to B. Upon A's death, B and not C owns Blackacre. [Braswell v. Braswell, *supra*, §176]

  4. **Abolition of Doctrine:** [§182] The Doctrine of Worthier Title, unlike the Rule in Shelley's Case, apparently is still applied in many jurisdictions, though most of the cases applying it have arisen in jurisdictions which subsequently abolished the Doctrine. It has been abolished in, among other states, California, Illinois, Massachusetts, Minnesota, New York, North Carolina, Tennessee, and Texas. Uniform Probate Code section 2-710 abolishes the Doctrine. Where it has been abolished, the heirs of O take the future interest limited to them under the instrument. [Hatch v. Riggs National Bank, 361 F.2d 559 (D.C. Cir. 1966)]

    a.   **New York law:** [§183] New York has abolished the Doctrine of Worthier Title, but at the same time, New York enacted a statute that permits the settlor of a trust to revoke the trust when he has created a remainder in his heirs but otherwise owns all the equitable interests in the trust. [N.Y. Est. Powers & Trusts Law §6-5.9] Thus, in the context of revocation of trusts (*see supra*, §179), New York law comes to the same result reached under the Doctrine of Worthier Title, even though the Doctrine has been abolished.

Proceed to the Review Questions for Chapter II.

III. RIGHTS AND LIABILITIES OF OWNERS OF FUTURE INTERESTS

A. DISCLAIMER

1. **Disclaimer Permitted:** [§184]   Any person given or devised a possessory or future interest has the right to accept or reject the interest. An intended donee or devisee cannot be forced to accept property against his will. Almost all states have enacted disclaimer statutes, which regulate disclaimers of interests in property. Sometimes the term *"renunciation"* is used instead of "disclaimer," but the terms are synonymous.

   a. **Reasons for disclaimer:** [§185]   A person may disclaim a gift or devise for any number of reasons, but disclaimer usually happens in one of four situations: First, the donee of a life estate may disclaim in order to pass the property on to the remaindermen, who need it more. Second, the donee may disclaim to avoid being treated as owner for income and estate tax purposes, or to achieve some other tax advantage. Third, the donee may disclaim in order to prevent the donee's creditors from reaching the property. Fourth, a surviving spouse may disclaim the devises to her under a will and elect a statutory forced share.

2. **Uniform Disclaimer Acts:** [§186]   The National Conference of Commissioners on Uniform State Laws has promulgated three uniform disclaimer acts. The Uniform Disclaimer of Property Interests Act (incorporated into the Uniform Probate Code as section 2-801) is the broadest in reach and covers all transfers of property. Narrower acts include the Uniform Disclaimer of Transfers by Will, Intestacy or Appointment Act and the Uniform Disclaimer of Transfers under Nontestamentary Instruments Act. Nearly all states have enacted legislation identical with or a reasonable facsimile of one of the uniform acts. The approach taken by these acts is to dispose of the disclaimed interest as if the disclaimant had *predeceased the decedent or donor.*

   a. **Effect of disclaimer:** [§187]   Uniform Disclaimer of Property Interests Act section 4 provides: If the transferor has not provided for another disposition, the property devolves as if the disclaimant had predeceased the decedent. "Any future interest that takes effect in possession or enjoyment after the termination of the estate or interest disclaimed takes effect as if the disclaimant had died before the event determining that the taker of the property or interest had become finally ascertained and his interest is indefeasibly vested. A disclaimer relates back for all purposes to the date of death of the decedent, or of the donee of the power, or the determinative event, as the case may be." This way of treating a disclaimer, adopted in nearly all states, has an important effect on the acceleration of future interests.

   b. **Time of disclaimer:** [§188]   At common law, a disclaimer had to be made within a reasonable time. Most statutes today fix a definite time for filing disclaimers. The Uniform Disclaimer of Property Interests Act section 2 requires that the disclaimer "be delivered, as to a present interest, not later than nine [9] months after the death of the deceased owner or deceased donee of a power of appointment and, as to a future interest, not later than nine [9] months after the event determining that the taker of the property or interest has become finally ascertained and his interest is indefeasibly vested."

(1) **Internal Revenue Code:** [§189]   The Internal Revenue Code provides that the disclaimant makes a taxable gift of the property disclaimed unless the disclaimer is made either nine months after the decedent's death or nine months after the disclaimant reaches 21, whichever is later. [I.R.C. §2518(b)]

3. **Effect on Future Interest:** [§190]   When a life estate is disclaimed, it may affect a future interest as discussed below.

a. **Acceleration**

(1) **Common law:** [§191]   Orthodox doctrine holds that vested remainders accelerate into possession when the prior life estate is disclaimed, but contingent remainders do not. [Rest. §233] In some cases, this does not result in carrying out the testator's perceived intent, so courts may pay less attention to the classification of remainders than to what they think the testator would have wanted in this situation. They may accelerate a remainder that standard classification calls contingent on the ground that the testator would have wanted acceleration. For example, where T devises property "to W for life, remainder to my children who survive W," and W disclaims, courts may accelerate the remainder (eliminating the requirement of surviving W) on the theory that T intended to postpone the remainder merely to let in the life tenant. [Estate of Reynolds, 158 N.W.2d 328 (Wis. 1968)] On the other hand, a court may refuse to accelerate a remainder where it believes the donor would not intend it. [Aberg v. First National Bank, 450 S.W.2d 403 (Tex. 1970)]

(2) **Statutes:** [§192]   The Uniform Disclaimer statutes have superseded the common law. Under these acts, a disclaimant is treated *for all purposes* as having predeceased the decedent. Thus, remainders contingent upon surviving the life tenant who disclaims accelerate on the theory that the life tenant is dead. Similarly, where a contingent remainder is created in the issue of the life tenant who has no issue, and the life tenant disclaims, the life tenant is treated as having predeceased the decedent without issue. The remainder to the life tenant's issue, if later born, cannot take effect. [*In re* Estate of Gilbert, 156 Misc. 2d 379 (1992)]

b. **Sequestration:** [§193]   At common law, if a surviving spouse elected to disclaim what was given her by will and take a statutory forced share against the will, the principle of sequestration might apply. The principle is this: Unless the testator indicates to the contrary, any interest disclaimed by the spouse will be sequestered and used for the benefit of those harmed by the election to take against the will. [Rest. §234]

(1) **Example:** T devises Blackacre (worth $20,000) to W for life, remainder to B. T devises his residuary estate (worth $100,000) to C. W disclaims the life estate and elects to take her statutory forced share of one-third of T's estate ($40,000). W's share is paid out of the residuary estate devised

to C. In an attempt to compensate C for the loss caused by W's election, W's life estate in $20,000 is sequestered for C. C is entitled to possession of Blackacre during W's life. B is neither enriched nor harmed by W's election and the sequestration of W's life estate for C. [Sellick v. Sellick, 173 N.W. 609 (Mich. 1919)]

(2) **Modern disclaimer legislation:** [§194]   Under modern disclaimer legislation, W's disclaimer is related back to T's death *for all purposes*, and W is treated as having predeceased T. B's remainder accelerates into possession. Hence, modern disclaimer legislation apparently has abolished the principle of sequestration.

B. TRANSFERABILITY [§195]

The transferability of possibilities of reverter and rights of entry was dealt with earlier, at §§47, 55-58, and is omitted here. The following discussion focuses on the transferability of other future interests.

1. **Assignment During Life**

   a. **Vested future interests:** [§196]   Vested remainders and reversions are assignable by inter vivos conveyance. They have always been thought of as "things" capable of assignment.

   b. **Contingent remainders and executory interests**

      (1) **Common law:** [§197]   At common law, contingent interests, which were thought of not as "interests" or as "things" but as "merely possibilities of becoming things," were not assignable. In addition, transfer of these interests was thought to stir up litigation; it was a form of maintenance.

         (a) **Exceptions:** [§198]   There were three exceptions to the rule of nonassignability:

            1) **Release:** [§199]   A contingent interest can be released to the holder of the interest that will be divested if the contingency occurs. This avoids possible litigation, rather than stirring it up.

            2) **Estoppel:** [§200]   If an owner of a contingent interest assigns it by warranty deed and the interest later vests, the owner-assignor is estopped to plead that he owned no interest at the time of the conveyance, and the grantee acquires the interest.

            3) **Valuable consideration:** [§201]   If the transfer is for a valuable consideration, the transfer is enforceable in equity as a *contract to transfer* the interest when it vests and becomes assignable. If the interest vests, equity gives specific performance.

         (b) **Still followed:** [§202]   A few states still follow the old common law view that contingent interests are inalienable, subject to the three exceptions noted above. These states apparently include Arkansas, Georgia, Illinois, Indiana, Tennessee, and possibly others. In a few states, future interests contingent as to "event" are assignable inter vivos, but future interests contingent as to "person" are not.

(2) **Modern law:** [§203]   In a large majority of states, contingent remainders and executory interests are assignable by an inter vivos conveyance. A contingent interest is today recognized as an existing estate and is not a mere expectancy. The modern trend is to make all interests in property alienable. [Rest. §162]

2. **Transfer at Death:** [§204]   Reversions, remainders, and executory interests are descendible in the same manner as possessory interests. Future interests in land descend to the owner's heirs. Future interests in personal property are distributed to the owner's next of kin. Of course, any future interest contingent upon the owner's surviving to the time of possession is not descendible. Reversions, remainders, and executory interests are devisable on the principle that whatever is descendible is devisable.

3. **Creditors' Rights**

   a. **General principle:** [§205]   The general principle is that creditors can reach whatever interests in property a person can voluntarily alienate. This general principle applies to future interests, so that the law stated immediately above is relevant in determining creditors' rights. The fact that the future interest may bring little on judicial sale is usually deemed irrelevant. In some states there are deviations from this general principle, noted below.

   b. **Vested interests:** [§206]   Vested interests, including defeasibly vested interests, are transferable, and therefore, a judgment creditor can reach vested interests and sell them to pay the judgment.

   c. **Contingent interests:** [§207]   If contingent interests are alienable under state law, creditors can reach them. If the state follows the common law rule (contingent interests alienable only by release, by estoppel, or for a valuable consideration), contingent interests cannot be reached by creditors.

   d. **Bankruptcy:** [§208]   Prior to 1978, the Federal Bankruptcy Act provided that creditors of a bankrupt could reach any interest that the bankrupt could by any means transfer. Thus, contingent remainders were transferred to the trustee in bankruptcy if they were alienable, but not if they were inalienable. [*In re* Landis, 41 F.2d 700 (7th Cir. 1930)] The 1978 Bankruptcy Act abolished the test of alienability and provides that creditors can reach the "estate" of the debtor, which is defined to include "all legal and equitable interests of the debtor in property." [Federal Bankruptcy Act of 1978, 11 U.S.C. §541] Hence, all vested and contingent future interests are included in the bankrupt's estate, regardless of their alienability under local law, with one big exception. If the future interests are in a spendthrift trust, and the spendthrift trust is immune to creditors under local law, the future interests are not in the bankrupt's estate.

C. TAXATION

1. **Federal Estate Taxation:** [§209]   The federal government levies a tax upon the estate of a decedent who dies owning a *taxable estate* in excess of $600,000. The

taxable estate of a decedent means the *gross estate* minus debts and various deductions. The decedent's gross estate includes all property owned by the decedent at death *that passes by will or intestacy*. Included is the value of any future interest transferable (or transmissible) by the owner of the future interest. [I.R.C. §2033]

a. **Example:** O conveys a fund in trust "to A for life, remainder to B for life, remainder to C in fee simple." While A is alive, B dies. Upon B's death, the value of B's remainder for life is not included in B's federal gross estate because it is not a transmissible interest. No tax is payable. While A is alive, C dies. Upon C's death, the value of C's remainder in fee simple *is included* in C's federal gross estate because C can transmit the remainder to his heirs or devisees. A tax may be payable if C owns sufficient property to incur estate taxation.

b. **Transmissibility controls taxation:** [§210] The classification of a future interest as vested or contingent is irrelevant to federal estate taxation. The key to taxation is *transmissibility*, not whether the interest is vested or contingent. A transmissible contingent future interest is subject to federal estate taxation.

   (1) **Example:** O conveys a fund in trust "to A for life, then to B, but if B does not survive A, to C." Under standard classification, B has a vested remainder subject to divestment by C's executory interest. While A and B are alive, C dies intestate. C's executory interest passes to C's heirs, and C's executory interest is subject to federal estate taxation. While A is alive, B dies. B's defeasibly vested remainder is not subject to federal estate taxation at B's death because it is not transmissible to B's heirs or devisees. It is divested by C's heirs at B's death.

c. **Estate planning precept:** [§211] An estate planning precept is: *Never create a future interest transmissible at death.* Because of the possibility that the owner of a future interest may die before the interest becomes possessory, a transmissible future interest should not be created if federal estate taxation is a worry. Hence, estate planners usually make every future interest contingent upon surviving to the time of possession. Thus: O conveys a fund in trust "to A for life, then to B if B survives A; and if B does not survive A, to C if C survives A; and if B and C do not survive A, to D if D survives A." At the death of B, C, and D during A's life, no federal estate taxation will become payable.

d. **Valuation of a future interest:** [§212] When the value of a future interest is included in a decedent's federal gross estate, how is it valued? Suppose O conveys $100,000 in trust to pay the income to A for life, and on A's death to pay the principal to B. Subsequently B dies. What is the value of B's remainder?

   (1) **How to value a remainder:** [§213] To value a remainder we must know the number of years the right to receive the sum will be deferred. Since we do not know how long the life tenant will actually live, we assume the life tenant will die at the time predicted by a life expectancy (mortality) table. Mortality tables are published by the Internal Revenue Service. Assume that the trust fund is worth $100,000 today, and that A has a life estate and B a remainder. Assume also an interest rate of 6%.

How do we apportion this $100,000 present value between A's and B's interests? First, as for A, what is the present value of the right to receive $6,000 annually (6% of $100,000) for the life tenant's life expectancy? We seek a sum which, invested for the life tenant's life expectancy at 6%, will pay $6,000 for the given number of years and exhaust itself on final payment—in short, the price of an annuity. To simplify the problem let us assume A has a life expectancy of only three years. The right to receive $1 a year from now is not worth $1 now, but only $1 less the amount of interest that could be earned on it. Assuming a 6% rate of interest, the present value of $1 due at the end of one year is 94¢; the present value of $1 due at the end of two years is 89¢; and the present value of the right to receive $1 at the end of three years is 84¢. The present value of the right to receive $1 at the end of each of the three years is the sum of 94¢, 89¢ and 84¢, which is $2.67. Now what is the present value of the right to receive $6,000 for three years? $6,000 × 2.67 = $16,020, which is the present value of the life estate. The present value of a life estate and the present value of a remainder together equal the present value of the whole property. The remainder has a present worth of $83,980. The Internal Revenue Service provides tables by which future interests are valued, depending upon the age of the life tenant.

2. **Federal Gift Taxation:** [§214]   If a person owning a future interest makes a gift of it, such gift is subject to federal gift taxation. The future interest may not be transmissible at death, and hence excluded from taxation at death. If it is given away during life, however, it is subject to gift tax. It is valued as all future interests are valued, as illustrated above.

   a. **Example:** O conveys a fund in trust "to A for life, then to B for life." While A is alive, B conveys her life estate to C. The value of B's remainder is subject to federal gift tax.

D. FUTURE INTERESTS IN PERSONAL PROPERTY

1. **Future Interests in Consumables:** [§215]   Generally speaking, future interests can be created in any kind of property, but some kinds of property raise special problems. One kind of property in which it may be difficult to create a future interest is a consumable. Suppose that O bequeaths a case of fine wine "to A for life, remainder to B." The courts have held that a bequest of a consumable, such as wine, transfers absolute ownership to the intended life tenant, A, and that B takes nothing. A consumable is not limited to digestibles. A consumable is something destroyed by normal use. [Underwood v. Underwood, 50 So. 305 (Ala. 1909)]

   a. **Reasons:** [§216]   The reasons for the rule are that the courts are trying to avoid difficult problems about how much the life tenant can consume and are seeking some way to make the consumable exchangeable. It might make more sense to imply in the life tenant either a power to consume it all or to sell it, preserving the remainder in what is left. There seems to be no reason why B, in the above example, should not take whatever wine remains at A's death.

   b. **Power of sale:** [§217]   If the life tenant has a power of sale, express or implied, the remainder in a consumable is valid. It is inferred from an express power of sale that the grantor wanted the life tenant either to consume the item or sell it and use the proceeds. The usual case where the courts imply a power of sale is that of a residuary gift that includes consumables. For example, suppose that T, a farmer, devises the residue of his property to A for life, and the residue includes farm implements, chickens, hay, and other items found on a farm. A court may imply a power of sale and transfer the remainder to replacement property. Or a court may give the life tenant absolute ownership of the consumables.

2. **Absolute Gift with Unrestricted Power to Destroy Future Interest:** [§218] Where there is a bequest of personal property to an individual *absolutely*, with the unrestricted power of absolute disposal, any gift over of what remains at the individual's death is void. The purported gift over is thought to be repugnant to absolute ownership given the first taker. The rule is sometimes called the *rule of repugnancy*. [Sterner v. Nelson, 314 N.W.2d 263 (Neb. 1982); Fox v. Snow, 76 A.2d 877 (N.J. 1950)]

   a. **Example:** T bequeaths her savings account "to A, and if there is any amount left on deposit at A's death, then to B." A takes absolute ownership of the savings account; the gift over to B is void.

   b. **Life estate with power of alienation:** [§219] If the first taker is given a life estate with power to convey or appoint a fee simple, the rule of repugnancy does not apply. A gift over (a remainder) after a life estate is not repugnant to the life estate. To avoid the rule, courts sometimes construe what appears to be an absolute gift to A to be a life estate in A.

3. **Security for Personal Property**

   a. **Testator's intent controls:** [§220] When a testator bequeaths personal property to a legatee and creates a future interest in it, the possessory owner may be able to destroy the personal property or transfer it to a bona fide purchaser, destroying the future interest. To protect the future interest, the testator may require that security (a bond) be put up by the possessory owner. The testator's intention controls. If the testator's intent is unclear, the courts may apply the following rules, though the authorities are in some conflict.

      (1) **Specific articles:** [§221] Where specific articles are left to a legatee for life, security is not required unless there is a showing of danger of loss or injury to the property.

      (2) **General bequest:** [§222] Where the property is money, negotiable instruments, or other property easily convertible into money, the possessory owner must put up security even without a showing of danger.

   b. **Judicial discretion:** [§223] Most authorities regard the matter of exacting security as discretionary with the court. A variety of factors are considered, including the kind of property, the value of the property, the financial solvency of the possessory owner, the power, if any, of the possessory owner to consume or to appoint, the hostility of the possessory owner to the future interest owner, the residence of the possessory owner in or out of state, and the probable duration of the possessory interest. [Scott v. Scott, 114 N.W. 881 (Iowa 1908)]

(1) **Language in will:** [§224]   Language in a will indicating that the possessory owner is to have wide power over the property may indicate an intention that security not be exacted. For example, a bequest of personal property to testator's wife "for her own individual benefit and support without any hindrance on the part of any person" has been held to indicate that a bond was not required. [Colburn v. Burlingame, 190 Cal. 697 (1923)]

Proceed to the Review Questions for Chapter III.

IV. CONSTRUCTION OF INSTRUMENTS

A. BROAD RULES OF CONSTRUCTION

1. **In General:** [§225]   Rules of construction are laid down by courts to use in construing ambiguous instruments. They are designed to carry out the average person's intent and, if that intent is difficult to ascertain, to further other policies such as promoting alienability of property. Certain broad rules of construction appear in the cases. These are of limited value where they give way to more specific rules of construction.

2. **Preference Against Partial Intestacy:** [§226]   It is usually assumed that a person who makes a will intends to dispose of all property owned. Thus, the will is construed so as to avoid intestacy as to any part of the testator's estate. This maxim arose in English ecclesiastical courts, which had jurisdiction over wills of personal property. Because failure to make a will (given orally to a priest in early days) was thought to indicate that a person died without a last confession, ecclesiastical courts naturally presumed against intestacy.

   a. **Heir protected:** [§227]   An opposite maxim—"it takes express language to disinherit an heir"—is sometimes voiced when the court wishes to find an intestacy. This maxim grew up in English law courts with jurisdiction over wills of land. The law courts had a strong preference for protecting "the heir" (the oldest son), a preference which, together with primogeniture, reinforced the strength of the upper class.

3. **Preference for Maximum Validity:** [§228]   If a court has a choice between a valid construction and an invalid construction, it should choose the valid construction. Unhappily, this preference is not always displayed in cases involving the Rule Against Perpetuities.

4. **Preference for Blood Relatives:** [§229]   If an instrument is ambiguous, it will be construed to give property to blood relatives rather than to strangers. Equal distribution among persons similarly related to the transferor is also preferred.

5. **Preference for Legislative Scheme:** [§230]   When distribution is to be made to members of a class, a court may prefer to distribute to those members of the class as would take, and in such shares as they would receive, under the applicable law of intestate succession. The theory is that the legislature is the best body to determine the average person's intent with respect to who comes within a class and how much each gets.

6. **Preference for Technical Meaning:** [§231]   When an instrument is drawn by a lawyer, it is presumed that the words are used in their technical sense. When an instrument is drawn by a nonlawyer, this presumption is not very strong.

7. **Preference for General Plan:** [§232]   Where the transferor indicates a *general plan* for distribution, the court may interpret words in an ungrammatical or unusual way to carry out the plan. A general plan usually involves a plan for a per stirpes distribution of property among the testator's issue or a plan for keeping property within the bloodline.

B. PREFERENCE FOR VESTED INTERESTS

1. **Common Law:** [§233]   If an interest might be classified as vested or contingent, the common law preferred to classify it as vested. Courts found that vested remainders had certain advantages (*see supra,* §§95-99). They were alienable. They accelerated into possession when the life estate ended, thus preserving continuity of possession. They could not be destroyed by the life tenant acting together with the grantor. They were not subject to the Rule Against Perpetuities, which could play havoc with an estate plan. Hence, the courts preferred vested interests. This preference for vested remainders gave rise to a number of techniques of classification designed to effectuate the preference.

2. **The Surplusage Technique:** [§234]   To vest a gift, a court may strike out language in the instrument deemed mere *surplusage*. If the testator means the same thing without the included language, the language may be called surplusage. For example, if T devises property "to A for life, and then *on A's death* to B," the words "on A's death" merely refer to the termination of the life estate and do not state a condition precedent. Accordingly, B takes an indefeasibly vested remainder.

   a. **Condition stated both as condition precedent and divesting contingency:** [§235]   If an *age* condition attached to a gift to an *individual* is stated both as a condition precedent and as a condition subsequent, the statement of condition precedent is surplusage and is struck out. Suppose that T devises property "to A for life, then to B if B reaches 21, and if B does not reach 21 to C." The condition of B reaching 21 has been stated twice, both as a condition precedent and as a divesting contingency. The first statement, "if B reaches 21" can be ignored as surplusage. The testator's intent is the same if these words are struck out. But by striking these words, B is given a vested remainder subject to divestment, and not a contingent remainder. [Edwards v. Hammond, 83 Eng. Rep. 614 (1683); Hoblit v. Howser, 170 N.E. 257 (Ill. 1930)]

      (1) **Not applicable to class gifts:** [§236]   The surplusage rule of *Edward v. Hammond, supra,* does not apply to class gifts. With class gifts, it is said that the age condition is an *essential part of the description of the beneficiaries* and thus cannot be deemed surplusage. Thus suppose a gift "to A for life, then to such of A's children as reach 21, and if none reach 21, to B," the remainder to A's children is contingent because reaching 21 is an essential part of the description of the beneficiaries. The gift is not to the children of A but only to those who reach 21. A's children have a contingent remainder. [Festing v. Allen, 152 Eng. Rep. 1204 (1843)]

      (2) **Survivorship conditions:** [§237]   The surplusage theory of *Edwards v. Hammond* could logically apply to any condition stated both as a condition precedent and a condition subsequent. Nonetheless, courts have refused to extend the theory beyond age contingencies stated twice, on the ground that to do so would vest a large number of contingent remainders and make classification more unpredictable. Thus, in a gift "to A for life, then to B if B survives A, and if B does not survive A, to C," B has a contingent remainder. The words "if B survives A" (a survivorship condition), unlike "if B reaches 21" (an age condition), cannot be treated as surplusage.

3. **Power of Revocation or Appointment:** [§238]   A remainder limited in default of exercise of a power of revocation or appointment is not contingent upon nonexercise of the power. The exercise of the power is looked upon as a divesting event, not as a condition precedent. Thus, in a revocable trust, future interests are classified as if the power to revoke did not exist. [First National Bank of Cincinnati v. Tenney, 138 N.E.2d 15 (Ohio 1956)] Similarly, if T devises property "to A for life, remainder as A by will appoints, and in default of appointment to B," B takes a vested remainder subject to divestment by A's exercise of the power of appointment. If B dies before A, B's remainder passes to B's heirs or devisees. [Doe *dem.* Willis v. Martin, 100 Eng. Rep. 822 (1790)]

C.   REQUIREMENT OF SURVIVAL

1. **Basic Rule:** [§239]   The basic rule is that if there are no express words requiring the taker of a future interest to survive to the time of possession, none will be implied. This owes something to the preference for vested interests and something to the belief that the rule carries out the average transferor's intent. [First National Bank of Bar Harbor v. Anthony, 557 A.2d 957 (Me. 1989); Boone County National Bank v. Edson, 760 S.W.2d 108 (Mo. 1988)]

   a. **Example:** T devises Blackacre "to A for life, remainder to B." B dies before A. B's remainder passes under B's will or, if B dies intestate, to B's heirs.

   b. **Unrelated condition precedent:** [§240]   Suppose that T devises property "to A for life, then to A's children who survive A, and if A dies without children, to B." B then dies. A then dies without children. Does B's estate take? Yes. There is no condition expressed requiring B to survive A. The presence of an unrelated condition precedent (A dying without children) is not a basis for implying an additional condition precedent requiring B to survive A. [Estate of Ferry, 55 Cal. 2d 776 (1961); Hofing v. Willis, 201 N.E.2d 852 (Ill. 1964); Tapley v. Dill, 217 S.W.2d 369 (Mo. 1949); First National Bank of Cincinnati v. Tenney, *supra*; Bomberger's Estate, 32 A.2d 729 (Pa. 1943)]

      (1) **Minority view:** [§241]   In a few states, there is an implied condition of survival on a *class gift* where there is a condition precedent unrelated to survival. Thus, in the above example, if the gift over had not been to B but to B's children, a condition of surviving A would be implied. However, this is distinctly a minority view. [Lawson v. Lawson, 148 S.E.2d 546 (N.C. 1966)]

2. **Class Gifts**

   a. **Gifts to single-generational classes:** [§242]   The basic rule is applied in classes composed of a single generation such as to gifts to "children" or "brothers and sisters." Thus suppose that T devises property "to A for life, remainder to A's children." A has a child, B, who survives T but predeceases A. A has another child, C, who survives A. At A's death the property is equally divided between B's estate and C. There is no requirement that a child survive to the time of possession in order to take. [*In re* Stanford's Estate, 49 Cal. 2d 120 (1957); *but cf. In re* Trust of Walker, 116 N.W.2d 106 (Wis. 1962)]

b. **Gifts to multi-generational classes:** [§243]   Where a gift is to a class that may be composed of different generations, survivorship to the time of possession is required. Thus, suppose that T devises property "to A for life, remainder to A's issue." Contrast the remainder to "issue" with a remainder to A's "children." Where the class gift is to "issue," which includes several generations, survivorship to the time of possession is required. The word "issue" or "descendants" connotes a requirement of survival, and any of A's issue who predecease A do not take. The theory is that if a child predeceases A, the testator wants such child's issue to take in his place. [Altman v. Rider, 291 S.W.2d 577 (Ky. 1956); Weller v. Sokol, 318 A.2d 193 (Md. 1974)]

c. **Gifts to "heirs":** [§244]   Suppose that T devises property "to A for life, remainder to A's heirs" (and the Rule in Shelley's Case, *see supra*, §145, is abolished). Since no one is heir of the living, A's heirs are ascertained at A's death and must be living at that time. (Other rules relating to gifts to heirs are discussed *infra*, §§299-305.)

d. **Gifts to "surviving" persons:** [§245]   Suppose that T devises property "to my wife for life, then to my *surviving* children." It is not clear whether the children must survive the testator or the wife. The majority of cases hold that the children must be surviving at the time of distribution. If any child dies before the wife, leaving issue, such issue do not share. [*In re* Gautier's Will, 3 N.Y.2d 502 (1957)] But some courts hold that if a child predeceases the wife *with issue*, "surviving" means surviving testator. This construction leads to equality of distribution among the lines of descent, so that one line is not cut out. [Nass' Estate, 182 A. 401 (Pa. 1936)]

3. **Divesting Language Read Strictly:** [§246]   If a vested remainder subject to divestment is created, courts ordinarily read the divesting language strictly as written and do not expand it to cause divestment in events other than those stated. Where, for example, the testator devises property "to A for life, then to A's children, the issue of any then deceased child to take such child's share," the divesting gift to issue operates to divest a child *only* if a child dies with issue. Any child of A who dies *without issue* before A is not divested of his share. [Security Trust Co. v. Irvine, 93 A.2d 528 (Del. 1953); *In re* Krooss, 302 N.Y. 424 (1951); Houston Estate, 201 A.2d 592 (Pa. 1964)]

a. **Example:** As in the example above, T devises property "to A for life, then to A's children, the issue of any then deceased child to take such child's share." A has three children, B, C, and D. B dies before A leaving issue; B's vested remainder is divested by B's issue. C dies before A without issue; C's vested remainder passes to C's estate. D survives A. At A's death the property goes in one-third shares each to B's issue, C's estate, and D. Note that C can devise her third to whomever she wishes, but B, who leaves issue, has no power to deprive his issue of a third. [Warner v. Warner, 237 F.2d 561 (D.C. Cir. 1956)]

4. **Alternative Dispositions to A *or* Her Children:** [§247]   Where there is a devise of a remainder "to A *or* her children," the word "or" implies that A must survive the life tenant. If she does not, her children take in her place. If A predeceases the life tenant without children, A's estate does not take. The property goes to the residuary devisee or the testator's heirs. [Old Colony Trust Co. v. Barker, 126 N.E.2d 188 (Mass. 1955); Robertson v. Robertson, 48 N.E.2d 29 (Mass. 1943)] *Note well:*

Carefully *distinguish* a remainder "to A's children, the issue of any child who predeceases the life tenant to take her share," which does require a child to survive the life tenant, and is divested only if a child dies with issue, *from* a remainder "to A's children or their issue," which requires a child to survive the life tenant.

5. **Divide-and-Pay-Over Rule:** [§248]   Suppose that T bequeaths property in trust "to pay the income to A for life, then to divide and pay over the corpus to A's children." Where there is no language of gift except a direction to the trustee to divide and pay over, some cases have held there is an implied requirement that it be divided among A's children surviving at distribution. [*In re* Crane, 164 N.Y. 71 (1900)] The great majority of jurisdictions have rejected the divide-and-pay-over rule.

6. **Apt Language:** [§249]   Where the testator somewhere else in the will expressly requires survivorship with respect to another gift, there is a presumption that testator knows how to use apt language to require survivorship. Hence, when the testator requires survival elsewhere, but does not expressly require survival for the gift at hand, survivorship is not required. The inference is that testator intends something different when he shows he knows how to require survivorship and does not do so. [Old Colony Trust Co. v. Tufts, 168 N.E.2d 86 (Mass. 1960)]

   a. **Example:** T devises Blackacre "to A for life, then to A's children who survive A." T devises Whiteacre "to B for life, then to B's children." B's children do not have to survive B in order to take because in the devise of Blackacre T has shown he knows how to require survivorship, but T did not require it in the devise of Whiteacre.

7. **Age Conditions:** [§250]   *Clobberie's Case*, 86 Eng. Rep. 476 (1677), laid down three rules of construction that are widely followed today.

   a. **Gift "at" a designated age:** [§251]   If T bequeaths property "to A at 21," A will take nothing unless A lives to 21. There is an implied requirement of survivorship by the use of the word "at." Hence "at 21" equals "if A reaches 21."

   b. **Gift "payable at" a designated age:** [§252]   If T bequeaths property "to A, payable at 21" or "to A, to be paid at 21," there is no implied condition that A must live to 21. The use of the word "payable" means attainment of age 21 relates merely to the time when possession is to be enjoyed. If A dies under 21, A's administrator is entitled to the property at A's death, unless someone would be harmed by such accelerated payment. If someone else is entitled to the income until A reaches 21, for example, A's administrator is not entitled to the property until the time A would have reached 21 had A lived. A's gift is said to be *vested with payment postponed*. [*In re* Mansur's Will, 127 A. 297 (Vt. 1925)]

   c. **Gift of income vests the principal:** [§253]   If T bequeaths property "to A at 21, with income to be paid to A in the meantime," A does not have to survive to 21 in order to take the property. The gift of the *entire income* indicates T was postponing possession of the corpus only, and did not intend to require survival for ownership of the corpus. A's gift is vested with possession postponed. [Clay v. Security Trust Co., 252 S.W.2d 906 (Ky. 1952)]

Rule	**Example**
Unless expressly required, remainderman is not required to survive to time of possession.	(1) "To A for life, remainder to B." B dies before A. B's remainder passes to B's heirs or devisees. (2) "To A for life, remainder to A's children." A has a child, B. B dies before A. B's remainder passes to B's heirs or devisees.
Exception: In a gift to multi-generational class, remainderman must survive to time of possession.	(1) "To A for life, then to A's issue." A has a child, B. B dies. B drops out of the class. B's share goes to B's children, or if B has no children, to A's other issue. (2) "To A for life, then to A's heirs." A has a child, B. B dies. B cannot be an heir of A.
A remainder contingent on an event other than survivorship is not also contingent on survivorship.	"To A for life, then to B, but if B dies before A, to C." C dies, survived by A and B. C's executory interest passes to C's heirs or devisees.
A divesting gift divests only on the event stated.	"To A for life, then to A's children, the issue of any deceased child to take such child's share." A has two children, B and C. B dies before A without issue. B is not divested. B's share passes to B's estate. C dies before A with issue. C's share is divested by C's issue.
A gift to A payable at a given age is vested with possession postponed; A's heirs or devisees take if A dies under the age.	"$5,000 to A payable at 21." After the gift is made, A dies at 17. A's estate is entitled to the $5,000.

(1) **Amount for support:** [§254]   If A is not given all the income until 21 but is given only the amount needed for support, and the trustee can withhold the rest, most cases hold that the bequest of principal is vested with possession postponed. The gift of *some* income indicates an intent to vest the gift of principal immediately upon testator's death. [Coddington v. Stone, 9 S.E.2d 420 (N.C. 1940)] However, if A dies under 21 A's administrator is not entitled to get the money until A would have reached the designated age, had A lived. If the whole income is given, the administrator is entitled to the principal at A's death under 21.

(2) **Discretionary trust for a class:** [§255]   If a trustee is directed to pay income to members of a *class* as the trustee determines until the members of the class reach a designated age (a spray trust), *Clobberie's Case, supra*, does not apply. There is no intent to confer a present benefit on any one person. [*In re* Parker, 16 Ch. D. 44 (1880)]

8. **Uniform Probate Code:** [§256]   In 1990, the Uniform Probate Code ("UPC") was amended to effect a revolutionary change in the law of future interests. New section 2-707 provides that, unless the trust instrument provides otherwise, *first*, all future interests *in trust* are contingent on the beneficiary's surviving the distribution date. The common law's ancient preference for vested interests is reversed. *Second*, if the remainderman does not survive in the distribution date, a substitute gift is created in the remainderman's then surviving descendants. If the remainderman has no surviving descendants, the remainder fails, and the property passes on the life tenant's death to the testator's residuary devisees or heirs.

   a. **Reasons for change:** [§257]   The stated reason for making all future interests in trusts contingent upon survivorship is to avoid the cost of having such interests pass through the owners' probate estates. (*See supra*, §204.) This change, however, deprives the remainderman of the power to select who will take the property upon the life tenant's death.

   b. **Anti-lapse idea applied to remainders:** [§258]   Under the law of wills, if a devisee predeceases the testator, anti-lapse statutes give the devise to the devisee's descendants if the devisee bears a particular relationship to the testator (usually kindred). The UPC applies the anti-lapse idea to trust remainders, changing the requirement that a beneficiary survive the *testator* to a requirement that a remainderman survive to the *date of distribution* and applying it to all trust remainders and not just to remainders given the testator's kindred. [U.P.C. §2-707] This section applies to reversions as well as to remainders in trust, but not to legal future interests.

   c. **Complex statute:** [§259]   Because of the enormous variety of complicated trusts possible, section 2-707 invents a whole new future interests vocabulary to determine which of alternative future interests will be given effect under a variety of circumstances. Its complexities cannot be summarized here. They are explained in seven pages of closely analytical reasoning in the Official Comments. Because section 2-707 upends the law of remainders, creating a new body of law for lawyers to master for the future and leaving the old law applicable to existing instruments, it may not be popular with lawyers. It is too early to tell how many states will enact section 2-707.

D.   GIFTS OVER ON DEATH WITHOUT ISSUE

1. **The Ambiguities:** [§260] The ambiguities that lurk in the phrase "die without issue" are best seen by starting with a hypothetical devise. Suppose that O conveys property "to A and his heirs, but if A dies without issue, to B and her heirs." The ambiguities can be divided into two questions: (i) Did O intend an *indefinite failure of issue construction* or a *definite failure of issue construction*? (ii) Assuming the latter, did O intend a *successive* or *substitutional construction*?

2. **Indefinite and Definite Failure of Issue**

   a. **Indefinite failure of issue:** [§261] Indefinite failure of issue means, in the above example, whenever A and all of A's descendants are dead. Or, to put it differently, B or B's successor will take whenever A's bloodline runs out. This indefinite event may happen at A's death or hundreds of years from now or never. Under the indefinite failure of issue construction, Adam and Eve are not dead without issue because their descendants are still alive.

      (1) **Historical perspective:** [§262] The English courts strongly preferred the indefinite failure of issue construction, a preference understandable in light of English history. The phrase "if A dies without issue" was commonly used in the medieval period to introduce a remainder following a fee tail. Thus O, head of the family, might convey Blackacre "to A, my eldest son, and the heirs of his body, and if A dies without issue, to B, my second son, and his heirs." It was common for a parent to want the land to shift to a second son if the eldest son's line ran out. In this context it was clear that "if A dies without issue" meant if A's issue becomes extinct. The courts, having given the phrase that meaning, did not change it when the context was different. Words had fixed, plain meanings in those days. If you used a word, you used it with the fixed meaning assigned to it.

      (2) **Modern status:** [§263] The presumption of indefinite failure of issue has been rejected by statute or decision in almost all states. It is absurd today to assume that a person is making a gift over when the donee's bloodline expires. A statute abolishing the presumption of indefinite failure of issue may not be retroactive, however, so the old law may still be relevant. For example, a 1957 Massachusetts case applied the indefinite failure construction to a will of a testator who died in 1855! [Hayes v. Hammond, 143 N.E.2d 693 (Mass. 1957)]

   b. **Definite failure of issue:** [§264] Definite failure of issue means failure of issue at the death of the ancestor. In the above example, if A dies leaving issue at his death, B never takes. If A dies without leaving issue alive at his death, B takes. This construction is preferred in almost all states.

3. **Successive or Substitutional Construction:** [§265] If the court applies a definite failure of issue construction (almost certain today), the court must next decide between a successive or substitutional construction. Refer back to the example of "to A, but if A dies without issue, to B." A *successive construction* means that A and then B, *in succession*, take the property if at A's death A leaves no issue. A *substitutional* construction means that either A *or* B will take the property but not each in succession. If A's interest becomes possessory, B can never take. These two constructions are most easily understood by reference to two hypothetical cases.

a. **Gift over following fee simple:** [§266]   Suppose that T devises property "to A, but if A dies without issue, to B." This may mean "to A, but if A dies *before testator* without issue, to B," or it may mean "to A, but if A dies *before or after testator* without issue, to B." The first meaning is the *substitutional* construction, which views the gift over in this context as a substitute for lapse. If A survives T or leaves issue surviving T, B can never take. [Goldberger v. Goldberger, 102 A.2d 338 (Del. 1954)] The second meaning is the *successive* construction. B will succeed A in possession if A dies without issue after T dies. The substitutional construction makes the property more readily alienable, but appears to defeat the intent of the testator. The Restatement prefers the successive construction in this context [Rest. §267], but the states are split on which is preferable in this context.

b. **Gift over following life estate:** [§267]   Suppose that T devises property "to A for life, then to B, but if B dies without issue, to C." This may mean "if B dies *before A* without issue," which is a *substitutional* construction. C is substituted for B if B dies without issue before A dies. If B survives A, B takes an absolute fee simple. [Pyne v. Pyne, 154 F.2d 297 (D.C. Cir. 1946)] Or the above devise may mean "if B dies *before or after A* without issue," which is a *successive* construction. Under the latter meaning A, and then B, and then C may become possessors in succession. The substitutional construction makes the property marketable earlier, and is preferred by the Restatement. [Rest. §269] A substantial number of courts apply the successive construction in this context, however.

E.   CLASS GIFTS

1. **What Is a Class?** [§268]   A class gift is a gift to beneficiaries as members of an identifiable group and not to the beneficiaries individually. Class gifts raise unusual problems and have special rules applicable in certain situations. Rules of construction have evolved with respect to class gift terms to identify who is in the class and how much each class member takes. These rules can be overcome by the language of the instrument and also by circumstantial evidence.

   a. **Class designation only:** [§269]   A gift to a group of persons described only by a class term presumptively creates a class gift. *Examples*: "To the children of A," "to the issue of B," "to the nephews and nieces of C."

   b. **Class and individual designations:** [§270]   Suppose that T devises property "to A, B, and C, the children of my sister S." T has described the beneficiaries individually ("A, B, and C"), and has also used a class term ("children of S"). If T was group-minded, and intended the consequences of a class gift, the devise is to a class. Since T has used individual names, however, the usual presumption, barring additional circumstances, is that T intended a gift to A, B, and C individually.

   c. **Individual designations only:** [§271]   Suppose that T describes the beneficiaries only by their individual names, A, B, and C, and does not use a class designation. Ordinarily this is not a class gift. But circumstantial evidence may show that T intended the consequences of a class gift. If so, the gift may be treated as a gift to a class, even though no class term is used, particularly where the beneficiaries form a *natural group*, such as being in the same generation in relation to the testator.

(1) **Exact shares:** [§272]   The specification of the exact share each beneficiary is to take (*e.g.*, "one-third each to A, B, and C") is evidence that a class gift was not intended. [Dawson v. Yucus, 239 N.E.2d 305 (Ill. 1968)]

2. **Gift to "Children":** [§273]   Where there is a gift to "children" of A, the primary meaning of the term includes only immediate offspring of A, absent any expressions of contrary intent. Hence, presumptively, grandchildren and more remote descendants of A are excluded. [Matter of Gustafson, 74 N.Y.2d 448 (1989); Rest. 2d §§25.1, 25.7] Of course, if the remainder given to A's children is not subject to surviving the life tenant, a child who predeceases the life tenant can devise his share of the remainder to his child (a grandchild of A) or pass it by intestacy.

a. **Adopted children**

(1) **Stranger-to-the-adoption rule:** [§274]   In the nineteenth century, when adoption first was legally permitted, courts laid down a rule that although adopted children were included in a gift by the adoptor to his or her children, adopted children were presumptively not included in a gift to the adoptor's children by someone other than the adoptor (by a stranger to the adoption). The discrimination against adopted children rested both upon the inherited reverence for blood descent and upon a social stigma inflicted upon adoptees.

(2) **Modern law:** [§275]   The stranger-to-the-adoption rule has been repudiated in almost all states. But this repudiation has taken a tortuous route in some states, with courts changing their minds only as to prospective instruments, leaving the old law applicable to earlier instruments. Legislatures also frequently intervened to change the law, sometimes prospectively only, but sometimes also retroactively. With respect to older wills and trusts, it may be necessary to examine local law on the date the instrument came into effect. Today, with respect to any new instrument, adopted children of A are presumptively included in a gift to the children of A in virtually all states. [Estate of Coe, 201 A.2d 571 (N.J. 1964); *cf.* Rest. 2d §25.4—including adoptive children only if "raised" by A]

(3) **Adult adoptee:** [§276]   The courts are split over whether a person adopted by A as an adult is included in a gift to the children of A. Some hold that the word "children" includes persons adopted at any age, even as adults. Others hold "children" includes only children adopted when they are minors. [Minary v. Citizens Fidelity Bank, 419 S.W.2d 340 (Ky. 1967)] The UPC includes adopted children only if the child lived while a minor as a member of the household of the adopting parent or her close relatives. [U.P.C. §2-705]

(4) **Adopted child treated as child of natural parent:** [§277]   Where a child of A has been adopted by B, the question may arise whether a gift to the children of A includes the child adopted by B. The courts are split on the question. Extrinsic evidence of the donor's intent may be persuasive one way or the other. The Restatement provides that a gift to the children of A does not include a child of A adopted by another "if such

adoption removes the child from the broader family circle of the designated person." [Rest. 2d §25.5]

b. **Children born out of wedlock:** [§278]   At common law, an illegitimate child was considered filius nullius, the child of no one, and consequently, an illegitimate child of A did not share in a gift to the children of A. A presumption against the inclusion of nonmarital children in a gift to the children of A probably still holds in a majority of states, but the law on this is in a state of flux. It appears to be moving toward presumptively including nonmarital children. The Restatement provides that children born out of wedlock are presumptively included in a gift to the children of a designated person. [Rest. 2d §25.2]

c. **Stepchildren:** [§279]   Stepchildren of A are not included in a gift to the children of A, unless evidence shows the donor intended to include them. [Rest. 2d §25.6]

d. **Uniform Probate Code:** [§280]   The UPC provides that adopted persons and persons born out of wedlock are included in class gifts in accordance with the rules of intestate succession. Thus, if a person would take by intestacy from A, such person is treated as being a child of A for purposes of class gifts to the children of A. [U.P.C. §2-705]

3. **Gift to "Grandchildren":** [§281]   Where a gift is made to the "grandchildren" of A, presumptively this includes only grandchildren and not great-grandchildren as well. [*In re* Welles's Will, 9 N.Y.2d 277 (1961)] The same sort of restrictive construction is given to gifts to "brothers and sisters" and "nephews and nieces." The gift is limited to persons who bear the specific relationship to the designated person. [Rest. 2d §25.8]

4. **Gifts to "Issue" or "Descendants":** [§282]   Gifts to the "issue" of A or to the "descendants" of A include all descendants of A (including adopted or nonmarital children if they would be included in a gift to the children of A or to the children of A's children). The fundamental question is what share each descendant takes. The law on this varies considerably from jurisdiction to jurisdiction.

a. **Per capita distribution:** [§283]   Under English law, when a gift was made to the "issue" of A, each descendant of A—whether child, grandchild, or great-grandchild—was entitled to an equal share. The property was divided per capita among all descendants. This rule has been repudiated in virtually all American jurisdictions, which do not distribute per capita unless the gift so expressly provides. In this country, the presumption is that a per stirpes distribution is intended, though per stirpes may be defined differently from state to state. [*See* Petry v. Petry, 186 App. Div. 738 (1919)—following English per capita rule, *superseded by* N.Y. Est. Powers & Trusts Law §2-1.2—adopting per stirpes distribution]

b. **Per stirpes distribution**

(1) **Classic or English per stirpes distribution:** [§284]   In England, when property is distributed among A's issue per stirpes, the property is divided into as many equal shares as there are (i) living children of A, if any, and

(ii) deceased children of A who leave issue then living. Each living child of A is allocated one share, and the share of each deceased child who leaves issue then living is divided in the same manner. Thus, the division into stocks (or stirps) is made at the level of A's children, whether any are then alive or not, with the issue of deceased children representing them.

(a) **Example:** T devises property "to the issue of A." A had two children, B and C, both of whom predeceased T. B left one child, D, who survives T. C left two children, E and F. E predeceased T, leaving two children, G and H. Thus, there are living at T's death D (child of B), F (child of C), and G and H (children of E and grandchildren of C). The property is first divided into two shares, one for B's line and one for C's line. D takes B's one-half by representation. C's one-half is divided into two shares, one for F and one to be divided between G and H. Hence, the property goes one-half to B, one-quarter to F, and one-eighth each to G and H. This is sometimes known as a "straight" or "strict" per stirpes distribution.

(b) **Meaning of right of representation:** [§285] The phrase "by right of representation" traditionally has meant the same thing as a per stirpes distribution. Issue represent deceased parents in the same way as they do under a per stirpes distribution (however per stirpes is defined in the particular jurisdiction). But the UPC has given it a different meaning (*see infra* §290).

(c) **Wills law mirrors intestacy law:** [§286] In England, the intestacy statute divides the decedent's property into as many shares as there are children of the decedent alive or dead but leaving issue surviving the decedent (as above). The issue of any deceased child succeeds to the child's share. Thus distribution of a devise to the issue of A per stirpes calls for the same distribution as the issue of A would take if A died intestate.

(2) **Modern per stirpes distribution:** [§287] In the large majority of states in this country, the legislatures and courts have defined per stirpes in a different way. Instead of dividing the property into shares at the level of A's children, whether any are dead or alive, as the English do, the majority of American states divide the property into shares at the generational level where a descendant of A is alive. Representation then occurs below that level. In the example above, under the modern per stirpes method, the property is divided at the level of A's grandchildren, since no children of A are alive. There are three grandchildren and thus three shares. D, a living grandchild, takes one-third. F, a living grandchild, takes one-third. E's one-third is divided between G and H by representation.

(a) **Called per capita with representation:** [§288] Sometimes the modern per stirpes method of distribution is called "per capita with representation," particularly by academic writers. But judges and lawyers call it "per stirpes," even though it differs from the English per stirpes system.

(b) **Wills law mirrors intestacy law:** [§289] The modern per stirpes distribution system is provided by the intestacy statutes of most states. The interpretation of wills and trusts thus mirrors intestate distribution, as it did in England. The Restatement says that "per stirpes" or "right of representation," used in a will, are to be given the same meaning as under the intestacy statutes of the particular state. [Rest. §303]

c. **New developments:** [§290] In recent years, this rather simple picture of the meaning of "per stirpes" and "representation" has become far more complex. The Restatement (Second) of Property section 28.2, adopted in 1988, abandoned the position of the First Restatement (1940) that these terms were to be defined by reference to intestacy law. It provides that a gift to "issue" is to be distributed by the modern per stirpes system, and a gift to "issue per stirpes" is to be distributed according to the classic English per stirpes system. The UPC was amended in 1990 to draw a distinction between a gift to "issue" and to "issue by representation," on the one hand, and to "issue per stirpes" on the other. The UPC provides that a gift to "issue" or to "issue by representation" is to be referred to the intestacy law for meaning, which provides for distribution per capita at each generation (a novel invention of the UPC). [U.P.C. §§2-106, 2-708, 2-709] On the other hand, a gift to "issue per stirpes" is to be distributed according to the classic per stirpes method. New York now follows the UPC for gifts to "issue" or "issue by representation," but calls for a modern per stirpes distribution of a gift to "issue per stirpes." [N.Y. Est. Powers & Trusts Law §2-1.2] In California, a gift to "issue" is distributed by the intestacy law, which adopts the modern per stirpes system. A gift to "issue per stirpes" or "issue by right of representation" is distributed by the classic per stirpes system. [Cal. Prob. Code §§245, 246] These new developments have greatly weakened national uniformity on this matter.

5. **Gifts to "A and her Children" (Rule in *Wild's Case*):** [§291] If there is a devise "to A and her children" or "to A and her issue," the question arises as to what interests are created in A and in A's children. *Wild's Case*, 6 Co. Rep. 16b (1599), laid down two rules of construction to deal with this problem.

   a. **First resolution of *Wild's Case*:** [§292] If there is a devise of land "to A and her children" or "to A and her issue," and A has *no children* at the date of testator's death, A takes a *fee tail*. If the fee tail is abolished, A takes whatever estate is substituted by statute for the fee tail, often ending up with a fee simple. This constructional rule made sense in feudal times in the heyday of the fee tail, but makes little sense today when the fee tail has been abolished. It may still be followed in a few states.

   b. **Second resolution of *Wild's Case*:** [§293] If there is a devise of land "to A and her children" or "to A and her issue," and A *has children* at testator's death, A and her children share equally as *co-tenants*. At common law, A and her children would share equally as joint tenants. Today A and her children share as tenants in common.

      (1) **Class closing:** [§294] If the gift to A and her children is an immediate gift, and not a postponed gift, the class closes at testator's death and unborn children of A are cut out. (*See infra*, §§306 *et seq.*)

(2) **Modern status:** [§295]   The second resolution is followed in a majority of states and has been extended to inter vivos grants as well as to devises and to personal property as well as to land. [*In re* Parant's Will, 39 Misc. 2d 285 (1963)] The Restatement repudiates both resolutions in *Wild's Case*. [Rest. 2d §28.3] It provides that a transfer to "A and her children" creates a life estate in A, with remainder to A's children.

6. **Gifts to "A and the Children of B":** [§296]   If there is a devise to "A and the children of B," the question arises whether this is a gift to one class, composed of A and the children of B, each member taking an equal share, or is a gift of one-half to A and one-half to the children of B.

   a. **Same degree of relationship:** [§297]   If A and the children of B all stand in the same degree of relationship to the donor (*e.g.,* all are nephews or nieces), they form a natural group that presumably the donor would treat equally. In this case, they usually are treated as composing one class. [*In re* Moss, [1899] 2 Ch. 314; McCartney v. Osburn, 9 N.E. 210 (Ill. 1886)]

   b. **Different degree of relationship:** [§298]   If A is of a different generational relationship to the donor than are the children of B, presumably the gift is one-half to A and one-half to be divided among the children of B. [Osburn's Appeal, 106 Pa. 637 (1883)]

      (1) **Example:** T devises property "to my brother A and the children of my deceased sister B." Because A is related to T in the second degree, and the children of B in the third degree, A probably will take one-half. On the other hand, if A were a nephew of T, A probably would take a share equal to that of each child of B. [Rest. 2d §28.1, comment g]

7. **Gifts to "Heirs":** [§299]   The word "heirs" refers technically to those persons who would take the indicated ancestor's *real property* by descent under the intestacy laws if the ancestor were to die intestate. The words "next of kin" refer to those persons who would take the indicated ancestor's *personal property* by distribution under the intestacy laws if the ancestor were to die intestate. In almost all jurisdictions, the identical persons succeed by intestacy to an ancestor's real and personal property, and in those jurisdictions "heirs" and "next of kin" refer to exactly the same persons.

   a. **Spouse as heir:** [§300]   At common law, a spouse was not an heir, but had only dower or curtesy rights in land. If the decedent left no blood kin, the land escheated. Today, in all states, the property will not escheat to the state if the decedent leaves a surviving spouse, although the position of the spouse in relation to blood kin varies from state to state. Therefore, in all states, a surviving spouse may be an heir. [Harris Trust & Savings Bank v. Jackson, 106 N.E.2d 188 (Ill. 1952)]

   b. **Time heirs are ascertained:** [§301]   The general rule is that heirs are ascertained at the death of the ancestor. Thus if T devises property "to A for life, remainder to the heirs of B (a living person)," the heirs of B are determined at B's death. If B had died before T, the heirs of B would be determined as if B had died immediately before T. [Estate of Woodworth, 18 Cal. App. 4th 936 (1993); Matter of Dodge Testamentary Trust, 330 N.W.2d 72 (Mich. 1982)]

Class Designation	Who Is Included
Children of A	All children of A, including adopted children (but maybe not adopted adults).
Issue of A	Issue of A take by a system of representation (dead children are represented by their children). Majority rule is issue take by modern per stirpes system. But the system varies in many states and may depend on whether gift is to "A's issue" or to "A's issue per stirpes."
A and her children	If A has children at time of gift, A and her children take as tenants in common under *Wild's Case*.
Heirs of A	Heirs of A are ascertained at A's death, unless rule of incongruity applies, in which case heirs would be ascertained as if A died at time of distribution.

(1) **Rule of incongruity:** [§302]   In situations where it appears incongruous to determine heirs at the death of the ancestor, the court may determine heirs of the ancestor as if the ancestor died at the time of distribution. Suppose that T devises property "to A for life, remainder to T's heirs," and T's sole heir is A. It would seem incongruous to give A the remainder when A is also given the life estate. Hence, a court is likely to determine T's heirs as if T died immediately after the life tenant, thus excluding A as an heir of T. [*In re* Latimer's Will, 63 N.W.2d 65 (Wis. 1954); *but see* Old Colony Trust Co. v. Stephens, 190 N.E.2d 110 (Mass. 1963)—determining T's heirs at T's death; *cf. In re* Easter's Estate, 24 Cal. 2d 191 (1944)] When the taker of the prior interest is only one of several heirs, however, the usual meaning of the word "heirs" is followed. The incongruity is not so strong as to require departure from the technical meaning of "heirs."

(2) **Statutory change:** [§303]   The UPC provides that where there is a gift to the "heirs" of A, the heirs of A shall be ascertained as if A died at the time of distribution. [U.P.C. §2-711] Many states have similar statutes. The purpose of these statutes is to avoid creating transmissible and taxable future interests in the heirs of A, ascertained at A's death, who die before their remainder becomes possessory. (*See supra*, §210.)

c. **Doctrine of Worthier Title:** [§304]   When the grantor purports to create a remainder in the grantor's heirs, the Doctrine of Worthier Title may be involved. Under this doctrine, the remainder is void, and the grantor has a reversion. (*See supra*, §172.)

d. **Rule in Shelley's Case:** [§305]   When an instrument creates a life estate in A and purports to create a remainder in A's heirs, the Rule in Shelley's Case, if not abolished, may be involved. Under this Rule, the remainder in A's heirs becomes a remainder in A. (*See supra*, §145.)

F.   CLASS-CLOSING RULES

1. **How Class Closes:** [§306]   A class is either open or closed. It is open if it is legally possible for other persons to come into the class. It is closed if it is not legally possible for other persons to come into the class. *Persons not in the class when it closes cannot share in the gift.* They are excluded. A class may close in one of two ways: (i) physiologically, or (ii) by the rule of convenience.

2. **Physiological Closing:** [§307]   A class closes physiologically when the designated parent of the class dies. Assume a gift "to A for life, remainder to B's children." The class of B's children closes physiologically at B's death.

   a. **Child in womb:** [§308]   When a class closes, any member of the class then conceived who is later born alive is a member of the class. Here, as elsewhere in property law, a child is treated as in being from the time of conception, if later born alive.

   b. **Adopted children:** [§309]   When an adopted child claims to be within a class, the child must be adopted before the class closes. *Remember:* To say the "class is closed" is to say no one can come in thereafter.

3. **Rule of Convenience:** [§310]   A class may close under the "rule of convenience" earlier than it would close physiologically. The *rule of convenience* is as follows:

When property is to be divided among a class, *the class will close whenever any member of the class is entitled to demand possession of his share*. The rule of convenience is a rule of construction and will not apply if the transferor expressly indicates an intention to keep the class open after the time of distribution.

a. **Reasons for rule:** [§311]   The reason for the rule of convenience is that the rule makes it possible to distribute property without worrying about unborn class members. When one person is entitled to distribution of a share, we do not know how much to give the person unless we close the class. We could extract a security bond from the distributee, and recalculate shares if another member is born later, but this remedy would be costly. So we close the class and exclude the unborn. It is the simplest and least costly alternative. It also probably embodies what the average donor would want if the problem had been considered. In addition, the rule of convenience makes property alienable earlier.

(1) **Example:** T bequeaths property "to A for life, remainder to B's children." B has one child, C, alive at T's death. At A's death, even though B may still be alive, the class will close under the rule of convenience because C can then demand her share. The property will be distributed among B's children born or conceived before A's death. If the class would not close until the death of B, the property could not be distributed to C without C's giving security to refund a portion to afterborn children or without a trustee being appointed. So afterborns are excluded.

(a) **Note:** If C dies during A's life, C's share goes to C's estate. The class closes at A's death because C's administrator may demand possession of C's share at that time. There is no express condition that B's children survive A, and none is implied.

(2) **Delay in distribution:** [§312]   A delay in distribution will not prevent the class from closing. The class will close when a beneficiary has the *right* to demand distribution, and not when the beneficiary actually demands distribution or when distribution actually occurs.

b. **Immediate gifts:** [§313]   Where there is an immediate gift to a class when the instrument takes effect, and at least *one member* of the class can demand possession of a share, the class closes immediately.

(1) **Example:** T bequeaths $10,000 "to the children of A." At T's death A is alive and has one child, B, alive. B takes the whole $10,000. Two years after T dies, C is born to A. C does not share in the bequest. [Loockerman v. McBlair, 6 Gill 177 (Md. 1847)]

(2) **Exception:** [§314]   Where there is an immediate gift to a class by will, as in the above example, but *no member of the class* is alive at testator's death, no one can demand possession at testator's death. In this case the class will stay open until it physiologically closes. The firstborn child of A will not take the entire gift. It is assumed in this situation that testator intended to benefit all children of A, and not merely the firstborn. [Rest. 2d §26.1(2)]

(3) **Specific sum gift:** [§315]   Where there is an immediate bequest of a *specific sum* to each member of a class, the class closes at testator's death, regardless of whether there are any members of the class then alive. *Rationale:* If the class did not close then, the distribution of the residue might be held up for years until the class closes physiologically. [Rogers v. Mutch, 10 Ch. D. 25 (1878)]

(a) **Example:** T bequeaths "$1,000 to each child of A." At T's death A is childless. The class closes at T's death, and no child of A can ever take.

(b) **Contrary intent:** [§316]   If T indicates a contrary intent, the class will stay open. Thus if T bequeaths "$1,000 to each child of A, whether born before or after my death," the class will not close until A's death. T's executors will have to hold back from the distribution of the residue a sum sufficient to pay these possible bequests, or exact a bond from the residuary legatee, or make other arrangements to protect the children of A born after T's death. [Earle Estate, 85 A.2d 90 (Pa. 1951)]

c.   **Postponed gifts:** [§317]   Where a gift is postponed until the termination of a prior estate or until a specific condition happens, the class will close whenever any member has the right to demand distribution of his share. Of course, no member can demand distribution until any prior estate has terminated.

(1) **Preceding life estate:** [§318]   Suppose that T bequeaths property "to A for life, remainder to the children of B." If B dies before A, the class will close physiologically at B's death. If A dies before B, the class will close under the rule of convenience at A's death: (i) if a child of B is then alive, or (ii) if a child of B predeceased T and the gift did not lapse but went to that child's issue under a lapse statute, or (iii) if a child of B was alive at T's death, or was born thereafter, and such child predeceased A. In all these cases, the child (or the child's issue, or the child's administrator) is entitled to possession at A's death. This closes the class. [Britton v. Miller, 63 N.C. 268 (1869)]

(a) **Exception:** [§319]   If no members of the class have been born at the expiration of A's life estate, all children of B, whenever born, share. [Rest. 2d §26.2(2)]

(2) **Age contingency:** [§320]   Suppose that T bequeaths property "to such children of A as shall reach 21." A has a child, B, age 18, and a child, C, age 12. As soon as a class member reaches 21 (be he B or C or some afterborn child), he can demand his share and the class closes. Suppose that after B reaches 21, D is born to A. Then C dies at age 19. C's share goes to B, as the other member of the class who qualified. D, born after the class closed, does not share.

(3) **Vested with payment postponed:** [§321]   Suppose that T bequeaths property "to the children of A payable at 21." A has a child, B, age 18, and a child, C, age 12. The class will close when B reaches 21, or if B dies under that age, when B would have reached 21 had B lived. At that time, B or B's administrator can demand possession of B's share. [*In re* Evans' Estate, 80 N.W.2d 408 (Wis. 1957)]

CLASS-CLOSING RULE OF CONVENIENCE

Rule: Class closes, excluding afterborns, when any member of class can demand possession.

Examples: Immediate Gifts	Examples: Postponed Gifts
(1) T's will devises $5,000 "to the children of A." A has a child, B. The class closes at T's death. B takes the whole $5,000.	(1) "To A for life, then to the children of B." B is alive, with a child, C. A dies. The class closes at A's death, and C takes all.
(2) T's will devises $5,000 "to each child of A." A has a child, B. B takes $5,000, and afterborn children take nothing.	(2) "To A for life, then to the children of B who reach age 21." B is alive, with a child C, age 13. A dies when C is age 15. Two years later, D is born to B. Eight years later, E is born to B. The class closes when C reaches 21. D is within the class, but E, born two years after C reaches 21, is excluded.

(a) **Earlier closing:** [§322]   If B dies under 21, the class will not close at B's death, but only when B would have reached 21 had B lived. Earlier closing is not permitted where the gift is vested with possession postponed if earlier closing would harm someone else. Earlier closing might cut out some child of A born after B dies but before B would have reached 21 had B lived.

(4) **Life estate and age contingency:** [§323]   Suppose that T bequeaths $100,000 "to A for life, remainder to B's children who reach 21." The class will close under the rule of convenience when A dies **and** when a child of B has reached 21. Assume that at A's death B has three children—C, age 18, D, age 15, and E, age 10. One year after A's death, B has another child, F. **Three years after A dies, C reaches 21. The class closes.** Four years after A's death, B has still another child, G. G does not share because G was born after the class had closed. C, D, E, and F are members of the class. When C reaches 21, $25,000 is distributed to C. $75,000 is held for D, E, and F if they reach 21. If D dies under 21, $8,334 is distributed to C at that time, the remaining $66,666 is held for E and F if they qualify.

(5) **Gift when "youngest" reaches 21:** [§324]   Suppose that T bequeaths a sum "to the children of A, to be distributed when the **youngest** reaches 21." "Youngest" is ambiguous because it does not tell us when the determination of who is youngest shall be made. The Restatement says "youngest" refers to the person in the class who was the youngest on the date no living class member was under the stated age. [Rest. 2d §26.2 comment o] Thus, the class will close when all living members have attained the stated age. [Lux v. Lux, 288 A.2d 701 (R.I. 1972)]

d. **Gifts of income:** [§325]   The rule of convenience applies to gifts of principal. A gift of income is ordinarily treated as a separate gift of each income payment. The income is distributed to those members of the class born before the income accrues. [*In re* Wenmoth's Estate, 37 Ch. D. 266 (1887)]

(1) **Example:** T bequeaths a sum in trust "for A for life, then for the children of B for their lives." After A dies, as each item of income accrues, the class will close with respect to that item of income (*e.g.*, dividend, interest, rent). B's children share in the income accruing after their respective births.

G.   IMPLIED GIFTS

1. **General Rule:** [§326]   Generally, a court will not imply a gift that is not expressly made. Sometimes, however, the courts are convinced that the testator's intent can be carried out only by implying a gift. Except for the situations dealt with below, the circumstances under which a court will imply a gift to fill in a gap in disposition are hard to generalize. Cases implying gifts tend to emphasize the testator's general plan or the desire of testator to keep property in bloodlines. But the facts vary greatly. All that can be said is that a court is reluctant to imply a gift, but, if sufficiently motivated, it will. [*In re* Thall, 18 N.Y.2d 186 (1966)]

2. **Implied Gift to Issue:** [§327]   Where a life estate is created, followed by a remainder to another if the life tenant dies without issue, courts may imply a remainder

to the life tenant's issue. Thus, if T devises property "to A for life, and if A dies without issue surviving her, to B," there is a gap in the disposition if A dies with issue. Courts may infer that T intended A's issue to take in this circumstance and imply a gift to A's issue if A dies with issue. [Estate of Blake, 157 Cal. 448 (1910)]

3. **Death of One of Several Life Tenants:** [§328]   Suppose that O transfers property "to X's children, A, B, and C, for their lives, and on the death of the survivor, to D." What happens to the property upon the death of A, leaving B and C alive? The instrument does not clearly provide who is to take the income that A was receiving. There are at least four possible solutions to this problem.

    a.   **Reversion:** [§329]   It may be found that O intended (i) that A, B, and C take only one-third of the income each and (ii) that D take the corpus only on the death of A, B, and C. If so, there is a gap in the income disposed of, and this goes back to O as reversioner. When A dies, O gets one-third of the income. When A and B die, O gets two-thirds of the income. When A, B, and C die, D gets the corpus. Courts usually reject this solution on the ground that the donor intended to make a complete disposition of the property and retain no interest.

    b.   **Fractional vesting of remainder:** [§330]   It may be found that O intended to vest D's remainder in possession fractionally. Thus D would receive one-third of the corpus when A dies, and a second one-third when B dies. Few courts have come to this solution unless the income is given to the life tenants for their "respective lives," or other language is used indicating fractional vesting of the remainder.

    c.   **Life estate pur autre vie:** [§331]   It may be found that O intended A's share of the income to go to A's estate until the death of the survivor of A, B, and C. In this case, each of the life tenants has a life estate measured by the lives of A, B, and C, and on A's death, his estate has a life estate pur autre vie. This solution, too, has not been favored by courts.

    d.   **Remaining life tenants divide income:** [§332]   The most common solution is to hold that the income is to be divided among the surviving life tenants until the death of the survivor of A, B, and C. When A dies, B and C divide the income between them, and the survivor takes the entire income. The court may rest upon the theory that the donor intended to create (i) a joint tenancy in A, B, and C for their joint lives and the life of the survivor, (ii) a class gift with the survivors of the class being entitled to the income, or (iii) cross-remainders among the life tenants. [Dewire v. Haveles, 534 N.E.2d 782 (Mass. 1989)]

        (1)   **Implied cross-remainders:** [§333]   The joint tenancy theory and the class gift theory are easy enough to understand. The implied cross-remainders theory requires more explanation. Under this theory, cross-remainders are implied as follows: "One-third to A for life, then to B and C for their joint lives, then to the survivor of B and C for life; one-third to B for life, then to A and C for their joint lives, then to the survivor of A and C for life; one-third to C for life, then to A and B for their joint lives, then to the survivor of A and B for life." It looks complicated but if you

read it carefully you will see that the survivors of A, B, and C divide the income until the last one dies.

Proceed to the Review Questions for Chapter IV.

V. POWERS OF APPOINTMENT

A. CLASSIFICATION OF POWERS

1. **Terminology:** [§334]   The law of powers has its own terminology. Suppose that T devises property "to A for life, remainder as A appoints among her issue, and in default of appointment to B." T is *donor* of the power. A is *donee* of the power. A's issue are *objects* of the power or *permissible appointees*. B is *taker in default* of appointment. If A exercises the power by appointing to her daughter D, D is an *appointee*. Powers may also be classified as *testamentary* or *inter vivos*, and as *general* or *special*.

2. **Testamentary or Inter Vivos:** [§335]   A power of appointment may be created so that it is exercisable only by a certain type of instrument. There are two general classifications, testamentary and inter vivos.

   a. **Testamentary power:** [§336]   A power that may be exercised by *will alone* is a *testamentary* power. The purpose of the donor is to prevent exercise during the donee's life. Thus, the donee may neither make an appointment during life nor contract to appoint by will.

      (1) **Example:** T devises property "to A for life, then among A's issue in such shares as A appoints by will, and in default of appointment to A's issue per stirpes then living." By deed, A appoints the property to her son, B. The appointment of the remainder by a deed is invalid. However, since A could transfer her life estate, B takes a life estate for A's life. [*In re* Estate of Curtis, 307 A.2d 251 (Pa. 1973)]

   b. **Inter vivos power:** [§337]   A power that may be exercised by a *deed alone* is an *inter vivos* power. So too is a power exercisable by *deed or will*. The crucial fact is that the power is exercisable by deed, which gives the donee present control over the property.

      (1) **Example:** T devises property "to A for life, then among A's issue in such shares as A by deed or will appoints." A has an inter vivos power. A may appoint the property by a deed or by a will.

      (2) **Presently exercisable power:** [§338]   Most inter vivos powers are presently exercisable, that is, they may be exercised upon creation. However, an inter vivos power may be created so as to be exercisable only after a specific act or event occurs.

         (a) **Example:** T bequeaths a fund in trust "to pay the income to the children of A, with power in A to appoint the principal among the children of A when the youngest child alive reaches age 21." When the condition occurs, the power becomes exercisable. This permits A to divide up the principal among A's children after they become adults.

3. General and Special Powers

a. **General:** [§339]   A general power of appointment is a power exercisable in favor of the ***donee, the donee's estate, the donee's creditors,*** or the ***creditors of the donee's estate***. [I.R.C. §2041(b)(1)] The essence of a general power is that the donee may benefit herself pecuniarily by its exercise, and may appoint to herself or for her benefit if she chooses.

   (1) **Example:** T devises property "to A for life, then as A appoints by will." A holds a general power. By will A can appoint to anyone, including A's executor or creditors. By appointing to her creditors, A can benefit herself.

b. **Special:** [§340]   A special power is a power to appoint to persons other than the donee, the donee's estate, the donee's creditors, or the creditors of the donee's estate. The essence of a special power is that the donee cannot benefit herself by exercising the power. A special power is sometimes called a nongeneral power. [Rest. 2d §11.4]

   (1) **Discretionary power in a trustee:** [§341]   A trustee may be given discretion to distribute income or principal to beneficiaries. This discretion is a special power of appointment, but it must be exercised in accordance with fiduciary principles. A power in a trustee attaches to the office and can be exercised by a successor trustee. A nonfiduciary power of appointment is personal and can be exercised only by the donee, and not by the donee's heirs, executor, or assigns. [Dormer's Estate, 35 A.2d 299 (Pa. 1944)]

B. THE THEORY THAT DONEE IS NOT OWNER

1. **Relation-Back Doctrine:** [§342]   The exercise of a power by the donee is viewed as filling in blanks in the instrument creating the power. The theory is that the appointees take from the donor, not from the donee, of the power. This is called the "relation-back doctrine." Although this doctrine described well how powers were viewed at early English law, in modern times it has not always been followed where a general power is involved. A general power approximates ownership, and in a number of circumstances courts now treat the donee of a general power as owner of the appointive property. (*See infra*, §§344, 350, 400, 406, 488.)

2. **Federal Estate and Gift Taxes**

a. **Relation-back doctrine:** [§343]   Estate and inheritance taxes are generally imposed upon the *succession* of title at death. Suppose that T devises property "to A for life, then as A appoints by will." A by will appoints to B. Under the relation-back theory, B succeeds to title from T, not from A. Therefore, if the relation-back theory were followed, a death transfer tax would be paid at T's death, and no tax would be paid at A's death. Federal and state estate taxation statutes do not follow this theory.

b. **Federal estate tax:** [§344]   The federal estate tax law includes in the donee's taxable estate any property over which the donee holds a ***general*** power of appointment. It does ***not*** include any property over which the donee holds a *special* power. Thus the tax laws treat the donee of a general power as owner, but do not treat the donee of a special power as owner. [I.R.C. §2041]

(1) **Tax planning:** [§345]   Since a life estate coupled with a *special* power is not taxed at the donee's death, special powers are very useful in estate planning to give flexibility without any estate tax cost.

(2) **Limited by standard:** [§346]   The Internal Revenue Code provides that a power of the donee to consume or invade property "limited by an ascertainable standard relating to the health, education, support or maintenance" of the donee is not a general power. [I.R.C. §2041(b)(1)(A)] Thus, it is possible for the donee to be given a power to appoint to herself for the specified limited purposes without adverse tax consequences.

(a) **Example:** T devises property in trust for A for life, with the power in A "to withdraw corpus if necessary to support her in the style of living *to which she is now accustomed.*" This power is limited by an ascertainable standard and is not a general power under the Code. Upon A's death, the property is not included in A's estate under section 2041.

c. **Federal gift tax:** [§347]   Generally speaking, a federal gift tax is imposed on a transfer made during life that would be taxable if made at the death of the transferor. The same distinction between general and special powers made in the federal estate tax is made in the federal gift tax. The donee of a general power is treated as owner of the property. The donee of a special power is not. If a general power is exercised by the donee during life, a gift tax is payable. [I.R.C. §2514(b)]

(1) **Release:** [§348]   A *release* of a general power by the donee is treated as an exercise of the power, and a gift tax is payable upon release. A *disclaimer* by the donee is not deemed a release of the power. A disclaimer must occur within nine months after the power is created or the donee reaches 21. (*See infra*, §§360-361.)

3. **Creditors of the Donee**

a. **General power unexercised**

(1) **Majority rule:** [§349]   The rule in most states without statutes on the subject is that the creditors of the donee of an *unexercised general* power may not reach the property. [Irwin Union Bank & Trust Co. v. Long, 312 N.E.2d 908 (Ind. 1974); Quinn v. Tuttle, 177 A.2d 391 (N.H. 1962)]

(a) **Rationale:** Under common law, the property does not belong to the donee of a power. The donee is merely authorized to pass ownership from the donor to the appointee. Until the donee exercises the power she has not accepted control that gives her the equivalent of ownership.

(b) **Criticism:** This rule is out of tune with reality. The donee of a general inter vivos power presently exercisable has the equivalent of full ownership. All she has to do is sign her name to a document making an appointment. She is no further from ownership than a person who deposits money in a bank and has to write a check to withdraw it. As for a general testamentary power, by analogy to general debtor-creditor principles, the creditors should be able to reach whatever the debtor can voluntarily convey. Despite this criticism, the Restatement (Second) adopts the majority rule. [Rest. 2d §13.2]

(2) **Statutes:** [§350] In an increasing number of states, statutes provide that the creditors of a donee of a general power of appointment may reach the property whether or not the power is exercised. If the power is a testamentary power, creditors may not reach the property until the death of the donee since she cannot appoint until that time. [Cal. Civ. Code §1390.3]

(3) **Bankruptcy:** [§351] The Bankruptcy Act of 1978 provides that the trustee shall be vested with all powers that the bankrupt might have exercised for her own benefit, but not those that she might exercise solely for some other person. [11 U.S.C. §541(b)] Thus, the trustee is vested with any inter vivos general powers, but not with any testamentary powers or special powers.

b. **General power exercised**

(1) **Majority rule:** [§352] In most states creditors of the donee of a general power may reach the property if the donee *exercises* the power. The donee is exercising dominion over the appointive assets that is in its practical aspects the same as dominion over her own property. Because of this exercise of dominion, equity seizes the appointed property for the benefit of the donee's creditors. [*In re* Masson's Estate, 142 Cal. App. 2d 510 (1956); Clapp v. Ingraham, 126 Mass. 200 (1879)]

(a) **Extent:** [§353] Creditors may reach the appointive assets only if the donee's own assets are insufficient to pay her debts. The donee's own assets must be used first to pay debts.

(b) **Restraint against creditors:** [§354] If the donor provides, in the instrument creating the power, that under no circumstances shall the assets be appointed to the donee's creditors or subjected to their claims, such a provision is void. A general power may not be limited so as to defeat the equitable doctrine that the appointive property be dealt with as an asset of the donee's estate for the satisfaction of debts. [State Street Trust Co. v. Kissel, 19 N.E.2d 25 (Mass. 1939)]

c. **Special power:** [§355] The donee of a special power may not appoint the property to herself or for her benefit, and her creditors may not reach the property.

4. **Choice of Law:** [§356] If the donor and donee are domiciled in different states, or if the appointive assets are located in a third state, which state law governs questions

relating to the power? Is the exercise related back so that the law of the donor's domicile governs?

a. **Land:** [§357]   If the appointive property is land, the law of the state where the land *is located* determines questions of the validity of creation and exercise of the power.

b. **Personal property:** [§358]   With respect to personal property, the standard rule is that the law of the donor's domicile governs the creation and exercise of the power. The law of the donee's domicile does not govern. The relation-back theory is applied. If the donee exercises the power in a way not permitted by the donor's domicile, even though permitted by the donee's domicile, the exercise is invalid. [Beals v. State Street Bank & Trust Co., 326 N.E.2d 896 (Mass. 1975)]

   (1) **Donor's contrary intent:** [§359]   The standard rule gives way if the settlor of an *inter vivos trust* indicates that the law of some other state, either the law of the donee's domicile or the law where the trust is administered, shall govern the trust. Since the settlor could take the property to another state and establish a trust there, the settlor of an inter vivos trust may stay where he is and specify that the law of another state governs the creation and exercise of the power. Some states and the UPC permit the settlor of a *testamentary trust* to choose the law governing the exercise of the power. [*See* U.P.C. §2-703]

C. RELEASE OF POWERS AND CONTRACTS TO APPOINT

1. **Release of Power:** [§360]   A power of appointment may be released in whole or in part by the donee, except to the extent that the donor has manifested an intent that it not be releasable. A complete release makes indefeasible the interest of the taker in default if the interest is subject to no other condition. [District of Columbia v. Lloyd, 160 F.2d 581 (D.C. Cir. 1947); Rest. 2d §14.1]

   a. **Disclaimer compared:** [§361]   A release should be distinguished from a disclaimer of the power. The donee of a power may disclaim the power before she accepts it, but once having accepted the power, the donee can extinguish it only by release or exercise.

   b. **General power presently exercisable:** [§362]   A general power presently exercisable may be released by the donee. This may have the effect of vesting indefeasibly the gift in default of appointment. Thus, in one sense, by releasing the power the donee has appointed to the takers in default.

      (1) **General turned into special:** [§363]   A general power may be released in part, turning it into a special power. Thus A, donee of a general power, may release the power to appoint to anyone other than A's issue. A now has a special power. [Beals v. State Street Bank & Trust Co., *supra*]

   c. **Special power:** [§364]   A special power of appointment may be released by the donee. It may be released even though the takers in default are different persons from the permissible appointees. In effect, then, by releasing the power, the donee of a special power may "appoint" to the takers in default.

Is Donee Treated as Owner of Property Subject to Power?

Situation	Answer	Example
Taxation	Yes	Donee is treated as owner for federal estate and gift taxation.
Creditors	No	Creditors cannot reach appointive property unless donee exercises power.
Conflict of laws	No	Law of donor's domicile, not law of donee's domicile, governs.
Release	Yes	Donee may release power, but donee of testamentary power may not contract to exercise it.
Exercise by residuary clause	No	In most states, power is not exercised by a residuary clause in donee's will.
Anti-lapse statute	Yes	If donee appoints to a relative who predeceases donee, relative's issue take under usual anti-lapse statute.
Invalid appointment	Maybe	If donee intends to capture property for her estate if appointment invalid, it goes to her estate.
Perpetuities	Yes/No	Donee of general inter vivos power is treated as owner; perpetuities period begins to run from date of appointment. Donee of general testamentary power is not treated as owner; perpetuities period begins to run from date of creation of power.

(1) **Example:** T devises property "to A for life, then as A appoints among her children, and in default to A's children equally." A has three children— B, C, and D. During A's life, B dies, survived by a wife. A wishes B's wife to take one-third of the property at A's death. A may not appoint to B's wife, but A may release the power, vesting one-third of the remainder indefeasibly in B's estate.

(2) **Released in part:** [§365]   Any releasable power may be released with respect to the whole or any part of the appointive property and may also be released in such manner as to reduce or limit the permissible appointees.

d. **Testamentary power:** [§366]   A testamentary power may be released inter vivos even though this may defeat the intent of the donor that the donee hold the discretionary power until death.

2. Contracts to Appoint

a. **General power presently exercisable:** [§367]   A donee of a general power presently exercisable may make a present appointment. Therefore, she may contract to exercise the power in a particular way. [Rest. 2d §16.1]

b. **Special power:** [§368]   A contract to exercise a special power in a way to benefit a non-object is void and unenforceable. What the donee may not do by appointment she may not do by contract to appoint.

(1) **Example:** A has a power to appoint among her children. In return for $5,000 given A (a non-object of the power), A contracts to appoint $8,000 to her child B. This contract is unenforceable by specific performance or damages. If A does not appoint to B, B's only remedy is to claim restitution of the $5,000 paid. [Rest. 2d §16.1, comment g]

c. **Testamentary power:** [§369]   A contract to exercise a testamentary power is void. *Rationale:* If the donee can validly contract inter vivos to exercise a testamentary power in a specified way, the donee has in effect exercised the power inter vivos. This would defeat the donor's intent in creating a power exercisable only by will. [*In re* Estate of Brown, 33 N.Y.2d 211 (1973); Seidel v. Werner, 81 Misc. 2d 220 (1975); Rest. 2d §16.2]

(1) **No damages allowed:** [§370]   A contract to exercise a testamentary power is wholly void. Neither damages nor specific performance is allowed. Restitution might be allowed if the promisee was ignorant of the law and not consciously wrongful.

(2) **Appointment in compliance with contract:** [§371]   If the donee of a testamentary power makes a contract for its exercise and then dies appointing the property in accordance with the contract, the appointment is valid.

(3) **Contract treated as release:** [§372]   All powers of appointment are releasable, and in some cases a contract to exercise a testamentary power, though unenforceable as a contract, is given effect as a release when that is the intent of the donee.

(a) **Example:** A has a testamentary power to appoint $90,000 among her children, and the children are takers in default. There are three children—B, C, and D. Suppose that A contracts with B that A will not exercise the power in such a way as to cause B to take less than $20,000. Since there are three children, A could have carried out her wishes by releasing the power over $60,000, vesting $20,000 shares in remainder in each child. A's contract will be treated as a release over $60,000. A now has a power of appointment over only $30,000.

(b) **Compare effects of contract and release:** [§373]   Where the effect of the contract is not substantially the same as a release, the contract will not be treated as a release. Thus, suppose that A is donee of a special testamentary power to appoint among her children, with a gift in default to A's children equally. A has two children. The effect of a release would be to vest the remainder in default in the two children. If A contracts to appoint all the property to one of her two children, the contract cannot be treated as a release because A intended all the property to go to only one child by the contract, not to both children. It does not have substantially the same effect as a release. If, on the other hand, A contracts to appoint equally to all children, the contract will be treated as a release. [Seidel v. Werner, *supra*, §369]

D.   EXERCISE OF POWERS

1.   Formalities

a.   **General rule:** [§374]   In most cases, a power of appointment may be exercised only by an instrument legally effective to transfer the appointive property, *i.e.*, a delivered deed or a duly executed will.

b.   **Formalities prescribed by donor:** [§375]   If the creating instrument specifies requirements as to the manner, time, and conditions of the exercise of a power of appointment, the power may be exercised only by complying with those requirements.

(1)   **Specific reference:** [§376]   If the donor directs that a power be exercised by an instrument that makes specific reference to the creating instrument, the power may be exercised only by an instrument containing the required reference. The reason for requiring specific reference is to prevent inadvertent exercise.

(2)   **Strict compliance:** [§377]   The Restatement (Second) provides that a "specific reference" requirement must be strictly complied with. [Rest. 2d §17.1] Some cases are in accord. [Estate of Smith, 585 P.2d 319 (Colo. 1978); First National Bank v. Walker, 607 S.W.2d 469 (Tenn. 1980)] Other courts are more flexible, permitting extrinsic evidence to show the intent of the donee to exercise the power. [Motes/Henes Trust v. Motes, 761 S.W.2d 938 (Ark. 1988)]

(a)   **Example:** T devises property in trust "for A for life, then as A by will appoints by specific reference to this power." Subsequently A dies, devising to B "all the rest of my property, including all property over which I have a power of appointment." Under the strict approach favored by the Restatement, A has not exercised the power over T's property because A did not specifically refer to that power by a reference to "the power created by T's will," or similar language. Under a more flexible approach, analyzing the donee's probable intent in view of her estate planning objectives, A may be held to have exercised the power.

c. **Exercise by residuary clause:** [§378]   In most states, a residuary clause or other similar clause in a will is presumed *not* to exercise powers. *Rationale:* Property subject to a power is not donee's "property." Thus, if the will of A, donee of a power, devises "all my property" to B, the power is not exercised and B does not take the appointive property. [*In re* Proestler's Will, 5 N.W.2d 922 (Iowa 1942); U.P.C. §2-608]

   (1) **Contrary intent:** [§379]   The states are split over whether extrinsic evidence is admissible to overcome the presumption of nonexercise by a residuary clause. The UPC provides that such evidence is not admissible [U.P.C. §2-608], but in most states evidence that the testator intended to exercise the power by the residuary clause, including extrinsic circumstances, is admissible to rebut the presumption of nonexercise [Bank of New York v. Black, 139 A.2d 393 (N.J. 1958); Dollar Savings & Trust Co. v. First National Bank, 285 N.E.2d 768 (Ohio 1972); Rest. 2d §17.3].

   (2) **Minority rule:** [§380]   In a few states, including New York, general (and maybe even special) powers are presumptively exercised by a residuary or similar clause. *Rationale:* The donee likely did not distinguish between "her property" and "property subject to the power." [*In re* Smith, 279 A.D. 140 (1951); Beals v. State Street Bank & Trust Co., *supra*, §358—applies minority rule, but Massachusetts adopted majority rule in 1978 (*see* Mass. Gen. Laws ch. 191, §1A(4))]

2. **Limits on Exercise of General Power:** [§381]   Generally, a donee must exercise the power within the limits prescribed by the donor.

   a. **Creation of limited interest:** [§382]   A general power of appointment may be exercised by appointing a limited interest in the property, such as a life estate, to another. The donee may appoint in further trust or impose conditions. Since the donee may appoint to herself (or to her estate) and by a second instrument (or second clause in her will) transfer the property as she pleases, there is no reason to say she may not create a limited interest by a direct appointment. The donee may also create new powers of appointment in others. [Rest. 2d §§19.1, 19.2]

3. **Limits on Exercise of Special Power:** [§383]   A special power must be exercised in accordance with the instrument creating the power, and the donor may impose restrictions upon the way the power may be exercised.

   a. **Creation of limited interest:** [§384]   Unless the donor has expressed a contrary intent, the donee of a special power may appoint limited interests to objects of the power or appoint in further trust. [Rest. 2d §19.3]

b. **Creation of new power**

(1) **Creation of general power:** [§385]   Unless the donor provides to the contrary, the majority holds that the donee of a special power may exercise it by creating a general power in an object of the power. A general power is tantamount to appointing a fee simple. [Rest. 2d §19.4(1)] A few courts hold, however, that the donee may not appoint by creating a general power in an object of the power because this is an attempted "delegation" of the power, and powers may not be delegated.

(2) **Creation of special power:** [§386]   Unless the donor provides to the contrary, the majority holds that a donee of a special power may exercise it by creating a special power in any person to appoint to an object of the original special power. [Rest. 2d §19.4(2)] But the donee may not create a special power to appoint among persons who are not objects of the original power.

(a) **Example:** T devises "to A for life, remainder as A appoints among A's issue." A appoints to her daughter, B, for life, remainder as B appoints among B's issue. This is a valid appointment since the only objects of the new power are B's issue (who are within the class of A's issue). The creation of the power in B would not be valid if B were given the power to appoint "to B's issue or to such charities as B shall select."

c. **Nonexclusive powers:** [§387]   A special power is either exclusive or nonexclusive. If the donor intends that the donee be able to exclude one or more of the class of objects, perhaps appointing all the property to one object, the power is exclusive. If the donor intends that all members of the class benefit, but that the amount of each share shall be determined by the donee, the power is nonexclusive.

(1) **Presumption:** [§388]   The presumption is that the donor intends the power to be exclusive. [Harlan v. Citizens National Bank of Danville, 251 S.W.2d 284 (Ky. 1952)] However, courts often have found that the presumption is overcome by particular language in the creating instrument. Thus, a power in A to appoint "to *such* of A's children as A shall appoint" is exclusive, but a power to appoint "*among* A's children" has been held to be nonexclusive. [*Cf.* Estate of Kohler, 344 A.2d 469 (Pa. 1975)]

(2) **Invalid appointment:** [§389]   If the power is nonexclusive and the donee excludes one or more permissible appointees, the appointment is ineffective and the property passes in default of appointment.

(3) **Illusory appointment:** [§390]   Suppose that the power is nonexclusive and the donee attempts to circumvent the requirement that no object be excluded by appointing $1 to two of three objects of the power and the remainder to the third object of the power. Under the doctrine of "illusory appointments," each appointee must receive a *substantial* share, not merely a nominal share. The illusory appointment doctrine is rejected by the Restatement and by most courts. [*See* Rest. 2d §21.2]

E. INVALID OR INEFFECTIVE APPOINTMENTS

1. Appointments to Non-Objects of Special Power

a. Appointments to objects and non-objects: [§391]   The donee of a special power may not appoint to non-objects of the power. If the donee of a special power appoints to a class composed of objects and non-objects, the appointment to the non-objects is void. The appointment to objects is also void if the donee's scheme of disposition is more closely approximated by allowing both parts to pass in default of appointment. [Estate of DuPont, 379 A.2d 570 (Pa. 1977)]

(1) **Example:** T devises property "to A for life, remainder to such of A's children as A appoints, and in default of appointment to A's children equally." A has a child, B. A appoints to her child, B, "for life, remainder to B's issue who survive B." The appointment to B's issue is void because such issue are non-objects of the power.

b. Fraudulent appointment: [§392]   As stated above, any direct appointment to a non-object is void. Indirect techniques by which the donee of a special power attempts to benefit a non-object may also be held void as "fraudulent appointments." Fraud in the usual sense is not involved. The term means only that equity will set aside the appointment.

(1) **Appointment in consideration of benefit to non-object:** [§393]   If the donee of a special power appoints to an object and the donee's purpose is to benefit a non-object, the appointment is void to the extent it was motivated by the purpose of benefiting non-objects. The intent to benefit a non-object may be shown by extrinsic evidence. [Rest. 2d §20.2]

(a) **Example:** A, donee of a special power to appoint among A's children, appoints by will all of the property to one of A's children, B. Child B has promised A that B will give half the appointive property to A's spouse, W. The appointment is fraudulent. The entire appointment to B may be void on the theory that A's whole purpose in appointing to B was to benefit W. [*In re* Carroll, 274 N.Y. 288 (1937); Horne v. Title Insurance & Trust Co., 79 F. Supp. 91 (S.D. Cal. 1948)]

2. Failure to Exercise Special Power: [§394]   If there is no gift in default of appointment by a special power, and the donee fails to exercise the power, the property will pass to the objects of the power if the objects are a *defined limited class*. In the absence of a contrary manifestation of intent, it is assumed that the donor intends the objects of the power to have the benefit of the property. [Rest. 2d §24.2]

a. Example: T devises property "to A for life, then among A's children as A by will appoints." There is no gift in default. A dies intestate. It is inferred that T has a general intent to benefit A's children and desires them to take the property if A fails to appoint.

b. Theory: [§395]   Some courts reach this result by describing the donee's power as an "imperative" power, which the donor intends must be exercised. If the donee won't exercise the power, the court will exercise the power in favor of the objects equally. Other courts reach the result by implying a gift in default to the objects of the power. [Loring v. Marshall, 484 N.E.2d 1315 (Mass. 1985)]

c. **Survivorship may be required:** [§396]   If the power is not exercised and an object of the power does not survive the donee, the question arises whether the object's estate will take in his place, or the object's issue will take by virtue of an anti-lapse statute, or the object's share will lapse. The cases are divided: (i) Some hold that the object's share lapses, on the theory that the donee could not appoint to the object's estate or issue. [Daniel v. Brown, 159 S.E. 209 (Va. 1931)] (ii) Others hold that the object's share, implied as a gift in default, is a vested remainder passing to the object's estate. [Bridgewater v. Turner, 29 S.W.2d 659 (Tenn. 1930)] (iii) The Restatement (Second) provides that the object's share passes to the object's issue under an anti-lapse statute, and if no issue are living, the share lapses. [Rest. 2d §24.2]

(1) **Example:** T devises property "to A for life, then to such of A's children as A appoints by will." There is no default clause. A has three children, B, C, and D. B dies, leaving a child, E. C dies, leaving a wife, F. A dies intestate. Under holding (i) above, D takes all the property. Under (ii), D, E, and F divide the property equally. Under (iii), E and D divide the property.

d. **Appoint to only one member:** [§397]   Sometimes the donee is directed by the donor to select one member of the class to take the property. If the donee fails to make the selection, there is authority that the members of the class share equally. [Bridgewater v. Turner, *supra*] But there is contrary authority that equal division is forbidden when the donee is directed to select one object. [Waterman v. New York Life Insurance & Trust Co., 237 N.Y. 293 (1923)]

3. **Appointments to Deceased Persons:** [§398]   If an appointee dies before the donee, an appointment by the donee to the appointee lapses. Thus suppose that A, donee of a power, executes a will appointing the property to B. B then dies. A then dies. B cannot take the property because B is dead. The appointment is ineffective unless an anti-lapse statute applies.

a. **Anti-lapse statute:** [§399]   Almost every jurisdiction has an anti-lapse statute. Typically it provides that if the legatee is kin of the testator the gift does not lapse but goes to the legatee's issue.

(1) **General power:** [§400]   Although anti-lapse statutes by their terms usually apply only to *devises* and *bequests* of property by the *testator*, they have been held to apply also to the exercise of a general power of appointment. Thus, "testator" is construed to include the "donee of a general power," and "bequest" to include "appointment." *Rationale:* A general power is the substantial equivalent of ownership. The lapse statute carries out the inferred intent of the donee. [Thompson v. Pew, 102 N.E. 122 (Mass. 1913)]

(a) **Example:** A has a *general* testamentary power, which A exercises in favor of her daughter, B. B dies before A, leaving a son, C, alive. C survives A. C takes the appointive property.

(2) **Special power:** [§401]   If the person who would take under the anti-lapse statute comes within the class of permissible appointees (*e.g.*, if, in the above example, A had a *special* power to appoint to A's "issue"), it is arguable that the anti-lapse statute should apply. The theory is that the statute, by sending the property to C, will carry out the presumed intent of the donee. There are few cases on this point. On the other hand, an anti-lapse statute does not apply to the exercise of a special power if the property would pass to persons who are not permissible appointees of the power. In the preceding example, if A had a *special* power to appoint to her "children," C (A's grandson) could not take the property. An anti-lapse statute cannot operate to carry the property to persons who are not permissible appointees. [Daniel v. Brown, *supra*, §396; *but see* Rest. 2d §18.6—takers substituted by an anti-lapse statute are regarded as objects of the power]

4. **Allocation of Assets:** [§402]   When the donee of a power blends her own property with the appointive property and exercises the power in an *invalid way*, the donee's own property and the appointive property will be allocated, if possible, to give maximum effect to donee's intent. (Allocation is sometimes known as "marshaling.") [Rest. 2d §§22.1, 22.2]

   a. **Example:** A is the donee of a special testamentary power over a $50,000 trust to appoint among her children. A also owns outright $120,000. An introductory clause to A's will declares that the will disposes of A's own property and of the property subject to the power. A's will gives $80,000 outright to her child, B. A's residuary clause gives the residue to charity. Since the charity cannot take the trust property, the trust property ($50,000) is allocated to B. B also takes $30,000 of A's own property. The charity takes the rest.

   b. **Blending requirements:** [§403]   Allocation is permitted where the donee has blended her own property and the appointive property. If the donee has indicated that specific property is to pass to a named taker, allocation does not apply, even if the gift fails.

      (1) **Introductory clause:** [§404]   If the donee blends the appointive property with her own, the blended fund is selectively allocated. Blending occurs, for example, where, in an introductory clause in her will, A states: "I devise and bequeath by this will my property and all property over which I have a power of appointment."

      (2) **Residuary clause:** [§405]   If the donee exercises the power in her residuary clause, blending it with her own property, the assets will be allocated. In the preceding example, allocation would occur if A's residuary clause read: "I give the residue of my estate and any property over which I have a power of appointment $80,000 to B and the rest to Charity." The trust property would be allocated to B.

5. **Capture by Donee:** [§406]   Ordinarily, if the donee of a power makes an ineffective exercise, the property goes in default of appointment. If there is no gift in default, the property reverts to the donor or the donor's estate. An important exception to this is the capture doctrine. This doctrine provides: If the donee of a *general* power of appointment ineffectively exercises the power, but *manifests an intent to*

assume control of the appointive property for all purposes, the property is captured in the donee's estate. It does not go in default of appointment or revert to the donor. The court must find in the donee's will language or acts from which it can infer donee means this: "I am exercising this power but if this exercise is not valid I want this property to be part of my estate." [Rest. 2d §23.2]

a. **Theory:** [§407]   The donee of a *general* power could have appointed first to her estate, then disposed of the assets as her own. The capture doctrine supplies this result when circumstances indicate the donee intended it. The capture doctrine applies even though there is a gift in default of appointment. The question is whether the donee intended to capture the property; if so, the property does not pass in default of appointment.

b. **Ineffective exercise:** [§408]   The power is usually ineffectively exercised because the appointment violates the Rule Against Perpetuities or the appointment is to a person then dead.

c. **Blending clause:** [§409]   Intent to capture the property may be found from a clause blending the donee's own property with the appointive property. This shows an intent of the donee to treat the property as her own. (*See supra*, §§403-405.)

d. **Appointment in trust:** [§410]   It has been held that an appointment in trust indicates an intent to capture the property, because the donee would be the new settlor of the trust. Any resulting trust would be for the donee. [Talbot v. Riggs, 191 N.E. 360 (Mass. 1934)]

e. **Special power:** [§411]   The doctrine of capture has no application to special powers, because the donee by definition is excluded from the benefits of a special power. The donee of a special power may not appoint the property to her estate.

Proceed to the Review Questions for Chapter V.

VI. THE RULE AGAINST PERPETUITIES

A. INTRODUCTION

1. **Statement of Rule:** [§412]   The classic formulation of the Rule was laid down by John Chipman Gray, a Harvard professor, who in the late nineteenth century wrote the authoritative book on the Rule: ***No interest is good unless it must vest, if at all, not later than 21 years after some life in being at the creation of the interest***. Hence, any future interest in real or personal property is void if there is ***any possibility***, however remote, that the interest may vest more than 21 years after the death of persons alive at the creation of the interest. The Rule is a rule against remote vesting.

   a. **Why the period is lives in being:** [§413]   The judges fixed upon the period of lives in being plus 21 years as the limit of dead hand control for this reason: It was reasonable, they thought, for a testator to be able to tie up property for the lives of family members known to the testator. He could assess their capacity for managing property, and could make wise judgments as to their abilities. But the testator could not assay the abilities of persons born after his death. Therefore, the testator's judgment was given effect only during the lives of persons he knew.

      (1) **Addition of 21 years:** [§414]   The judges then extended the period of testator's control to 21 years after lives in being, which covers the minority of persons in the next generation. This permitted, as Professor Leach said, "a man of property . . . [to] provide for all those in his family whom he personally knew and the first generation after them upon attaining majority." [6 Amer. Law Prop. §24.16] The 21-year period is not limited to actual minorities, however. It is a period of years that can be used regardless of minorities.

   b. **Must vest or fail within period:** [§415]   The classic statement of the Rule says an interest "must vest, ***if at all***," within lives in being plus 21 years. The words "if at all" mean that the interest must vest ***or fail*** within the period. If the interest may remain contingent beyond this period, it is void.

      (1) **Example:** T devises property "to A for life, and then to B if B becomes a lawyer." B is age two. B's interest will vest, ***if at all***, during B's lifetime—when B becomes a lawyer. B is the validating life.

      (2) **Compare:** T devises property "to A for life, and then to A's first child to become a lawyer." B, a child of A, is in law school. The interest in "A's first child to become a lawyer" will not necessarily vest within the life of B, because B may die tomorrow or fail the bar exam. Nor will the interest necessarily vest within A's life or 21 years after A's death. A may have an afterborn child, C, who becomes a lawyer more than 21 years after the deaths of A and B. The gift to "A's first child to become a lawyer" is void.

   c. **What might happen is test:** [§416]   Observe that the Rule Against Perpetuities is a rule of proof about what ***might*** happen. To win, the claimant of an interest must prove that the interest will *necessarily* vest or fail within 21 years after the death of some person alive when the instrument becomes effective. For the person attacking the interest to win, he must prove that there is a possibility that the interest *might* vest too remotely. Whichever party can make the required proof wins. In the example given first above, B is the party who can make the required proof, and B wins. In the comparative example, the party arguing for invalidity can make the required proof, and he wins.

(1) **No wait-and-see:** [§417]   At common law we do not wait and see what happens. We do not, for instance, in the comparative example given above, wait and see whether a child of A becomes a lawyer within A's life or 21 years after A's death. An interest is determined to be void or valid at the time of creation, according to what might happen. Actual events that happen after creation are ignored.

   (a) **Modern wait-and-see:** [§418]   The common law Rule permits you to prove validity of an interest. Where it is shown to be invalid, a majority of states have adopted the wait-and-see test. This permits an invalid interest to be saved if it actually vests in time. In this summary, the common law Rule is treated first, followed by a discussion of wait-and-see. It is easier to learn both the common law Rule and the wait-and-see doctrine if they are treated in consecutive order. Even where wait-and-see has been adopted, it remains important to know the common law Rule. No instrument is properly drafted unless the interests created are certainly valid. Good lawyers do not wait and see.

2. **Interests Subject to the Rule:** [§419]   The Rule applies to *contingent remainders* and *executory interests*. It does not apply to vested remainders. Nor does it apply to future interests in the grantor (reversion, possibility of reverter, and right of entry), which are treated as part of the grantor's estate and vested from the beginning.

   a. **Duration of trusts:** [§420]   The Rule is not a rule prohibiting trusts that may last longer than lives in being plus 21 years. It is solely a rule *against creation of contingent interests* that may remain contingent beyond the permissible period.

      (1) **Example:** O conveys to X in trust "to pay income to A for life, then to A's children for their lives, then to pay the principal to B." A has no children. The conveyance is entirely valid. A may have children born after the conveyance, and the life estate in A's children may last for the life of an afterborn child of A, which may be more than 21 years after A's death, but all interests are valid. The life estate in A's children vests at A's death. The remainder in B is vested at creation. The Rule indirectly limits the duration of trusts, however, by requiring that all future interests in the trust must vest or fail within the period.

   b. **Charitable trusts:** [§421]   Charitable trusts are not subject to the Rule Against Perpetuities. They may endure in perpetuity.

3. **When Period Begins to Run:** [§422]   The validity of an interest is determined as of the time of the *creation* of the interest. "Lives in being" must be persons alive

at that time. Generally, the perpetuities period (lives in being plus 21 years) begins to run whenever the transferor makes an irrevocable transfer.

a. **Will:** [§423]   If the interest is created by will, the period begins at testator's death. The "lives in being" used to validate the devise must be persons alive at the testator's death.

b. **Irrevocable deed:** [§424]   If the interest is created by deed, or by an irrevocable deed of trust, the period begins at the time the deed is delivered with intent to pass title. The "lives in being" used to prove validity must be persons alive at that time.

c. **Revocable trust:** [§425]   If a trust is revocable by the settlor, the period begins at the date the trust becomes irrevocable (either at the settlor's death or when the trust is amended to make it irrevocable). *Rationale:* The policy of the Rule is not offended if one person has the power to convey a fee simple absolute and destroy the interests in trust. The property is not tied up. [Cook v. Horn, 104 S.E.2d 461 (Ga. 1958); Ryan v. Ward, 64 A.2d 258 (Md. 1949)]

   (1) **Example:** By deed O transfers property in trust "to pay the income to O for life, then to O's children for life, then to convey the principal to O's grandchildren." O retains the power to revoke the trust. The remainder in O's grandchildren is valid. The perpetuity period begins to run at O's death, when the power of revocation ceases. At that time, all of O's children are in being. Hence the remainder to O's grandchildren will vest at the death of O's children, all of whom are in being when the trust becomes irrevocable.

      (a) **Irrevocable trust:** [§426]   If the above trust were an irrevocable inter vivos trust, the remainder to O's grandchildren would be void. O might have another child conceived after the trust is set up, and the remainder to grandchildren might not vest until the death of such afterborn child.

B. ANALYSIS OF THE RULE

1. **Meaning of Vest:** [§427]   A remainder or executory interest is vested when it either *vests in possession or turns into a remainder vested in interest*.

   a. **Vest in possession:** [§428]   An interest is vested in possession when it becomes possessory.

   b. **Vest in interest:** [§429]   A remainder is vested in interest when it is owned by an ascertained person and is not subject to a condition precedent (*see supra*, §78).

      (1) **Vested upon creation:** [§430]   A remainder vested upon its creation satisfies the Rule Against Perpetuities (*see supra*, §420).

      (2) **Vesting after creation:** [§431]   A contingent remainder or executory interest that will necessarily turn into a vested remainder or fail within the perpetuities period satisfies the Rule.

      (a) **Example:** T devises property in trust "for A for life, then to A's children for their lives, then to B, but if B is not then living, to C." B's remainder is vested subject to divestment upon creation. It is valid. C's executory interest will divest B's vested remainder, turning into a vested remainder itself, if B dies before the remainder becomes possessory. Therefore it will vest or fail within B's life and is valid.

   c. **Exception—class gift:** [§432] There is one major exception to the above rules, the class gift. A *gift to a class* is not vested under the Rule Against Perpetuities *in any member of the class until the interests of all members have vested*. Or to put it differently, a class gift is not vested under the Rule Against Perpetuities until the **class has closed** and **all conditions precedent have been satisfied** for every member of the class. If the gift to one member of the class might vest too remotely, the whole class gift is void. This is known as the "all-or-nothing" rule. (*See infra,* §472.)

      (1) **Example:** T devises property "to A for life, then to A's children for their lives, then to A's grandchildren." A has a grandchild, B, alive. By common law classification, the remainder is vested in B subject to open and let in later born grandchildren. *But it is not vested for purpose of the Rule Against Perpetuities*. The remainder, a gift to a class, is entirely void. It will not vest under the Rule until the class of grandchildren is closed (*i.e.,* when all A's children die), and since A can have an afterborn child, the class of grandchildren may close at the death of an afterborn person. (Compare the similar two-generation trust in §431, where the remainder in fee is given to an individual rather than to a class, and is valid.)

   d. **Vested with possession postponed:** [§433] A gift can be vested with possession postponed rather than subject to a condition precedent. This occurs almost entirely in cases where there is a provision postponing payment until the beneficiary reaches a designated age. The principles laid down in *Clobberie's Case* (*see supra,* §250) are applicable under the Rule Against Perpetuities.

 2. **Validating Lives:** [§434] The persons who enable a claimant to prove validity of the gift have traditionally been called the "measuring lives." The modern term for these persons is "validating lives," which emphasizes their function—enabling a claimant to prove validity of a gift.

   a. **Relevant lives:** [§435] In seeking a validating life, you should narrow the candidates to persons who might qualify in making the required proof. You will find a validating life, if you find one at all, *only among persons who can affect vesting of the interest*. All other persons are irrelevant to this search. The question thus becomes: Who can affect vesting?

      (1) **Who can affect vesting:** [§436] The persons who may affect vesting include: (i) the preceding life tenants, (ii) the beneficiaries of a contingent interest, (iii) any ancestor who can affect the identity of the beneficiaries (such as A in a gift to A's children, and A and A's children in a gift to A's grandchildren), and (iv) any person who can affect any condition

precedent attached to the gift. If there is no person among the relevant lives by whom the requisite proof can be made, the interest is void unless it must vest or fail within 21 years.

(2) **Example:** T devises property "to Mary, and if Mary's line of descendants runs out, to the daughters then living of Elizabeth." Elizabeth has four daughters living at T's death. The relevant lives are Mary, Elizabeth, and the four living daughters. Try each life to see if the gift will vest or fail at her death. You will find that it will not necessarily vest or fail within the lives of any of the relevant persons and is void. There are no validating lives, no "lives in being" referred to by the Rule. [Jee v. Audley, 29 Eng. Rep. 1186 (1787)]

(a) *Mary cannot be a validating life* because her line of descendants *might not* run out at her death. It might not run out until centuries hence. Therefore, the executory interest will not necessarily vest or fail at her death.

(b) *Elizabeth cannot be a validating life* because the gift will not vest or fail at Elizabeth's death.

(c) *The daughters of Elizabeth now living cannot be the validating lives*, because the gift to "daughters then living" (which can include afterborn daughters) will not necessarily vest or fail within the lives of the presently living daughters. The present daughters might die tomorrow, Elizabeth might have another daughter, and the gift vest in the afterborn daughter.

(d) *Here is what might happen:* Assume T dies in 2000. In 2002 Elizabeth has a daughter, Faith. In 2003 Mary has a son, Alex. In 2004 a plane crash wipes out Mary, Mary's issue alive in 2000, Elizabeth, and the daughters of Elizabeth alive in 2000. Faith and Alex are left. Alex dies childless in 2050. Mary's line of descendants has then run out. Faith claims the property. This is more than 21 years after the death of persons alive in 2000 who are connected with this gift.

b. **Not mentioned in instrument:** [§437]   The validating lives need not be mentioned in the instrument. Suppose that T (testator) devises property by his will "to my grandchildren who reach 21." This is valid because all of T's grandchildren will become 21 within 21 years after the death of all of T's children. T's children are the validating lives.

c. **Artificial validating lives:** [§438]   The validating lives need not have any interest in the property nor family connection to the beneficiaries. Such validating lives are called "artificial" or "extraneous" lives. It is sometimes useful, particularly in drafting a provision terminating a complicated trust, to specify artificial measuring lives.

(1) **Example:** "This trust shall terminate 21 years after the death of the survivor of the issue of Joseph P. Kennedy now living, and the principal shall be distributed to my issue then living per stirpes." The Kennedy issue

now alive are the validating lives. All interests in the trust will vest within their lives plus 21 years. Since the Kennedy descendants are numerous, chances are the last to die will live at least to age 80. Thus the trust will probably run for 100 years or so.

(2) **Royal lives:** [§439]   The English sometimes use "royal lives" to measure the duration of a trust. For example, a trust may be created to last until 21 years after the death of the survivor of Queen Elizabeth's issue now alive. [*In re* Villar, [1929] 1 Ch. 243—holding valid as measuring lives 120 living issue of Queen Victoria] Descendants of royalty are usually prominent, and it is not too difficult to ascertain when they die.

(3) **Healthy babies:** [§440]   It is possible to select a number of healthy babies as validating lives, *e.g.*, "to my issue alive at the death of A, B, C, D, E, F, and G (being babies born in Mt. Hope Hospital this week)."

d. **Reasonable number:** [§441]   The validating lives must be reasonable in number. They must not be so difficult to trace as to make evidence of their deaths unreasonably difficult to obtain. A bequest "to A's issue after the death of the last person now alive" is void.

e. **Nonhuman lives:** [§442]   Only human beings can be used as validating lives. Corporations, turtles, dogs, and trees cannot be used as validating lives. This problem usually is raised in an honorary trust for a pet. For example, T bequeaths $5,000 "to A and her heirs, to use for the care of my dog Trixie." Trixie cannot be used as a validating life, and the bequest is void. Any honorary trust for a pet is void if it can endure longer than the perpetuities period.

f. **Periods of gestation:** [§443]   Any actual periods of gestation are included within the permissible perpetuities period. For purposes of the Rule, a person is treated as in being from the time of conception.

(1) **Example:** T devises property "to my children for their lives, then to my grandchildren who reach 21." At T's death, his wife is pregnant and four months later gives birth to A. At the death of A, A's wife is pregnant and three months later gives birth to B. The gift to T's grandchildren is good, and B shares in it if B reaches 21.

g. **Twenty-one year period:** [§444]   The 21-year period cannot precede the measuring lives. The measuring lives must be in being at the date the instrument becomes effective, not 21 years later. (*See supra*, §413, for the reason for this.)

(1) **Example:** T bequeaths a fund in trust "to accumulate the income for 21 years, then to pay the income to my grandchildren alive at that time for their lives, and on the death of the survivor to pay the principal to their children." The gift of income (a life estate) to the grandchildren is valid because it vests at the end of 21 years. The gift of principal to their children is void because it may vest at the death of one of T's grandchildren born after T's death. [Thomas v. Harrison, 191 N.E.2d 862 (Ohio 1962)]

3. **Consequences of Violating Rule:** [§445]   Any interest that violates the Rule Against Perpetuities is stricken from the instrument. The valid part remains standing. [Lovering v. Worthington, 106 Mass. 86 (1870)]

    a. **Effect on defeasible interests:** [§446]   If a divesting gift is stricken, the preceding gift is left standing and becomes indefeasible. Thus suppose that T devises property "to A for life, then to A's children, but if any of A's children becomes a lawyer, to B." B's interest is void because an afterborn child of A may become a lawyer more than 21 years after A's death. Strike out B's gift. A's children now have a vested remainder subject to open up and let in more children born to A, but not subject to divestment by B. [Rust v. Rust, 211 S.W.2d 262 (Tex. 1948)]

    b. **Infectious invalidity:** [§447]   The general rule of striking out only the invalid interest is subject to one exception known as "infectious invalidity." If the court finds that the invalid interest was such an integral part of the transferor's scheme that if it is invalid the transferor would have preferred a valid interest also to fail, the valid interest will fail. The bad interest "infects" the good. The rule is designed to carry out the transferor's presumed intent. [New England Trust Co. v. Sanger, 149 N.E.2d 598 (Mass. 1948)]

C. APPLICATION TO DEFEASIBLE FEES

1. **Exemption of Possibility of Reverter and Right of Entry:** [§448]   The Rule Against Perpetuities does *not* apply to possibilities of reverter and rights of entry, which are regarded as vested interests, but it does apply to executory interests. This exemption of possibilities of reverter and rights of entry from the Rule has led to some strange results.

2. **Determinable Fee:** [§449]   Any executory interest following a determinable fee that violates the Rule Against Perpetuities is *struck out*, as with a blue pencil, leaving the determinable fee standing. Whatever is left after striking out the void interest is given effect as written.

    a. **Example:** O conveys Blackacre "to the School Board *so long as* it is used for school purposes, and if the land shall cease to be used for school purposes to A and her heirs." A's executory interest will not necessarily vest, if at all, within A's life but may be transmitted at A's death to her heirs or devisees and then on and on to their heirs or devisees. It might not become possessory for centuries. A's executory interest is void. The language "and if the land shall cease to be used for school purposes to A and her heirs," which is the language giving A an executory interest, is struck out. This leaves standing, "to the School Board so long as it is used for school purposes." This language gives the Board a determinable fee, which is not increased by striking out A's interest. Since the Board has only a determinable fee, which will automatically end when the land ceases to be used for school purposes, O has a *possibility of reverter*. [First Universalist Society v. Boland, 29 N.E. 524 (Mass. 1892); Institution for Savings v. Roxbury Home for Aged Women, 193 N.E. 301 (Mass. 1923); *cf.* Brown v. Independent Baptist Church of Woburn, 91 N.E.2d 922 (Mass. 1950)—where determinable fee was created by will, the possibility of reverter passed by the residuary clause rather than to testator's heirs (*see supra*, §44)]

b. **Exception—gift over from one charity to another charity:** [§450] If there is a gift to Charity A followed by a divesting gift to Charity B if a specified event happens, the executory interest in Charity B is exempt from the Rule Against Perpetuities. Thus in the above example, if O had conveyed Blackacre "to the School Board so long as it is used for school purposes, then to the Red Cross," the conveyance would be entirely valid. The reason for this exception is that charities are favorites of the law. A charitable trust can last forever. There is no objection to shifting enjoyment from charity to charity through time. *But note:* This exception applies *only* if *both* the possessory estate and the future interest are in charitable organizations.

3. **Fee Simple Subject to an Executory Limitation:** [§451] The example of the determinable fee above should be compared with a fee simple subject to an executory limitation. The difference in language is very slight but the difference in results is startling. Suppose that O conveys Blackacre "to the School Board, *but if* Blackacre shall cease to be used for school purposes to A and her heirs." The executory interest in A is void under the Rule Against Perpetuities for the same reason that A's executory interest in the preceding example is void. The language creating the executory interest—"but if Blackacre shall cease to be used for school purposes to A and her heirs"—is struck out. This leaves a conveyance "to the School Board," which of course gives the Board a fee simple absolute. [Proprietors of the Church in Brattle Square v. Grant, 69 Mass. 142 (1855); Peveto v. Starkey, 645 S.W.2d 770 (Tex. 1982)]

D. THE CLASSIC ABSURD CASES

1. **What-Might-Happen Test:** [§452] An interest is void under the Rule if *by any possibility*—however remote—the interest might vest beyond the permitted period. If a situation can be imagined in which the interest might not vest or fail within the perpetuities period, the interest is void. The remote possibilities test has resulted in some classic absurd cases that have brought the Rule into disrepute. The following pitfall cases illustrate this aspect of the Rule.

a. **The fertile octogenarian:** [§453] The law *conclusively* presumes that a person can have a child until he or she is dead. Thus suppose that T devises property "to my sister A for life, then to A's children for their lives, then to A's grandchildren in fee." A is age 80, has had a complete hysterectomy, and will not have any more children. We must assume, however, that it is *possible* for A to have another child conceived after T's death. On the basis of this assumption, the gift to grandchildren is void. It will not vest until the death of the survivor of A's children, and that surviving child might be a child not yet born. Thus, there is a possibility of remote vesting. [Connecticut Bank & Trust Co. v. Brody, 392 A.2d 445 (Conn. 1978); New England Trust Co. v. Sanger, *supra*, §447; North Carolina National Bank v. Norris, 203 S.E.2d 657 (N.C. 1974)]

(1) **Subsequent events:** [§454] Suppose that before litigation A dies without having any more children. We are then certain the remainder will vest at the death of persons in being. However, facts occurring after T's death are irrelevant. The validity of an interest is judged on the basis of facts existing at T's death only. [Jee v. Audley, *supra*, §436]

INVALID GIFTS

Example	Validating Life	Explanation
"To A for life, then to A's first child to become a lawyer."	None	A's first child to become a lawyer may be an afterborn child who becomes a lawyer more than 21 years after A dies.
"To School Board so long as it is used for a school, then to A."	None	A's interest may vest in A's heirs or devisees hundreds of years from now. A's interest is stricken. Possibility of reverter is left in grantor.
"To School Board, but if it ceases to be used for a school, to A."	None	A's interest void for reason given above. A's interest is stricken. School Board has a fee simple absolute.
Option "to A and her heirs."	None	Option may not be exercised within lives in being plus 21 years.

VALID GIFTS

Example	Validating Life	Explanation
"To A for life, then to B if B returns from Rome."	B	Condition must happen within B's life if at all.
"To A for life, then to A's children for life, then to B."	B	B's remainder is vested upon creation.
"To A for life, then to A's children for life, then to B if B is living, and if not living, to C."	B	Either B's or C's remainder will vest within B's lifetime.

(2) **Minority view:** [§455]   A few decisions have held that extrinsic evidence is admissible to show that a person cannot have a child. [*In re* Bassett's Estate, 190 A.2d 415 (N.H. 1963); *In re* Lattouf's Will, 208 A.2d 411 (N.J. 1965)] And statutes in several states have changed the conclusive presumption of fertility. They usually provide that women over 55 presumptively cannot have children and that evidence of infertility of a specific person is admissible in any case. The statutes usually provide that the possibility of adoption shall be disregarded. [N.Y. Est. Powers & Trusts Law §9-1.3(e)]

(3) **Saving by construction:** [§456]   In the example above, the remainder to A's grandchildren can be saved if it is construed as given only to the children of A's presently living children. The class of grandchildren would then close at the death of presently living persons. This construction makes a lot of sense where A is beyond child-bearing years, and T undoubtedly assumed A would not have any more children. Traditionally, courts have construed instruments "remorselessly," giving words their usual meaning, and paying no heed to the consequences under the Rule Against Perpetuities. In view of the modern movement to pull the claws of the Rule and carry out the testator's intent, it may be expected that courts will more and more avoid the Rule by construction. [Wright's Estate, 131 A. 188 (Pa. 1925)]

b. **The precocious toddler:** [§457]   If the law assumes a person can have a child until dead, what is the youngest age a person can have a child? This has never been settled. In *In re Gaite's Will Trusts*, [1949] 1 All E.R. 459, the court had before it a bequest that would be void only if it assumed that a person under the age of five could have a child. The court validated the bequest by construing a child born to a person under the age of five as not coming within the terms of the bequest (because illegitimate), thus avoiding the interesting question posed above.

c. **The unborn widow:** [§458]   The law assumes that a woman described as "A's widow," when A is alive, may refer to an afterborn woman. Thus suppose that T devises property "to my son A for life, then to his widow for her life, then to A's issue then living." The remainder to A's issue is void. It may vest at the death of A's widow, and A's widow may be a woman not now alive. If A is presently married, his present wife may die or be divorced, and A may marry some young woman not now alive who likes older men. [Dickerson v. Union National Bank of Little Rock, 595 S.W.2d 677 (Ark. 1980); Pound v. Shorter, 377 S.E.2d 854 (Ga. 1989); Perkins v. Igleheart, 39 A.2d 672 (Md. 1944)]

(1) **Construction:** [§459]   It is possible to save the remainder by construing "A's widow" to mean "A's present wife." Under such a construction "A's widow" would be a life in being at the creation of the interest, and the remainder would be valid. But very few courts have ever saved the gift by construction.

(2) **Statutory changes:** [§460]   In some states, statutes have been passed to deal with the unborn widow problem. They usually provide that an individual described as a spouse of a living person is presumed to be in being at the time the instrument becomes effective. [N.Y. Est. Powers & Trusts Law §9-1.3(b)]

d. **The slothful executor:** [§461]   The law assumes that a probate estate may not be closed within the perpetuities period. Thus suppose that T devises her property "to my issue per stirpes living at the distribution of my estate." The devise is void. Even though it is highly unlikely that the distribution of T's estate will be delayed beyond lives in being plus 21 years, it is possible. In that event, the class would not close and "issue" would not be definitely ascertained within the perpetuities period. [*In re* Campbell's Estate, 28 Cal. App. 2d 102 (1938); *cf.* Ryan v. Beshk, 170 N.E. 699 (Ill. 1930)]

(1) **Minority views:** [§462]   It has been held in one case that equity will require that the estate be distributed within a reasonable period of time and such a period will necessarily be less than 21 years. [Belfield v. Booth, 27 A. 585 (Conn. 1893)] In several states, statutes provide that an interest contingent upon probate of a will, settlement of the estate, or similar administrative contingency shall be presumed to occur, if at all, within 21 years after the creation of the interest. [N.Y. Est. Powers & Trusts Law §9-1.3(d)]

e. **The magic gravel pit:** [§463]   Suppose that T devises land to trustees "to work the gravel pits, and when they are worked out to sell the land and divide the proceeds among T's issue then living." Even though the pits are actually worked out in six years, the gift is void because it is possible for the pits to be worked in excess of lives in being plus 21 years. [*In re* Wood, [1894] 3 Ch. 381]

f. **Wars that never end:** [§464]   Suppose that in 1943 T, an immigrant from Germany, devises property to her issue living in Germany "when World War II ends." It has been held that the devise violates the Rule since the interest will not necessarily vest or fail within lives in being plus 21 years. The fact that World War II actually lasted less than 21 years is irrelevant. It *might* have gone on like the Hundred Years' War between England and France. [Brownell v. Edmunds, 209 F.2d 349 (D.C. Cir. 1953)]

2. **Alternative Contingencies:** [§465]   Under the doctrine of alternative contingencies, if the grantor makes a gift upon alternative contingencies, one of which might happen too remotely but the other of which must happen, if at all, within the perpetuities period, the gift is valid if the second (valid) contingency actually occurs. It is void if the first (invalid) contingency actually occurs. [First Portland National Bank v. Rodrique, 172 A.2d 107 (Me. 1961)]

a. **Example:** T devises property "to A for life, then to A's widow for life, then (1) on the death of A's widow or (2) on the death of A if A leaves no widow, to A's issue then living." T has made a gift to A's issue upon two separate contingencies. The gift upon the first contingency (the death of A's widow) is void. The gift upon the second contingency (the death of A unmarried) is valid. If A actually dies without a widow, A's issue will take at A's death. But if A dies leaving a widow, the gift to A's issue is void.

b. **Grantor must separate contingencies:** [§466]   Traditionally the alternative contingencies doctrine applies only if the grantor expressly separates the contingencies. The court will not separate the contingencies for him. In the above example, if contingency (2) had been omitted from the words of the devise, the gift to A's issue would be void in all events. But note that the second contingency is inherent in the gift to issue even if not expressly stated.

(1) **Reason for restriction:** [§467] The reason for requiring the grantor to expressly split the contingencies is to avoid jettisoning the what-might-happen test by slipping into the wait-and-see doctrine. If a court splits the contingencies in every gift into invalid events and valid events, it will end up with the wait-and-see doctrine.

(2) **Modern trend:** [§468] Several recent cases have treated the interest as vesting on separate contingencies inherent in the gift, even though the grantor did not split them. [Continental Cablevision of New England, Inc. v. United Broadcasting Co., 873 F.2d 717 (4th Cir. 1989)] The gift can be saved by this technique if the interest actually vests in time. The wait-and-see doctrine has been adopted in a majority of states. In view of the current popularity of wait-and-see, the alternative contingencies doctrine may come to be applied in jurisdictions that have not formally adopted wait-and-see, even though the contingencies are not expressly split by the grantor.

3. **Saving Clauses:** [§469] Because of the danger that even an experienced lawyer might overlook some remote possibility and violate the Rule, good estate planners—since the 1960s—insert a *saving clause* into any trust they draft. The saving clause terminates the trust, if it has not otherwise terminated under its terms, at the end of 21 years after the death of the survivor of a group of named persons. The named persons are usually the living beneficiaries of the trust or the settlor's living issue. If the trust terminates at the end of lives in being plus 21 years, no interest in the trust can violate the Rule. All interests will vest in possession, if at all, within the perpetuities period.

   a. **Example:** Here is an example of a saving clause: "Notwithstanding any other provision in this instrument, this trust shall terminate, if it has not previously terminated, 21 years after the death of the settlor's issue living at the date this instrument becomes effective. In case of such termination, the then remaining principal and undistributed income of the trust shall be distributed to the settlor's issue then living per stirpes."

   b. **Extraneous lives:** [§470] A saving clause need not use family lives to measure the duration of a trust. It can use extraneous lives (*supra*, §438). Extraneous lives are rarely used, however, unless they are from a prominent family easy to keep track of.

E. GIFTS TO CLASSES

1. **Class Must Be Closed:** [§471] A remainder in a class vested subject to open is not vested under the Rule Against Perpetuities. Under the Rule, the *class must be closed* for the gift to be treated as vested. Thus, if a testator devises property "to A for life, remainder to A's children," and A has a child, B, alive, the remainder is vested in B subject to open (*see supra*, §82), but it is not vested under the Rule *until the class closes*. Since the class will necessarily close at A's death, the remainder is valid.

2. **All-or-Nothing Rule:** [§472] A class gift is wholly void if the interest of any member might vest too remotely. The gift must be valid for all, or it is valid for none. Therefore, a class gift is not vested until: (i) the class has closed (all takers are ascertained) and (ii) all conditions precedent for *every* member of the class are met. [Leake v. Robinson, 35 Eng. Rep. 979 (1817)]

    a. **Example of class closing too remotely:** [§473] T devises property "to A for life, then to A's children for their lives, then to A's grandchildren in fee." The class of A's grandchildren will not close until A's children all die. At that time it will be impossible for them to have more children. Since A may have a child in the future (conclusive presumption), the class may not close until the death of an afterborn child. The remainder to A's grandchildren is void. [Ward v. Van der Loeff, [1924] A.C. 653; Connecticut Bank & Trust Co. v. Brody, *supra*, §453]

    b. **Example of condition precedent:** [§474] T devises property "to A for life, then to A's children who reach 25." The class will close at A's death, but the problem is the age condition. A might die two years from now, leaving a child age one. Since the condition precedent respecting that child will not be resolved for 24 more years, the class gift fails. [*In re* Lee's Estate, 299 P.2d 1066 (Wash. 1954)]

3. **A Workable Test for Class Gifts:** [§475] In applying the Rule Against Perpetuities to class gifts, the task will be easier if you ask the following questions, in the order given:

    a. **When will the class close?** [§476] This is the *first major question*. If the class will surely close within the perpetuities period, you have tentatively validated the interest and can proceed to ask the second major question. If the class will not necessarily close within the perpetuities period, the gift is void and there is no need to ask the second major question.

        (1) **When will the class close physiologically?** [§477] To determine when a class will close, ask first when will it close physiologically? A class will close physiologically at the death of the parent of the class (*i.e.*, the class of "children of A" will close at A's death). If you find that the class will close physiologically within the period, you should proceed to the second major question. If the class will not close physiologically within the period, ask the following question.

        (2) **When will the class close under the rule of convenience?** [§478] If the class will close under the rule of convenience (*see infra*, §480) within the period, proceed to second major question. If the class will close neither physiologically nor under the rule of convenience within the period, the gift is void.

    b. **When will all contingencies be resolved?** [§479] This is the *second major question*, which you should ask only if you have found that the class will close within the period. If the class will timely close, and now, in answer to this question, you find that all contingencies will be resolved (one way or the other) within the perpetuities period, the class gift is good. If a condition precedent for any member of the class will not be resolved within the period, the whole class gift fails.

4. **Rule of Convenience:** [§480]   A class gift may be saved through the operation of the rule of convenience. This rule is: A class closes whenever any member of the class can demand possession of her share (*see supra*, §310). This is an extremely important rule to remember in applying the Rule Against Perpetuities. In applying the rule of convenience, what you are looking for, to save the gift, is some person *in existence* when the interest is created who is certain to have the right to demand possession within the perpetuities period. If that person exists, the class is certain to close within the period.

   a. **Example:** T devises property "to A for life, and on A's death to A's grandchildren." If A has one grandchild, B, alive at T's death, the gift to grandchildren is good. We are certain at T's death that the class will close at A's death because B (or B's administrator) will demand possession of B's share at A's death. A is thus the validating life. If A has no grandchild alive at T's death, the remainder is void because the class might not close until the death of an afterborn child of A. [Ward v. Van der Loeff, *supra*, §473]

   b. **Example:** T devises property "to A's grandchildren who reach 25." A survives T. If one grandchild of A is alive and age 25 or over at T's death, he can demand possession at T's death, thus closing the class at T's death. The gift is good because all members of the class (limited to lives in being) will necessarily reach 25 or die under that age within their own lives. If no grandchild is age 25 or over at T's death, the gift is void. All present grandchildren of A might die tomorrow, A might have another child and the claimant might be a child of an afterborn child of A. [Picken v. Matthews, 10 Ch. D. 264 (1878)]

5. **Gift to Separate Subclasses:** [§481]   If there is a gift to separate subclasses of a younger generation, each gift to a subclass may be tested separately under the Rule. This is sometimes known as the doctrine of separate shares or as the doctrine of *Cattlin v. Brown,* 68 Eng. Rep. 1319 (1853), the case in which it originated.

   a. **Example:** T devises property in trust "to A for life, then to A's children for their respective lives, and *as each child dies* to pay the share of the principal from which such child was receiving the income to such child's children." At T's death A has one child, B, alive. One year later a child, C, is born to A. Here the gift is not to one big class of A's grandchildren, to be divided in equal shares among them, but a gift to B's children on B's death and a gift to C's children on C's death (and to other children of afterborn children upon the parent's death). Each subclass of grandchildren will close upon the death of the respective parent. Hence a gift to issue of B (a life in being) is valid because the gift will vest upon B's death. On the other hand, a gift to the issue of C (an afterborn child) is void. [American Security & Trust Co. v. Cramer, 175 F. Supp. 367 (D.C. 1959)]

   b. **Key:** [§482]   The key to a gift to separate subclasses is finding that separate gifts vest at different times. In the above example, the separate gifts vest in possession at the death of *each* child of A, rather than all vesting at the death of *all* children of A. If the gift to A's grandchildren vested when *all* of A's children died, it would be void. [North Carolina National Bank v. Norris, *supra*, §453; Connecticut Bank & Trust Co. v. Brody, *supra*, §453—both refusing to apply separability doctrine since remainders vested when **all** A's children died rather than when **each** of A's children died]

c. **Vesting in interest:** [§483]   The separate shares doctrine applies when gifts to subclasses vest in interest at different times as well as when they vest in possession. When a subclass closes, and there are no unsatisfied conditions precedent, it is vested in interest.

(1) **Example:** Suppose that T devises property "to A for life, then to A's children for their lives, then to A's grandchildren **by right of representation**." The number of children (and therefore the number of shares) will be fixed at A's death. At the death of each child of A, his or her children's share will vest in interest. Therefore, the gift to children of any child of A now in being is good. The gift to children of a child of A not in being is void. Assume A has one child, B, alive at T's death. After T's death, C is born to A. At A's death, the property is divided into two shares for the life tenants. When B dies, B's children take a remainder in one-half vested in interest indefeasibly. C's children's interest is void because it will not vest until the death of C, an afterborn. There is a reversion as to C's one-half, which goes to T's estate. [Second Bank-State Street Trust Co. v. Second Bank-State Street Trust Co., 140 N.E.2d 201 (Mass. 1957)]

6. **Per Capita Gifts:** [§484]   A separate gift of a **fixed sum** to **each** member of a class is not subject to the all-or-nothing rule. Each gift is tested separately. The amount each member of the class takes is not in any way affected by how many persons are in the class. [Storrs v. Benbow, 43 Eng. Rep. 153 (1853)]

a. **Example:** T devises a fund in trust "to pay $1,000 to each of A's grandchildren who reaches 21, whether born before or after my death." A and one child, B, survive T. Two years after T dies, C is born to A. The gifts of $1,000 each are valid for each child of B. Each child of B will reach 21 within 21 years of B's death. The gifts to the children of C, born after T's death, are void.

7. **Vested with Possession Postponed:** [§485]   Under *Clobberie's Case* (*supra*, §250), a gift is vested with possession postponed if the gift is "to be paid at" or "payable at" a specified age. The rules in *Clobberie's Case* are applicable under the Rule Against Perpetuities. If a class gift is vested with possession postponed, and the class will close within the perpetuities period, the gift is valid.

a. **Example:** T devises property "to A for life, then to A's children, payable at their respective ages of 25." The gift will vest in A's children at A's death, with possession postponed. It is valid because the class of A's children will close at A's death. Reaching 25 is not a condition precedent. If it were, the gift would be void (*see supra*, §474).

b. **Only issue is class closing:** [§486]   If a class gift is vested with possession postponed, the only issue is when the class will close. Reaching the age designated for possession is not a condition precedent.

INVALID GIFTS

Example	Validating Life	Explanation
"To A for life, then to A's children for their lives, then to A's grandchildren."	None	The class of grandchildren won't close until the death of all A's children, one of whom may not be now alive. (Fertile octogenarian case)
"To A for life, then to A's widow for life, then to A's issue then living."	None	Class of issue won't close until widow's death, who may be woman not yet born. (Unborn widow case)
"To my issue living when my estate is distributed."	None	Class of issue may close too remotely (distribution of estate).
"To A for life, then to A's children who reach 25."	None	A may die leaving a child under age 4 who doesn't satisfy condition within 21 years of A's death.
"To A for life, then to A's grandchildren who reach 25."	None	Even if A has grandchild age 25 at time of gift who can close class at A's death under rule of convenience, in that class may be an afterborn grandchild of A under the age of 4 (as above).

VALID GIFTS

Example	Validating Life	Explanation
Devise "to my grandchildren who reach 21."	T's children	All of T's grandchildren will reach 21 within 21 years of the death of T's children.
"To A for life, then to A's widow for life, then to A's children."	A	Class of A's children will close at A's death.
"To A for life, then to A's grandchildren."	May be valid or void	If A has a grandchild when gift made, remainder is valid. Class will close under rule of convenience at A's death. If A has no grandchild when gift made, remainder is void because class may not close until death of afterborn child of A.
To A's grandchildren who reach 25."	May be valid or void	If A has grandchild age 25 or more at time of gift, gift is valid. Class closes under rule of convenience at time of gift. If no such grandchild, gift is void.
"To A for life, then to A's children for their lives, then as each child of A dies, to pay that child's share of principal to that child's issue."	May be valid or void	Gifts to issue of children now alive are valid; class closes at death of person in being. Gifts to issue of afterborn children are void. (Gift to subclasses)
"To A for life, then to A's children, payable at 25."	A	Class closes at A's death; vested then with possession postponed.
"To A for life, then as A appoints by will." A appoints "to B for life, then to B's children."	May be valid or void	If B is alive when power created, gift to B's children is good. It vests at B's death. If B is not alive when power created, gift to children of B (afterborn) is void. (Second look doctrine)

(1) **Example:** T bequeaths a fund in trust "for A for life, then to B's grand-children payable at their respective ages of 25." B is alive. The class of B's grandchildren will physiologically close at the death of B's children, but this is too remote, because of the possibility of an afterborn child. If, however, a grandchild of B is four years of age or older at T's death, the class will close no later than 21 years after A's death under the rule of convenience. Such a grandchild (or her administrator if the grandchild dies under 25) will have the right to demand possession when A is dead and when the over-four-year-old grandchild reaches 25 (or, if the grand-child dies under that age, when she would have reached 25 had she lived). The gift is valid because of the existence of a grandchild four years of age or older.

F. APPLICATION TO POWERS OF APPOINTMENT

1. **Introduction:** [§487]   In applying the Rule Against Perpetuities to powers of appointment, there are three questions: *First*, is the power valid? If the power is not validly created, then it does not exist and cannot be exercised, and the second question is irrelevant. *Second*, is the exercise of the power valid? *Third*, is the gift in default of appointment valid? In answering these three questions, powers must be divided into two categories: (i) general powers presently exercisable (which are treated as the equivalent of absolute ownership under the Rule), and (ii) testamentary and special powers (which are treated as tying up property under the Rule).

2. **General Powers Presently Exercisable**

   a. **Basic principle:** [§488]   If a donee has a general power presently exercisable, the property is not tied up. Because the donee can appoint to herself, the donee has as much control over the property as she has over her savings account. Therefore, a *general power presently exercisable is treated the same as if the donee owned a fee simple*.

   b. **Validity of power:** [§489]   A general inter vivos power is valid if there is certainty that the power will *become exercisable*, or fail, within the perpetuities period. Once the power becomes exercisable, the property is no longer tied up. The fact that the donee may exercise the power after lives in being plus 21 years is irrelevant. The controlling thing is the first point in time when the power becomes exercisable, untying the property.

      (1) **Example:** T bequeaths a fund in trust "to A for life, then after A's death to A's children for their lives, and each child shall have the power to appoint his or her share of the principal by deed or will." The powers are valid, even if exercised by a child now unborn. The powers become *exercisable* at A's death. After that point in time, the property is no longer tied up, since each child of A may demand his share in fee simple.

   c. **Validity of exercise:** [§490]   When a general power presently exercisable is exercised, we treat the exercise as if the donee owned the property in fee simple. The perpetuities period begins to run from the date of exercise. The interests created must vest or fail within 21 years after the death of some life in being at the date of exercise.

d. **Validity of gifts in default:** [§491]   Gifts in default of appointment may be destroyed by the donee exercising the power. Future interests that may be destroyed at any time by one person making the property her own (appointing the property to herself) do not violate the policy against perpetuities. Hence the perpetuities period begins to run only when the general inter vivos power ceases.

e. **Revocable trust:** [§492]   An unconditional power to revoke a trust is treated as a general power presently exercisable. The property is not tied up until the power ceases. The perpetuities period begins to run on the interests in the trust when the power to revoke ends.

3. **Testamentary Powers and Special Powers**

a. **Basic principle:** [§493]   If a donee has a special power, she does not have the power to appoint to herself, only to others. If a donee has a testamentary power, she may appoint only by will. It is assumed that the property is tied up in these cases because the donee cannot appoint *now to herself*. Hence the donee is not treated as the owner of the property. The donor is treated as owner of the property, and the property is *deemed to be tied up from the date of the creation of the power*.

b. **Validity of power:** [§494]   A testamentary or special power is valid if it may not be exercised beyond the perpetuities period, which begins at the creation of the power. *If the power may be exercised beyond the perpetuities period, it is void ab initio.* [*In re* Hargreaves, 43 Ch. D. 401 (1890)]

(1) **Example:** T devises property "to A for life, then to A's children for their lives, and *as each child dies*, to pay the proportionate share of the principal on which such child was receiving the income as such child appoints by will, and in default of appointment to such child's issue." The testamentary powers given to children of A in being at T's death are valid because those powers cannot be exercised after the death of the respective donees, who are in being at T's death. The testamentary powers given to children of A not in being at T's death are void because such powers may be exercised at the death of unborn persons.

(2) **Powers given unborn persons:** [§495]   A testamentary or special power may not be given to an unborn person unless the exercise of the power is expressly limited to the perpetuities period.

(a) **Example:** In 1984, T devises property "to A for life, remainder as A appoints by will." In 1996, A dies, appointing "to B for life, remainder as B appoints among her children by deed or will." B was born in 1990. The special power created in B is void, as B was not in being in 1984, when the perpetuities period began.

(3) **Powers in discretionary trust:** [§496]   Discretionary powers in trustees to pay income or principal to the beneficiaries are treated as special powers of appointment under the Rule Against Perpetuities. Any such power that is exercisable beyond the perpetuities period is void.

c. **Validity of exercise**

(1) **Relation-back doctrine:** [§497]   The interests created by exercise of a testamentary or special power are read back into the instrument creating the power. The donee is viewed as the agent of the donor, filling in blanks in the donor's will or deed. The perpetuities period begins at the date the power was created. [Second National Bank of New Haven v. Harris Trust & Savings Bank, 283 A.2d 226 (Conn. 1971); Northern Trust Co. v. Porter, 13 N.E.2d 487 (Ill. 1938)]

(a) **Minority view:** [§498]   In a few states, the perpetuities period runs from the date of exercise of a *testamentary* power. There is no relation back. The theory is that at the moment of death the donee can do anything the owner of a fee simple can do. [Industrial National Bank of Rhode Island v. Barrett, 220 A.2d 517 (R.I. 1966)]

(2) **Second look doctrine:** [§499]   Although the exercise of a special or testamentary power is read back into the donor's instrument, facts and circumstances existing on the date of exercise are taken into account in determining the validity of interests created by exercise of the power. This is known as the "second look" doctrine. [*In re* Bird's Estate, 225 Cal. App. 2d 196 (1964); Marx v. Rice, 67 A.2d 918 (N.J. 1949)]

(a) **Example:** T devises property "to A for life, then as A appoints by will." A appoints by will "to B for life, remainder to B's children." This is treated as if T's will read "to A for life, then to B for life, then to B's children." If B was alive at T's death, the remainder to B's children is valid. If B was not alive at T's death, the remainder to B's children is void.

d. **Validity of gifts in default:** [§500]   The second look doctrine has been applied to a gift in default of appointment. We do not determine the validity of the gift in default until the power of appointment ceases.

(1) **Example:** In 1984, T devises property "to A for life, then as A appoints by will; and in default of appointment, to A's children for their lives, remainder to A's grandchildren." In 1996, A dies intestate. All of A's children were born before 1984. The remainder to A's grandchildren is valid by applying the second look doctrine to the gift in default. [Sears v. Coolidge, 108 N.E.2d 563 (Mass. 1952)]

4. Effect of Invalid Appointment

a. **General rule:** [§501]   If the donee makes an invalid appointment, the property passes to the taker in default, if any. If there is no gift in default, the property reverts back to the donor's estate.

b. **Capture:** [§502]   The general rule is subject to the doctrine of capture. Where the donee of a general power manifests an intent to take the property out of the creating instrument and capture it for her estate and the appointment fails, the property will pass to the donee's estate (*see supra*, §406). [Amerige v. Attorney General, 88 N.E.2d 126 (Mass. 1949)]

(1) **Special power:** [§503] Capture applies only to a ***general*** power by which the donee could appoint directly to her estate if she chose.

(2) **Residuary violation:** [§504] If the perpetuities violation is in the donee's residuary clause and capture applies, the appointive property goes to the donee's heirs. It would be reasoning in a circle to send the captured property back out under the residuary clause, which violates the Rule. The captured property would return to the donee's estate, which is where we started. [Fiduciary Trust Co. v. Mishou, 75 N.E.2d 3 (Mass. 1947)]

c. **Allocation:** [§505] The doctrine of allocation (*supra,* §402) may apply where the Rule is violated. The trust property subject to the power and the donee's own property will be allocated to achieve maximum effectiveness.

G. APPLICATION TO COMMERCIAL TRANSACTIONS

1. Options

a. **Traditional law:** [§506] The orthodox view of options is that an option creates in the optionee a specifically enforceable right to purchase the property on the terms provided in the option. Because specifically enforceable in equity, an option is regarded as an equitable interest in the property. An option is void if it may be exercised more than 21 years after some life in being at its creation. *Rationale:* With an option outstanding, an owner will not improve the land, and no one else will be likely to purchase it. Options tend to make land unimprovable and inalienable. [Central Delaware County Authority v. Greyhound Corp., 588 A.2d 485 (Pa. 1991)]

(1) **Example:** O gives "A, his heirs and assigns an option to purchase Blackacre for $10,000." This option is void because A or his successor in interest may exercise the option hundreds of years from now.

(2) **Personal option:** [§507] If the option is personal to a human (not corporate) optionee, the option is valid. The optionee is the measuring life.

(3) **Preemptive options:** [§508] A preemptive option gives the optionee the right of first refusal if the owner desires to sell. If the preemptive option may be exercised beyond the perpetuities period, the option is void.

(a) **Example:** O sells Blackacre to A by a deed that provides "whenever A or his heirs or assigns desire to sell Blackacre, O or her heirs have the right to repurchase Blackacre upon the same terms and conditions as A or his heirs or assigns might be willing to sell it to another person." The preemptive option in O is void. [Atchison v. City of Englewood, 463 P.2d 297 (Colo. 1969)]

(4) **Options in a lease:** [§509] Options to purchase contained in a lease further alienability. They encourage the tenant to improve the property and reap the capital gain by exercising the option. Options in a lease are not subject to the Rule Against Perpetuities. [Texaco Refining & Marketing, Inc. v. Samowitz, 570 A.2d 170 (Conn. 1990)]

b.   **Modern trend:** [§510]   Several recent cases have refused to apply the Rule Against Perpetuities to preemptive options, but have subjected them instead to the rule against unreasonable restraints on alienation. The latter rule offers a more flexible tool for determining what kinds of preemptive options are objectionable as a matter of policy. [Cambridge Co. v. East Slope Investment Corp., 700 P.2d 537 (Colo. 1985)—holding reasonable a preemptive option in condominium agreement giving association right of first refusal); Metropolitan Transportation Authority v. Bruken Realty Corp., 67 N.Y.2d 156 (1986)]

2.   **On-Completion Leases:** [§511]   A standard feature of shopping center development is the on-completion lease. Suppose that a developer leases a building not yet built to a merchant. The lease is to begin upon completion of the building. It has been argued that on-completion leases violate the Rule Against Perpetuities because the building may not be built within the perpetuities period. After all, it took centuries to build some English cathedrals. However, most courts hold on-completion leases valid, though their reasoning differs. The court may imply in the contract a provision that the building must be finished within a reasonable period of time and then hold as a matter of law that a reasonable period of time is less than 21 years. [Wong v. DiGrazia, 60 Cal. 2d 525 (1963)]

H.   REFORMS OF THE RULE

1.   **Introduction**

a.   **Reasons for reform:** [§512]   Beginning in the 1950s the Rule Against Perpetuities came under increasing attack, largely by academics. They alleged that the Rule is a technicality-ridden nightmare that strikes down perfectly reasonable gifts because of some remote possibility that will never happen. They made much of the "fertile octogenarian" cases, the "unborn widow," and other absurdities. They emphasized that the donor's intention should be carried out unless the intention violated public policy in fact. And finally, they argued that the traditional Rule unfairly penalizes persons who do not consult skilled estate planners but consult average lawyers not skilled in the Rule. These arguments have won the day, and as of 1996, the Rule Against Perpetuities has been reformed in every jurisdiction except Alabama, Arkansas, District of Columbia, Utah, and Wyoming. The reforms of the Rule have thus become an important part of the Rule itself. In most states, these reforms are prospective only, applying only to instruments becoming effective after the reform statute is enacted.

b.   **Types of reform:** [§513]   The reforms of the Rule can be generally classified among four types: (i) cy pres reformation of Rule violations; (ii) wait-and-see for the common law perpetuities period; (iii) wait-and-see for 90 years as provided by the Uniform Statutory Rule Against Perpetuities; or (iv) abolition of the Rule.

2.   **Cy Pres**

a.   **Full scale cy pres:** [§514]   Cy pres (pronounced SEE-PRAY) comes from the Law French and means "as near as possible." Under the cy pres doctrine, the court reforms an invalid interest so that it is given effect, within the limits of the Rule, to carry out the intention of the grantor as near as possible. The cy pres doctrine has been adopted in Mississippi, Missouri, Oklahoma, and Texas.

(1) **Example—fertile octogenarian:** [§515]   T devises property "to A for life, then to A's children for their lives, then to A's grandchildren." The gift to A's grandchildren is void because of the possibility that A will have more children (*see supra*, §453). The violation may be dealt with by construing "grandchildren" to mean "children of A's presently living children." Or, if A is still of child-bearing age, the court may insert a saving clause vesting the remainder in A's grandchildren 21 years after the death of A and A's presently living children, if it does not previously vest.

(2) **Example—unborn widow:** [§516]   T devises property "to A for life, then to A's widow for life, then to A's issue" (*see supra*, §458). The remainder in fee may be validated by construing widow to refer to A's present wife or to a woman presumably alive. Or the court may insert a saving clause providing that the gift to issue will vest in interest indefeasibly 21 years after the death of A, if A leaves a widow not alive at T's death.

(3) **Example—age contingency:** [§517]   T devises property "to A for life, then to A's children who reach 25." The gift to children is void under the Rule because of the possibility that A will leave a child under the age of four (*supra*, §474). The gift may be reformed by reducing the age contingency to 21 for all children of A. [Edgerly v. Barker, 31 A. 900 (N.H. 1891); Berry v. Union National Bank, 262 S.E.2d 766 (W. Va. 1980)] Or the gift may be reformed by reducing the age contingency only for those children under the age of four at A's death.

b. **Pros and cons:** [§518]   The cy pres doctrine permits immediate reformation of an interest, without waiting to see whether it is valid. This will avoid any problems resulting from not knowing whether an interest is valid or void under wait-and-see. On the other hand, cy pres does require a lawsuit to reform the offending instrument. And the court has a power "to fashion a will for the testator."

c. **Limited cy pres:** [§519]   Illinois and New York have adopted by statute specific cy pres correctives for the most frequent violations of the Rule. Age contingencies in excess of 21 that cause a gift to fail are reduced to 21 as to all persons subject to such contingency. The unborn widow is dealt with by a presumption that a gift to a spouse is a gift to a person in being. The fertile octogenarian is dealt with by a presumption that women over 55 are incapable of bearing children and the admission of extrinsic evidence of infertility in any case. Courts are also instructed to construe the instrument to avoid the Rule, if feasible. [765 ILCS §305/4; N.Y. Est. Powers & Trusts Law §§9-1.2, 9-1.3]

3. **Wait-And-See for the Common Law Perpetuities Period**

a. **The fundamental idea:** [§520]   The fundamental idea of the wait-and-see doctrine is to judge the validity of an interest by what actually happens, not by what might happen. If an interest is not valid initially, we wait out the perpetuities period applicable to the particular interest to see if the interest in fact vests within the period. States adopting wait-and-see for the common law perpetuities period include Kentucky, Mississippi, New Hampshire, Ohio, Pennsylvania, Rhode Island, Vermont, and Virginia. Iowa waits out the lives of persons on a statutory list closely resembling the lives that measure the common law perpetuities period.

b. **The measuring lives:** [§521]   Under the traditional what-might-happen test of the common law, it is not necessary to determine the particular perpetuities period that governs the validity of the contingent interest. But it is necessary to do so under wait-and-see. The lives that measure the wait-and-see period are the lives that can affect vesting, sometimes called the lives causally related to vesting. These are the lives that fix the common law perpetuities period applicable to the particular interest under the what-might-happen test. That is, the contingent interest will necessarily vest, if at all, within these lives; all other lives are irrelevant. These same relevant lives fix the period during which we wait to see if the interest actually vests.

(1) **Who can affect vesting:** [§522]   The lives that can affect vesting are determined by the common law meaning of vested. An interest is vested when it either *vests in possession* or *vests in interest*. An interest vests in interest when (i) the beneficiaries are ascertained and (ii) any condition precedent is satisfied. Accordingly, the lives fixing the common law perpetuities period—the lives we wait out—are:

(a) *The preceding life tenants* (who can affect vesting in possession and maybe vesting in interest);

(b) *The beneficiary* or beneficiaries of the *contingent interest*;

(c) *Any ancestor who can affect the identity of the beneficiary* or beneficiaries (such as A in a gift to A's children, and A and A's children in a gift to A's grandchildren); and

(d) *Any person who can affect any condition precedent* attached to the interest, or in case of a class gift, any person who can affect a condition precedent imposed on any member of the class or affect the size of a member's share.

(2) **Restrictions on measuring lives:** [§523]   There are two restrictions on who can be measuring lives, both part of the common law under the orthodox Rule.

(a) **Ascertainable but not traceable lives:** [§524]   If all persons in being who can affect vesting in the same way constitute an unreasonable number, so that their lives cannot reasonably be traced, they cannot be measuring lives even though they are ascertainable. [*Re* Villar, [1929] 1 Ch. 243]

(b) **Unascertainable lives:** [§525]   If all persons in being who can affect vesting in the same way cannot reasonably be ascertained within the perpetuities period, none of such persons can be measuring lives. [*Re* Moore, [1901] 1 Ch. 936] This principle rules out as measuring lives persons who have an *assignable power to affect vesting*, such as personal representatives in slothful executor cases, fiduciaries, and owners of defeasible fees. If these persons and their assignees could be measuring lives, it would be impossible to say when the perpetuities period ends. [Thellusson v. Woodford, 11 Ves. Jr. 112 (1804)]

(3) **The classic cases revisited:** [§526]   To illustrate who are measuring lives under wait-and-see, we can look again at some of the classic cases involving the Rule.

(a) **The fertile octogenarian:** [§527]   T bequeaths property "to A for life, then to A's children for their lives, then to A's grandchildren." At common law, the remainder to grandchildren is void because A is presumed to be capable of having another child (*supra*, §453). Under wait-and-see, the lives relevant to vesting of the remainder are A and all A's children and grandchildren living at T's death. A and A's children are relevant on two scores: they are preceding life tenants, and they can, by procreating, affect the identity of the remainder beneficiaries. A's grandchildren in being at T's death are relevant because they are beneficiaries.

(b) **The slothful executor:** [§528]   T bequeaths property "to my issue living upon the distribution of my estate." The gift is void at common law because of the possibility that the estate will not be distributed within lives in being plus 21 years (*supra*, §461). Under wait-and-see, the measuring lives are all of the testator's issue living at T's death. [*In re* Estate of Anderson, 541 So. 2d 423 (Miss. 1989)] The executor cannot be a measuring life for reasons given *supra*, §525.

(c) **Age contingencies:** [§529]   T bequeaths property "to A for life, then to A's children who reach 25." This is void at common law because A can leave, at her death, an afterborn child under the age of four (*supra*, §474). The wait-and-see lives are A and all of A's children living at T's death. A qualifies as a measuring life on two counts: A is the preceding life tenant, and A, by begetting a child, can affect the identity of the beneficiaries. The children of A in being at T's death are relevant lives because they are, or may become, beneficiaries.

(d) **Gifts to separate subclasses:** [§530]   T bequeaths property "to A for life, then for A's children for their lives, and *as each child of A dies*, to distribute such child's share to such child's issue." At T's death A is alive and has a child, B, alive. Two years later a child, C, is born to A. Under the separate shares doctrine, the remainder to B's issue is valid and the remainder to C's issue is void (*supra*, §481). Under wait-and-see, the measuring lives for the remainder to C's issue are A and B. A can affect vesting as a preceding life tenant and as an ancestor of the intended beneficiaries. B can affect the vesting of the remainder to C's issue because B can affect the size of the remainder (by dying before C without issue) as well as the time it becomes possessory. Therefore, the gift to C's issue will be valid if it vests within 21 years after the deaths of A and B. [Fleet National Bank v. Colt, 529 A.2d 122 (R.I. 1987)]

(e) **Defeasible fees:** [§531] T devises Blackacre "to the School Board, but if it ceases to use the land for a school, to A" (*supra*, §451). A's interest is void at common law. Under wait-and-see, A's interest is valid for the life of the beneficiary, A, plus 21 years. [*Cf.* North Bay Council, Inc., Boy Scouts of America v. Grinnell, 461 A.2d 114 (N.H. 1983)—holding option valid for life of beneficiary plus 21 years]

(4) **Limited wait-and-see:** [§532] Four states have adopted a limited version of wait-and-see. Maine and Maryland do not wait out the full perpetuities period, but only for the lives of the preceding life tenants. Illinois and Washington apply wait-and-see to trusts only and wait out the lives of the trust beneficiaries alive at the creation of the trust before declaring a remainder void.

(5) **Pros and cons:** [§533] The advantage of wait-and-see over cy pres is that a lawsuit is not required to deal with the perpetuities violation. In the great majority of cases the contingent interest will actually vest within the wait-and-see period. On the other hand, wait-and-see does make title uncertain for the wait-and-see period, and inconveniences may arise from the uncertainty of title.

(6) **Delayed cy pres:** [§534] Some of the states that have adopted wait-and-see for the common law perpetuities period provide for reformation of the instrument at the end of the waiting period if the contingent interest has not then vested. The instrument is reformed so as to most closely approximate the testator's intention. States applying delayed cy pres include Iowa, Kentucky, New Hampshire, Ohio, Rhode Island, Vermont, Virginia, and Washington.

4. **Wait-And-See for Ninety Years:** [§535] The Uniform Statutory Rule Against Perpetuities, promulgated in 1986, adopts a 90-year wait-and-see period. USRAP rejected waiting for the common law perpetuities period on the ground that the measuring lives might not be clear in every case and adopted a wait-and-see period approximating the longest period that could be obtained using extraneous measuring lives. The USRAP wait-and-see period is thus a proxy for a period measured by the lives of "twelve healthy babies plus 21 years." USRAP has been adopted in Alaska, Arizona, California, Colorado, Connecticut, Florida, Georgia, Hawaii, Indiana, Kansas, Massachusetts, Michigan, Minnesota, Montana, Nebraska, Nevada, New Jersey, New Mexico, North Carolina, North Dakota, Oregon, South Carolina, Tennessee, and West Virginia.

a. **Pros and cons:** [§536] A 90-year wait-and-see period is easier to administer than one measured by lives that must be accounted for and traced. On the other hand, USRAP rejects the fundamental policy underlying the common law: that a donor can tie up property only for the lives of persons he knows and can assay (plus 21 years) (*supra*, §413). It extends dead hand control for an arbitrary period of 90 years. This is a long extension in the practical reach of the dead hand.

b. **Effect of USRAP:** [§537] Under USRAP, a future interest cannot be declared invalid for 90 years after the instrument creating it takes effect. At the end of 90 years, any then contingent interest will be reformed by a court to most closely approximate the donor's manifested plan of distribution (delayed cy pres). Almost certainly the classic remote possibilities that have brought the Rule into disrepute will work themselves out within 90 years.

c. **Ninety-year perpetuities period:** [§538] Under USRAP, the drafter can choose to comply with the common law Rule Against Perpetuities period *or* to draft interests that will vest, if at all, within 90 years. In either case the instrument will be valid.

    (1) **Ninety-year trusts:** [§539] USRAP permits the creation of 90-year trusts. This makes it easy to create a long term "dynasty trust." Ninety-year dynasty trusts offer tax advantages under the federal generation-skipping transfer tax and may become popular among the rich. (*See infra*, §547.)

d. **Seeking the longer period:** [§540] Contingent interests in trust may endure for the common law perpetuities period or for 90 years under USRAP. Inasmuch as it may be uncertain which period will actually prove longer, the drafter of a long-term trust may draft a trust to endure for whichever period turns out to be longer. Under pressure from the United States Treasury, which objected to so prolonging trusts, USRAP was amended in 1990 to add section 1(e). USRAP section 1(e) provides that a trust created to last for specified lives in being plus 21 years *or* for 90 years, whichever period proves longer, can last no longer than 21 years after the specified lives expire. Section 1(e) has not been adopted in a number of USRAP states, where it remains possible to create a trust for the common law perpetuities period or for 90 years, whichever proves longer.

e. **Subsidiary effects**

    (1) **Noncharitable purpose trusts:** [§541] The Rule Against Perpetuities applies to noncharitable definite purpose trusts, such as a trust to provide free liquor at state bar meetings. If such a trust can extend beyond the perpetuities period, under the common law it is void. In USRAP jurisdictions, such trusts apparently can last 90 years before being declared void.

    (2) **Defeasible fees:** [§542] Where a defeasible fee is used to impose a land use restriction, an executory interest following it is void under the Rule if it might vest beyond the perpetuities period (*supra*, §451). Under USRAP, such an executory interest is valid for 90 years.

        (a) **Example:** O conveys Blackacre "to the School Board, but if it ceases to use the land for school purposes, to A and her heirs." Under the common law, A's interest is void. Under USRAP, A's interest is valid for 90 years.

    (3) **Accumulation of income:** [§543] Under the common law, income in a trust may be accumulated for the perpetuities period. [Gertman v. Burdick, 123 F.2d 924 (D.C. Cir. 1941)] Under USRAP, income from a trust can be accumulated for specific lives in being plus 21 years *or* for 90 years.

f. **Commercial transactions:** [§544]   USRAP exempts all commercial transactions from the Rule Against Perpetuities. Hence, under USRAP, options to purchase can endure forever. If options get out of hand, courts in USRAP jurisdictions may apply the rule against unreasonable restraints on alienation to them.

g. **Retroactivity:** [§545]   In most jurisdictions, USRAP is not retroactive, but applies only to instruments becoming effective after it is adopted. The same is true of common law wait-and-see, which is usually not retroactive. Therefore, the old common law will continue to apply to instruments effective before the wait-and-see doctrine is adopted.

5. **Abolition of Rule:** [§546]   The Rule Against Perpetuities has been abolished with respect to interests in trust in Idaho, South Dakota, and Wisconsin for many years. [Will of Walker, 116 N.W.2d 106 (Wis. 1962)] In 1995, Delaware joined these states by also abolishing the Rule Against Perpetuities as applied to personal property in trust. In these jurisdictions, trusts are permitted to endure forever.

a. **Federal taxes:** [§547]   Under federal tax law, each person can create a trust of up to $1 million, which will pass to succeeding generations free of federal estate tax and generation-skipping transfer tax for as long as is permitted under local state law. [I.R.C. §2631(a)] The exemption is $2 million for a married couple. This exemption provides a considerable incentive to establish long-term trusts, inasmuch as federal estate and generation-skipping transfer taxes are levied at approximately a 50% rate every generation. In USRAP states, tax-exempt dynasty trusts can continue for 90 years or for the common law perpetuities period. In Delaware, Idaho, South Dakota, and Wisconsin, tax-exempt dynasty trusts can go on forever.

I. SUSPENSION OF THE POWER OF ALIENATION (NEW YORK LAW)

1. **Background:** [§548]   In the nineteenth century, there was much uncertainty as to the real nature of the Rule Against Perpetuities. Some authorities—particularly John Chipman Gray—argued that it was solely a prohibition of *remote vesting*, a position now generally accepted. Others, however, contended that it was a prohibition of interests that *suspend the power of alienation* for too long a period. In 1830, New York wrote the latter rule into a statute and several other states followed suit. Since then, almost all these statutes, except New York's, have been repealed or held to be declaratory of the common law rule against remote vesting.

2. **New York Statutes**

a. **Suspension rule:** [§549]   The present New York statute provides: "Every present or future estate shall be void in its creation which shall suspend the absolute power of alienation by any limitation or condition for a longer period than lives in being at the creation of the estate and a term of not more than twenty-one years." [N.Y. Est. Powers & Trusts Law §9-1.1]

b. **When power suspended:** [§550]   The statute further provides: "The absolute power of alienation is suspended when there are no persons in being by whom an absolute fee or estate in possession can be conveyed or transferred."

(1) **Example:** O conveys Blackacre "to A for life, remainder to A's children for their lives, remainder in fee to A's grandchildren." The remainder to A's *children* suspends the power of alienation only during A's life, because on A's death, all of A's children are in being and can convey their interests. This remainder is valid. On the other hand, the remainder to A's *grandchildren* suspends the power of alienation during the lives of A's children, who are not all necessarily in being. Only on the deaths of all the children can all the grandchildren be ascertained. This remainder in fee violates the rule against suspension and is void.

    (a) **Note:** There is no violation of this rule merely because the ownership of the fee is split among several parties. For example, a conveyance by O "to A for life, then to B if the Washington Monument falls" is permissible. As long as the interest holders (A, B, and O) can join and convey a fee, the power of alienation is not suspended.

c. **Rule against remote vesting:** [§551] The New York statutes provide the rule against remote vesting (common law Rule Against Perpetuities) is also in force in New York [N.Y. Est. Powers & Trusts Law §9-1.1] To be valid, an interest must satisfy both the rule against suspension of the power of alienation and the common law Rule Against Perpetuities.

d. **Spendthrift trusts:** [§552] A spendthrift trust suspends the power of alienation. The income beneficiaries cannot convey their interests. Therefore, in New York, any spendthrift trust that may endure for longer than the permitted period is void.

(1) **Example:** O conveys in trust "to A for life, and then to A's children for their lives." The trust has *spendthrift* provisions forbidding alienation of income interests. The remainder to A's children is void because it may suspend the power of alienation beyond lives in being (A's life) and 21 years. A may have afterborn children, and hence, the class of A's children cannot be used as lives in being. If the trust were not spendthrift, the trust would be valid for the lives of A's children (*see supra*, §550). (The remainder to A's children is valid under the Rule Against Perpetuities. The life estate in A's children vests at A's death. But since the remainder must comply with both rules in New York, it is void.)

(2) **Statutory spendthrift trusts:** [§553] Prior to 1973, all trusts in New York that required the trustee to pay out or apply the income were, by statute, spendthrift. The settlor had no choice. Thus, any such trust was void if it could endure longer than the perpetuities period. [N.Y. Est. Powers & Trusts Law §7-1.5] In 1973, the statute was amended to permit the settlor of a trust to authorize the income beneficiaries to transfer their interests. Thus, present New York law is that every trust is a spendthrift trust unless the settlor expressly authorizes transfers of the beneficial interests. If the income beneficiary has the unconditional right to alienate his interest at any time, his interest does not suspend the power of alienation.

    (a) **Example:** In 1996, O conveys in trust "to A for life, then to A's children for their lives, then to A's grandchildren in fee." The trust instrument provides that the income beneficiaries may transfer their interest. The gift to A's children is good, because at the death of A they are all in being and can convey their interests. The gift to A's grandchildren violates the rule against suspension of the power of alienation as well as the Rule Against Perpetuities. (*Caveat:* If the trust instrument did not expressly provide that the beneficiaries may transfer their interests, the trust is spendthrift by statute. In that case, the life estate in A's children would violate the rule against suspension of the power of alienation.)

J. ACCUMULATION OF TRUST INCOME

1. **Common Law:** [§554]   Under the common law, income in a trust may be accumulated for the perpetuities period. A direction to accumulate income for a period in excess of lives in being plus 21 years is wholly void. [Thellusson v. Woodford, 32 Eng. Rep. 1030 (1805); Gertman v. Burdick, *supra*, §543]

   a. **USRAP:** [§555]   Under USRAP, income can be accumulated for 90 years or, in the alternative, for lives in being plus 21 years.

Proceed to the Review Questions for Chapter VI.

REVIEW QUESTIONS

CHAPTER I—CLASSIFICATION OF FUTURE INTERESTS

1. O conveys Blackacre "to A for life." Subsequently, O conveys her interest in Blackacre to B. What is the name of B's interest in Blackacre?   _____

2. T (testator) devises Blackacre "to A for life."

    a. T's will devises the residue of his property to B. What is the name of B's future interest?   _____

    b. If T's will does not contain a residuary clause, T's heirs will take Blackacre when A dies. If there is no residuary clause, what is the name of the heirs' future interest?   _____

3. O conveys Blackacre "to the City so long as it is used for a park." Does O have a reversion, a possibility of a reversion, a possibility of reverter, or a right of entry?   _____

4. O conveys "to A for life, and then, if B marries C, to B and his heirs so long as the land is used for a farm." What is the name of O's reversionary interest—

    a. Before B marries C?   _____

    b. After B marries C?   _____

5. O conveys "to A for life." Then A conveys "to B for B's life."

    a. What is the name of A's reversionary interest (to become possessory if B dies during A's lifetime)?   _____

    b. What is the name of O's reversionary interest?   _____

6. O conveys Blackacre "to A subject to the condition that if the land is used for nonresidential use during O's lifetime, O may reenter and terminate the estate."

    a. What kind of interest does O have?   _____

    b. If A uses Blackacre for a video store, does A's estate automatically end?   _____

    c. If O delays his entry for 10 years after A's use as a video store, and the jurisdiction has a 10-year statute of limitations to recover possession of land, will O be barred from entry?   _____

    d. Would your answer to c., above, be different if A had a fee simple determinable?   _____

7. O conveys Whiteacre "to School Board, but if it ceases to use the school for school purposes, O has a right of entry." Thereafter O conveys her interest in the land to A. O then dies intestate; O's heir is B. The School Board ceases to use the land for school purposes. Who owns the land?   _____

8. O conveys Greenacre "to Town Library so long as it is used for a library, and when it ceases to be used for a library, to the Board of Education." What is the name of the Board of Education's interest? _____

9. O conveys "to A for life, then to B for life, then to C and the heirs of his body."

   a. Is B's remainder vested? _____

   b. At common law, does O have a reversion? _____

   c. Under modern law, where a statute converts a fee tail into a fee simple, does O have a reversion? _____

10. O conveys "to A for life, then to A's widow for life, then to B." A is living and is married to C. Is any future interest contingent? _____

11. O conveys Blackacre "to A for life, then to the children of A." A has two children, B and C. B dies, devising all her property to D. C dies intestate, leaving E as his heir. A third child, F, is born to A. A dies. Who owns Blackacre? _____

12. O conveys "to A for life, remainder to B if B reaches 21." B is 18.

   a. What is the state of the title? _____

   b. If B reaches 21 during A's life, what is the state of the title? _____

13. O conveys "to A for life, and at A's death to the heirs of B." At the time of the conveyance, B has one child, C, living. Subsequently C dies, leaving a minor child, D, and a spouse, E, to whom C devises his property. Then B dies, devising all his property to his alma mater. B, a widower, is survived by his grandchild, D, and his daughter-in-law, E. Then A dies. Who owns the property? _____

14. O conveys "to A for life, then to B *if B survives A*, but if B does not survive A, to C."

   a. What future interests are created? _____

   b. If the italicized words "*if B survives A*" had been omitted from the conveyance, what future interests would be created? _____

   c. If C dies intestate, leaving D as her heir, and A and B survive C, what is the state of the title? _____

15. O conveys "to A 20 years from now." What future interest does A have? _____

16. O conveys "to A, but if A dies without issue living at the time of her death, to B." What interest does B have? _____

17. O conveys "to A for life, then to B, but if B dies before A without issue surviving B, then to C at A's death."

   a. Does O have a reversion? _____

   b. Suppose that B dies leaving a child, D; B's will devises all her property to her husband, E. Then D dies. Then A dies. Who owns the property? _____

18. O conveys "to A for life, remainder to B's children, but if all of B's children die under the age of 21, to C." A and B are alive.

    a. If B has no children, what future interests are created? _____

    b. If B has a child, D, age 5, what future interests are created? _____

    c. If B has a child, D, age 5, and one year after the conveyance A dies leaving B, C, and D surviving, what is the state of the title? _____

    d. If subsequent to the events in c., above, D dies at age 19, leaving her father, B, as her heir, and then C dies intestate, what is the state of the title? _____

19. T (testator) devises all her property "to my children for their lives, and upon the death of my last living child, to my grandchildren who are then living."

    a. What future interests are created if T is survived by two children but no grandchildren? _____

    b. What future interests are created if T is survived by two children and a grandchild? _____

20. T devises Blackacre "to A 20 years from now if A is then living." What is the name of A's interest? _____

CHAPTER II—RULES RESTRICTING REMAINDERS

In these problems, unless otherwise stated, it is assumed that the doctrine of destructibility of contingent remainders, the Rule in Shelley's Case, and the Doctrine of Worthier Title are in effect.

21. O conveys Blackacre "to A for life, then to the heirs of B." A then dies. Then B dies. Who owns Blackacre? _____

22. O conveys Blackacre "to A for life, then to A's children who survive A." A few years later, O dies intestate, leaving A as O's heir. What is the state of the title? _____

23. O conveys Blackacre "to A for life, then to B for life, then to B's first child to reach 21." No child of B is 21.

    a. Subsequently O conveys her reversion to A. What is the state of the title? _____

    b. Subsequent to a., above, B dies, leaving a child age 15. What is the state of the title? _____

24. O conveys Blackacre "to X in trust to pay the income from Blackacre to A for life, then to convey Blackacre to B if B reaches 21." Subsequently A dies; B is 15. What is the state of the title? _____

25. O conveys Blackacre "to A for life, then to B's children who survive B."

    a. B dies during A's lifetime, leaving children. Then A dies. What is the state of the title? _____

b.   A dies during B's lifetime. B has children at A's death. What is the state of the title? _____

c.   While A and B are alive, A conveys his life estate to B. What is the state of the title? _____

26.   T (testator) devises Blackacre "to A for life, then to A's children who survive A." A is T's sole heir. What is the state of the title? _____

27.   O conveys Blackacre "to A for life, then to B if B survives A, and if B does not survive A, to the heirs of C (a living person)." O subsequently conveys all her interest in Blackacre to B.

    a.   After O's second conveyance, what interest do the unascertained heirs of C have? _____

    b.   After O's second conveyance, B dies, leaving H as his heir. H then conveys all his interest in Blackacre to A. What is the state of the title? _____

28.   O conveys Blackacre "to A for 100 years so long as A lives, then to A's heirs." A then conveys her interest in the land to O. What is the state of the title? _____

29.   O conveys Blackacre "to A for life, then to the heirs of B (a living person)." Subsequently, A conveys her life estate to B. What is the state of the title? _____

30.   O conveys Blackacre "to A for life, then to A's widow for life, then to A's heirs."

    a.   What is the state of the title? _____

    b.   Can A convey a fee simple? _____

31.   O conveys Blackacre "to A for life, then to B if B survives A, and if B does not survive A, to A's heirs." What is the state of the title? _____

32.   O conveys Blackacre "to A for life, then to B for life, remainder to the heirs of B." What is the state of the title? _____

33.   O conveys Blackacre "to A and B for their lives, then to the heirs of A." What is the state of the title? _____

34.   O conveys Blackacre "to A for life, then to A's children." A has children. What is the state of the title? _____

35.   O conveys Blackacre "to A for life, then among A's heirs as A, their father, shall appoint, and in default of appointment to A's heirs equally." Does the Rule in Shelley's Case apply? _____

36.   O creates a trust "to pay the income to O for life, then to distribute the principal to O's heirs." Subsequently, O wants to revoke the trust. Can she? _____

37.   Suppose that in Question 36., the remainder were given "to O's issue." Can O revoke the trust? _____

38. O conveys Blackacre "to A for life, then to the heirs of O." Subsequently, O dies, devising all her property to B. O's heir is C. A dies. Who owns Blackacre? _____

CHAPTER III—RIGHTS AND LIABILITIES OF OWNERS OF FUTURE INTERESTS

39. T devises property in trust "for A for life, then to B if B survives A, and if B does not survive A, to C." T's residuary devisee is D. A disclaims the life estate.

   a. Who has what interests in the property at common law? _____

   b. Who owns the property if the jurisdiction has adopted the Uniform Disclaimer of Property Interests Act? _____

40. T devises property "for A for life, remainder to A's children who survive A, and if no children survive A, to B." The jurisdiction has adopted the Uniform Disclaimer of Property Interests Act. A, A's child C, and B survive T. A disclaims her life estate.

   a. Who is entitled to the property? _____

   b. If, one year after the disclaimer, D is born to A, does D share in the property? _____

41. T devises property "to A for life, then to B, but if B does not survive A, to C." During A's life, B transfers her future interest to D, and C transfers his future interest to E. The jurisdiction follows the old common law respecting inter vivos transfer of future interests.

   a. Is B's transfer to D valid? _____

   b. Is C's transfer to E valid? _____

   c. Would your answers to a. and b. be different if the modern (majority) law on alienability were in effect? _____

   d. Would your answers to a. and b. be different if T had devised the property in a spendthrift trust? _____

42. T devises property "to A for life, then to B if B survives A." The jurisdiction follows the common law that contingent remainders are not alienable inter vivos. B goes into bankruptcy. Is B's contingent remainder part of B's bankrupt estate and reachable by creditors? _____

43. T devises property in trust "for A for life, then to B if B survives A, and if B does not survive A, to C."

   a. B dies, leaving A and C surviving. Is B's remainder taxable under the federal estate tax? _____

   b. C dies, leaving A and B surviving. Is C's remainder taxable under the federal estate tax? _____

44. T devises property "to A for life, then to B, but if C returns from Rome to C."

    a.   B dies, leaving A and C surviving. Is B's remainder taxable under the federal estate tax? _____

    b.   C dies in Rome, leaving A and B surviving. Is C's executory interest taxable under the federal estate tax? _____

45. T bequeaths his farm to W for life, together with a horse and two fat hogs, with a remainder to B. W wants to sell the horse and the hogs. Can she? _____

46. T bequeaths his bank account to A absolutely, and whatever is in the account at A's death T bequeaths to B. At A's death, $5,000 remains in the account. Does this belong to B? _____

47. T bequeaths his bank account to A for life, remainder to B. A is given the power to withdraw and use whatever amount A needs for support and maintenance. At A's death, $5,000 remains in the account. Does this belong to B? _____

48. T bequeaths his grandmother's portrait and a $1,000 bond to A for life, remainder to B. B, who distrusts A, asks a court to require A to put up security for the portrait. Should it do so? _____

CHAPTER IV—CONSTRUCTION OF INSTRUMENTS

49. O conveys Blackacre "to A for life, then to B if B reaches 21, and if B does not reach 21 to C." B is age 14.

    a.   Is B's remainder vested or contingent? _____

    b.   If A dies when B is age 16, will B, C, or O go into possession? _____

50. T devises Whiteacre "to A for life, and then to such of my children as may be living at A's death, and to the children of those who may have died." T is survived by children B, C, D, and E and by a grandchild G, who is the child of T's child F, who predeceased T. Who must survive A in order to take? _____

51. O conveys a fund in trust "to A for life, remainder to A's children who survive A, and if there are none such, to my sister B." A has a child C. B dies. C dies. A dies. To whom should the trustee distribute the fund? _____

52. O conveys a fund in trust "to pay the income to the children of my dead brother, A, until they all attain the age of 21, and then to convey the principal to them; and if none of these children of A attain 21, then to convey the principal to B." At the time of the conveyance, A's living children are C, D, and E. C dies at age 6 and D dies at age 14. E attains the age of 21. Who is entitled to the principal of the trust? _____

53. O conveys property "to A for life, remainder to his issue per stirpes." A has children B and C, and C has a child D.

    a.   If B does not survive A, will B's estate share? _____

b.   If C survives A, will D share?   _____

54.   T bequeaths a sum in trust for A for life, "then to my surviving children." A
       child of T, named B, survives T but dies intestate during A's lifetime, leaving is-
       sue. Do B's issue share in the fund?   _____

55.   T bequeaths a sum in trust to pay the income to A for life, "then to pay the prin-
       cipal to A's children, the issue of any deceased child to take such child's share."
       After T's death, A's daughter B dies, survived by no issue, but survived by a hus-
       band, C, to whom B devises her property. Subsequently, A's son D dies, survived
       by a wife, E, and a daughter, F. D devises all his property to E. A then dies, sur-
       vived by a son, G, and by C, E, and F.

       a.   Who is entitled to the trust fund?   _____

       b.   Suppose that the limitation had read "then to pay the principal to A's chil-
               dren or their issue." Who is entitled to the trust fund?   _____

       c.   Assume the original limitation. Suppose that F died after T died but before
               D died. Would F share in the trust fund?   _____

56.   T bequeaths $600,000 in trust "to be given to A when she reaches 21, and in the
       meantime the trustee may in his discretion use so much of the income as is nec-
       essary to support A, and accumulate the rest for A at 21." If A dies under 21, is
       A's administrator entitled to the trust fund at A's death?   _____

57.   State X has a statute voiding any devise to charity made in a will executed less
       than 30 days prior to the death of the testator. T, domiciled in state X, executes a
       will and dies two days later. The will devises T's estate "to A for life," with a
       proviso that on A's death $5,000 shall go "to B, to be paid to her at the age of 21,
       but if B dies under 21 then this sum of money shall go to C Charity."

       a.   If B does not reach 21, is B's estate entitled to $5,000 at A's death? _____

       b.   If the gift over had been to D, an individual, rather than to C Charity,
               would your answer to the above question be different?   _____

58.   T devises property "to my daughter A, but if A dies without issue surviving her,
       to B." A survives T and then dies without issue. Who owns the property?   _____

59.   T devises property "to A for life, then to B, but if B dies without issue surviving
       her, to C." B survives T and A, but dies thereafter without issue. On B's death,
       who owns the property?   _____

60.   T devises property "to A's children." A has three children, B (legitimate), C
       (adopted), and D (illegitimate). Who takes the property?   _____

61.   T devises Blackacre "to A and her children."

       a.   At the time of T's death, A has no children. Who takes Blackacre? _____

       b.   At the time of T's death, A has one child, B. Who takes Blackacre? _____

62. T executes a will devising Greenacre "to A for life, then to B and the children of C." At the time of A's death, C has two children, D and E. B is T's brother and C is T's deceased sister. Who takes what shares in Greenacre?   _____

63. T devises property "to my son A for life, remainder to my heirs." A dies, devising all his property to his friend B.

    a.   A is T's sole heir at T's death. If T had died immediately after A, T's heir would be his brother C. At A's death, who owns the property?   _____

    b.   A and A's brother D are T's heirs at T's death. If T had died immediately after A, T's heir would be D. At A's death who owns the property?   _____

64. T bequeaths $100,000 "to my grandchildren." At T's death, T has one grandchild, A. Two months later, grandchild B is born. One year later, before the assets of T's estate are distributed, grandchild C is born.

    a.   Who takes the $100,000?   _____

    b.   If there had been no grandchildren of T alive at T's death, when would the class close?   _____

65. T devises Blackacre "to A for life, and then to the children of B who reach 21." At T's death, B has one child, C. Subsequently, B has another child, D. A dies. One year later, E is born to B. C then reaches age 21. One year later, F is born to B. D, E, and F later reach 21. Who owns Blackacre?   _____

66. T bequeaths $500 to each child of A. At T's death, A has no children. When will the class close?   _____

67. T devises property "to A for life, and if A dies without issue surviving him, to B." A dies leaving one child, C. Who takes the property?   _____

68. T devises property in trust to pay the income "to A, B, and C for their lives, and upon the death of A, B, and C, to pay the principal to their children." A dies. Who is entitled to A's share of the income?   _____

CHAPTER V—POWERS OF APPOINTMENT

69. T bequeaths a fund in trust "for A for life, then to such persons as A by will appoints, and in default of appointment, to A's issue per stirpes."

    a.   At A's death, may A's creditors reach the trust fund if A does not exercise the power?   _____

    b.   At A's death, is the trust fund included in A's gross estate under the federal estate tax?   _____

    c.   In the jurisdiction an anti-lapse statute provides: "If a devise is made to a relative of the testator who dies before the testator but leaves issue surviving the testator, such issue shall take the same estate which the person whose issue they are would have taken if he had survived the testator." A executes a will appointing the trust fund to B, who is a relation of A but no relation of T. B dies. A dies, survived by issue of B. Who takes the trust fund?

70. T, domiciled in New York, bequeaths a fund in trust "for A for life, then as A appoints by will." A dies, domiciled in Massachusetts. A appoints the trust fund in further trust in such a way as to violate the New York rule against suspension of the power of alienation (*see supra*, §548). Such a rule is not part of Massachusetts law. The law of which state applies?

71. A, donee of a general testamentary power of appointment, wants to release the power. The taker in default is B.

    a. Can A release the power?

    b. What effect will the release have upon B's interest?

72. T devises property "to A for life, remainder as A appoints by will, and in default of appointment to A's children equally." A has three children, B, C, and D.

    a. Upon divorce, A contracts with her husband, H, that she will appoint by will $10,000 to H's daughter E (A's stepdaughter). A then dies intestate. Is E entitled to $10,000?

    b. A contracts with B not to exercise the power in such a way as to deprive B of a one-fourth interest in the property. Subsequently A dies, appointing the property by will to E. Who takes the property?

73. A holds a special power of appointment that must be exercised by a specific reference to the instrument creating the power. A's will devises "to B all my property, including all property over which I hold a power of appointment." Does B take the appointive property?

74. A, donee of a general testamentary power of appointment over a trust fund, dies, leaving a will that contains various specific bequests of the donee's own property, and a residuary clause devising "all the rest of my property of whatever kind and description and wherever situated" to B. The power is not expressly mentioned in A's will.

    a. Does B take the trust fund?

    b. Suppose that the residuary clause expressly includes "all property over which I have a power of appointment." Suppose also that B had predeceased A, and no anti-lapse statute applies. Who takes the trust fund?

75. T devises property "to A for life, remainder to A's children in such shares as A by deed or will appoints, and in default of appointment, to A's children equally." A has three children, B, C, and D, all born before T died.

    a. A by will appoints all the property to B. Is this valid?

    b. A by will appoints a portion of the property to C for life, remainder as C appoints by will. Is C's general power valid?

76. A, donee of a special testamentary power to appoint among A's children, appoints the property to her daughter B upon condition that B give one-half the property to A's husband, H. A is survived by three children, B, C, and D.

   a.   What does H take?   _____

   b.   What does B take?   _____

77. T devises a fund in trust "for A for life, then for such children of A as A shall appoint." There is no express gift in default of appointment. A dies intestate, survived by two children, B and C. Who takes the trust fund?   _____

78. A has a general testamentary power over assets worth $100,000. A has assets of her own worth $150,000. A dies leaving a will providing, "I hereby devise, bequeath, and appoint all property which I own or over which I have any power of appointment as follows: I bequeath $125,000 to B; all the rest I give to C for life, then to C's children." C was not alive when the power was created and therefore the appointment to C's children violates the Rule Against Perpetuities. Can anything be done to save the gift to C's children?   _____

CHAPTER VI—THE RULE AGAINST PERPETUITIES

Answer by the common law Rule Against Perpetuities unless otherwise specified.

79. T bequeaths his law library "to the first child of A to become a lawyer." A survives T and has a daughter in law school. Is the bequest valid?   _____

80. T devises property "to A for life, then to B if B goes to the moon."

   a.   Is B's gift valid?   _____

   b.   Suppose the remainder had been given "to B if any person goes to the moon after my death." Would B's gift be valid?   _____

   c.   Suppose the remainder had been given "to the first of my children to go to the moon after my death." Would the gift be valid?   _____

81. O conveys Greenacre "to School Board so long as it is used for school purposes, then to A."

   a.   What estate does the School Board have?   _____

   b.   If the wait-and-see doctrine is applied in the jurisdiction, is A's interest void?   _____

82. T devises Whiteacre "to the School Board, but if it ceases to use the land for school purposes, then [gift over as specified below]." Is the gift over valid if A is alive and has two children at T's death and the gift over reads:

   a.   "To the children of A"?   _____

   b.   "To the children of A now living"?   _____

c. "To the children of A now living who are then living"? _____

d. "To the children of A then living"? _____

83. T bequeaths a fund in trust "for A for life, then for A's children for their lives, then [gift over of principal as specified below]." Is the gift over of principal at the end of the trust valid if it reads:

a. To B? _____

b. To B's children? _____

c. To A's grandchildren? _____

d. To A's heirs? _____

84. T devises one-half of his property in fee simple to his daughter A and the other one-half to a trustee in trust "to pay the income to my son B for life, then to B's children for their lives, then to pay the principal to B's grandchildren." A and B are T's sole heirs.

a. Is the gift of principal to B's grandchildren good? _____

b. If it is void, are any other gifts ineffective? _____

85. T devises Blackacre "to A for life, then to A's widow for life, then [gift over as specified below]." Is the gift over valid if it reads:

a. "To A's children in fee"? _____

b. "To A's issue in fee"? _____

c. "Upon the death of A, or upon the death of A's widow if he leaves one surviving, to A's children then living"? _____

86. O conveys property in trust "to pay O the income for O's life, then to pay the principal to O's grandchildren." Is the gift to O's grandchildren valid if:

a. O has no grandchild and the trust is revocable by O? _____

b. O has no grandchild and the trust is not revocable? _____

c. If O has one grandchild now alive? _____

87. T devises property "to A for life, remainder to A's children who reach 25." Is the remainder valid if:

a. A has no children at T's death? _____

b. A child of A is 25 at T's death? _____

88. T devises property "to A for life, then to the grandchildren of my sister B whenever born." B is alive at T's death. Is the gift to the grandchildren valid if:

a. There are no grandchildren alive at T's death? _____

b. There is one grandchild alive at T's death? _____

89. T devises property in trust "for A for life, then for A's children in equal shares for their lives, and on the death of each child of A, to distribute the share of the corpus upon which the child was receiving the income to the descendants of such deceased child per stirpes." At T's death, A is alive and has one child, B, alive. Two years after T dies, C is born to A. Then A dies.

   a. Upon B's death, will B's descendants take a share of the principal? _____

   b. Upon C's death, will C's descendants take a share of the principal? _____

   c. If the wait-and-see doctrine is applied in the jurisdiction, will C's descendants take a share of the principal upon C's death? _____

90. T bequeaths "$1,000 to each grandchild of A, whenever born." A has one child B, and A and B survive T. Two years after T dies, a child C is born to A. Will each of B's and C's children take $1,000 when born? _____

91. T devises Blackacre "to such of the grandchildren of A as shall attain the age of 25." Unless otherwise stated, assume that no grandchild of A has reached age 25. Is the gift valid if at T's death:

   a. A is dead? _____

   b. A and all of A's children are dead? _____

   c. A is alive and one grandchild of A is 25? _____

   d. A is dead and one grandchild of A is 25? _____

   e. A is dead and one grandchild of A is four? _____

92. T devises property in trust "for A for life, and then for A's children at their respective ages of 25, and after the death of A, the trustee shall pay the income in equal shares to A's children until they respectively attain 25." Is the devise wholly valid? _____

93. T devises property "to A for life, remainder to B's grandchildren, payable at their respective ages of 25." A and B are alive at T's death. Is the remainder valid if:

   a. B has no grandchildren at T's death? _____

   b. A grandchild of B is age two at T's death? _____

   c. A grandchild of B is age 10 at T's death? _____

94. T devises property "to A for life, then to A's children for their lives, and as each child of A dies, to distribute the share of the principal upon which such child was receiving the income to such persons as such child shall by will appoint." A

has a child, B, alive at T's death. Two years after T dies, a child C is born to A. A then dies.

a. C dies, appointing her share to her husband. Is the appointment valid? _____

b. B dies, appointing her share to D for life, remainder to D's children. D was not alive at T's death. Is the appointment wholly valid? _____

c. Would your answer to a., above, be the same if each child of A were given, at A's death, a presently exercisable general power of appointment over his or her share? _____

d. Would your answer to b., above, be the same if each child of A were given, at A's death, a presently exercisable general power of appointment over his or her share? _____

95. T devises property in trust "for A for life, and upon the death of A, the trustee may pay income to A's children in such shares as the trustee decides." Is the trustee's discretionary power valid? _____

96. T devises property "for A for life, then to such of A's children as A by will appoints, and in default of appointment, to A's children who reach 25." A has one child, B, age two at T's death. A dies intestate 10 years later, leaving B, his only child, surviving. Does B take the property? _____

97. O conveys to A and her heirs an option to buy Blackacre. Later O changes his mind and would like to get out of the bargain. May he? _____

98. T devises a fund in trust "to pay the income to my issue per stirpes for 90 years, and then to distribute the principal to my issue then living per stirpes." How long may this trust last:

a. Under common law wait-and-see? _____

b. Under USRAP? _____

ANSWERS TO REVIEW QUESTIONS

1. **REVERSION** — O retains a reversion by the initial conveyance, which O later conveys to B. The name of the future interest does not change when it is transferred. [§32]

2.a. **VESTED REMAINDER** — The takers under the residuary clause are transferees (same as grantees), so they must take a remainder or executory interest, not a reversion. [§26]

b. **REVERSION** — When property is not completely disposed of by will, T's heirs take in place of T, who is dead. They are substituted for T, and take any reversion the testator would have had. [§§34, 44]

3. **POSSIBILITY OF REVERTER** — A possibility of reverter is the future interest retained by the grantor when she creates a fee simple determinable. There is no such interest as a "possibility of a reversion." [§§23, 39]

4.a. **REVERSION** — Whenever a contingent remainder in fee simple is created, O has a reversion. [§33]

b. **POSSIBILITY OF REVERTER** — Once B's remainder vests, O's reversion is divested. But O then retains a possibility of reverter if the land is not used for a farm. [§37]

5.a. **REVERSION** — Under the hierarchy of estates, a life estate pur autre vie is lesser than a life estate. If B dies during A's life, A will be entitled to possession. [§§18, 32]

b. **REVERSION** — O will be entitled to possession when A dies, not when B dies if B dies before A. [§32]

6.a. **RIGHT OF ENTRY** — A has a fee simple subject to condition subsequent. [§8]

b. **NO** — The right of entry is optional. O may choose not to exercise it. [§49]

c. **PROBABLY** — The 10-year statute runs on the right of entry from time of breach in some jurisdictions. In others, the equitable doctrine of laches will probably bar O if A would suffer economic harm from O's slowness. [§61]

d. **YES** — In that case there would be no doubt that the statute of limitations barred O, since title automatically passed back to O upon breach, and A is an adverse possessor. [§61]

7. **SPLIT OF AUTHORITY** — In most jurisdictions, O can convey her right of entry to A, and A can enter against the Board. In a few jurisdictions, the attempted conveyance of a right of entry destroys it, and the Board has a fee simple absolute. In a few other jurisdictions, the right of entry is not transferable, but it is inheritable, and B can enter against the Board. [§§55-57]

8. **EXECUTORY INTEREST** — A future interest in a *grantee* after a determinable fee is an executory interest, not a possibility of reverter. [§§9, 109]

9.a. **YES** — There are no words of condition attached to it. The termination of the preceding life estate in A is not a condition precedent. [§79]

b. **YES**		O has not granted a vested fee simple. O has granted a remainder in fee tail to C, and when the fee tail expires the land will revert to O. [§§10, 18, 32, 76]
c. **NO**		O cannot have a reversion when O grants a vested fee simple in remainder to C. [§33]
10. **YES**		The secondary life estate in A's widow is contingent. The taker (widow) is presently unknown. C may not be A's widow. [§87]
11. **D, E, and F**		D, E, and F own Blackacre in equal shares. The remainder is vested in A's children when born. The share of any child who dies goes to that child's heirs or devisees. [§§82, 83]
12.a.		A has a life estate, B has a contingent remainder in fee simple, and O has a reversion in fee simple. [§§79, 89]
b.		A has a life estate, B has a vested remainder in fee simple. O's reversion disappears (is divested) when B's contingent remainder vests. [§75]
13. **D**		C, who predeceases B, is not B's heir; D, B's grandchild, is B's heir. E, a daughter-in-law, is not an heir. B has no interest in the property and cannot devise it to his alma mater. [§88]
14.a.		B and C have alternative contingent remainders in fee simple; O has a reversion in fee simple. [§§92, 93]
b.		B would have a vested remainder in fee simple subject to divestment; C would have an executory interest. [§108]
c.		A has a life estate, B has a contingent remainder in fee simple, and D has an alternative contingent remainder in fee simple. There is no condition that C survive anyone. [§§92, 93]
15. **EXECUTORY INTEREST**		The fee simple springs out from O 20 years from now. [§112]
16. **EXECUTORY INTEREST**		The fee simple will shift from A to B if the condition happens. [§108]
17.a. **NO**		O cannot have a reversion if O conveys a vested remainder in fee simple. B has a vested remainder in fee simple (subject to divestment). [§§33, 84]
b. **E**		B's remainder is not divested because the condition never happened. B can devise her remainder to whom she pleases. The condition did not happen because B left issue who survived B. The issue did not survive A, but that is not part of the condition subsequent. [§84]
18.a.		Contingent remainder in fee simple in B's children, contingent remainder in fee simple in C, and reversion in fee simple in O. [§§87, 89]
b.		Vested remainder in fee simple in D subject to open and subject also to complete divestment, and executory interest in C. [§85]

c.		D has a fee simple subject to divestment by the executory interest in C. [§§82, 97]
d.		B has a fee simple (inherited from D), subject to divestment by the executory interest in C's heir if B's children all die under the age of 21. B is alive and can have more children, so the condition may never happen. [§96]
19.a.		Contingent remainder in fee simple in grandchildren, reversion in fee simple in T's heirs. [§§87, 89]
b.		Contingent remainder in fee simple in grandchildren, reversion in fee simple in T's heirs. [§§89, 90]
20.	**EXECUTORY INTEREST**	It would not be treated as vested because of the condition that A be alive when the interest becomes possessory. [§112]
21.	**O**	O owns Blackacre. When A dies, the remainder in the heirs of B is contingent. It is destroyed. O's reversion becomes possessory. [§127]
22.	**A HAS A FEE SIMPLE**	Since A obtained the reversion subsequent to the life estate, the inherited reversion merges with A's life estate, destroying the intervening contingent remainder. [§133]
23.a.		A has a life estate, B has a vested remainder for life, B's first child to reach 21 has a contingent remainder in fee simple, and A has a reversion. The vested remainder in B prevents the merger of the life estate into the reversion. [§135]
b.	**A HAS A FEE SIMPLE**	When B's vested life estate terminates, the life estate in A merges into the reversion in A. [§131]
24.		The trustee has a legal fee simple. O has an equitable reversion. O is entitled to the income until B reaches 21, at which time the trust will terminate and B will be entitled to the property. If B dies under 21, O has the equitable fee simple. The doctrine of destructibility of contingent remainders does not apply to remainders in trust. [§139]
25.a.	**B'S CHILDREN OWN BLACKACRE**	When B dies, the remainder in B's children vests. It goes into possession at A's death. [§135]
b.	**O OWNS BLACKACRE**	When A dies, leaving B surviving, the contingent remainder in B's children who survive B is destroyed. [§127]
c.		B has a life estate pur autre vie (for A's life), B's children have a contingent remainder in fee simple, and O has a reversion. The conveyance by A did not affect the remainder because it was not made to O. [§131]
26.		A has a life estate, A's children have a contingent remainder in fee simple, and A has a reversion in fee simple. The life estate does not merge into the reversion at T's death, because the interests were created in A simultaneously. But A hereafter may convey the life estate and reversion to a third party, and they merge at that time, destroying the contingent remainder. [§133]

27.a.	**CONTINGENT REMAINDER IN FEE SIMPLE**	B's contingent remainder does not merge into the reversion now owned by B. [§131]
b.	**A HAS A FEE SIMPLE**	When B dies, his contingent remainder disappears, but his reversion passes to H. When H conveys the reversion to A, the contingent remainder in C's heirs is destroyed. [§131]
28.		O has a fee simple subject to a springing executory interest in A's heirs. [§§136, 141]
29.		B has a life estate, B's heirs have a contingent remainder, O has a reversion. The Rule in Shelley's Case does not apply to the remainder in B's heirs because B did not receive the life estate by the same instrument that created the remainder. [§150]
30.a.		A has a life estate, A's widow has a contingent remainder for life, and A has a vested remainder in fee simple by virtue of the Rule in Shelley's Case. There is no merger at the time of the conveyance. [§149]
b.	**YES**	*See* answer to Question 26. [§133]
31.		A has a life estate, B has a contingent remainder in fee simple, A has an alternative contingent remainder in fee simple, and O has a reversion in fee simple. [§158]
32.		A has a life estate, and B has a vested remainder in fee simple. [§152]
33.	**AUTHORITIES DIVIDED**	Some say A has the entire remainder in fee simple; others say A has only a remainder in an undivided half, with remainder in the other one-half in A's heirs. [§156]
34.		A has a life estate, and A's children have a vested remainder in fee simple. The Rule in Shelley's Case does not apply to a remainder given to children. [§163]
35.	**NO**	The reference to "father" indicates that "heirs" was intended to mean "children," and the Rule applies only to a gift to "heirs," which can include brothers and sisters if A leaves no children. [§165]
36.	**MAYBE**	If O has a reversion (presumed under the Doctrine of Worthier Title), O has all equitable interests in the trust and can revoke. But the Doctrine raises only a presumption of a reversion, which can be rebutted by evidence that O intended to create a remainder. [§179]
37.	**NO**	The Doctrine of Worthier Title does not apply to a remainder to O's "issue," but only to a remainder to O's heirs. [§176]
38.	**DEPENDS**	If the Doctrine of Worthier Title applies, O has a reversion, which O devises to B. B owns Blackacre. But if contrary evidence shows O intended to create a remainder in her heirs, C owns Blackacre. [§181]

39.a.   Orthodox theory says D is entitled to the income until A or B dies. Contingent remainders do not accelerate. But a court, reading T's intent, might give B the income until A or B dies, which event determines whether B or C takes the principal. This is likely if B is the child of A and C the grandchild. [§191]

b. **B**   B owns the principal. A, the disclaimant, is presumed to have predeceased T. Therefore B has survived A. [§192]

40.a. **C**   C takes the property indefeasibly. A, the disclaimant, is treated as having predeceased T for all purposes. Therefore, C has survived A. If C subsequently dies within A's lifetime, it is irrelevant. [§192]

b. **NO**   D does not share. A is treated as having predeceased T for all purposes. Therefore, A cannot have any more children who share in the property. [§192]

41.a. **YES**   B has a vested remainder. Vested remainders, even subject to divestment, are transferable inter vivos. [§196]

b. **DEPENDS**   The validity of the transfer depends upon whether C received consideration. C's executory interest is not transferable, but the transfer is enforceable in equity as a contract to transfer if given for a valuable consideration. [§201]

c. **YES**   In a majority of states, contingent future interests are alienable inter vivos. [§203]

d. **YES**   Future interests in a spendthrift trust cannot be transferred. [§208]

42. **YES**   B's remainder is included in the bankruptcy estate. [§208]

43.a. **NO**   B does not have a transmissible remainder. It disappears at B's death, since B does not survive A. [§210]

b. **YES**   C has a transmissible remainder. It passes to C's heirs or C's devisees. There is no requirement that C survive A or B. [§210]

44.a. **YES**   It is a transmissible interest passing to B's heirs, but it is still subject to divestment. However, because it can be destroyed by C returning from Rome, its *value* for federal estate tax purposes probably will be minimal. [§210]

b. **NO**   C's interest disappears at C's death in Rome, because he cannot ever meet the condition precedent. [§210]

45. **MAYBE AND YES**   Maybe as to the horse and yes as to the hogs. The hogs are consumables, and W has absolute ownership of them. The horse might be a consumable on the ground that its value wears out with age and use. Or the court might imply a power to sell the horse. It seems pretty silly to make W keep feeding a horse she doesn't want. [§215]

46. **NO**   B's gift of any remnant in the account is void under the rule of repugnancy. [§218]

47. **YES**   The rule of repugnancy does not apply where the first taker is given only a *life estate*, coupled with a power to consume. [§219]

48.	**PROBABLY NOT**	T did not require security, and bonding is very expensive. Although the court has discretion, unless there are unusually compelling reasons, B should take the risk. [§223]
49.a.	**VESTED**	The rule of *Edwards v. Hammond* eliminates the words "if B reaches 21," as surplusage. B has a vested remainder subject to divestment. [§235]
b.	**B**	Vested remainders are ready to go into possession whenever and however the life estate ends. [§233]
50.	**B, C, D, AND E**	The limitation says "my children as may be living at A's death." G does not have to survive because there is no express requirement of survival in the substitutional gift to children of deceased children, and none is implied from the word "children" in the substitutional gift. [§§239, 240]
51.	**B'S ESTATE**	B's remainder is subject to the condition precedent that A leave no surviving children, but it is not contingent upon B's survival. [§240]
52.	**C'S ESTATE, D'S ESTATE, AND E**	The interests in C and D are vested, and are not defeated by their failures to survive to 21 since the divesting event (failure of *any* child to attain 21) did not occur. [§246]
53.a.	**NO**	The word "issue" normally connotes a requirement of survival. [§243]
b.	**NO**	When the distribution is per stirpes, a person does not share if his parent is alive. [§§284, 287]
54.	**SPLIT OF AUTHORITY**	Most courts hold "surviving" means "surviving A," not "surviving T." Therefore, B's issue would not take B's share. However, to prevent the disinheritance of some of T's descendants (B's issue), there may be a strong pull to construe "surviving" to mean "surviving T" or to construe "children" to include "grandchildren" (another unusual construction). [§245]
55.a.	**C, F, AND G EQUALLY**	There is no implied requirement that A's children must survive A in order to take. Each share in the remainder is vested subject to divestment by issue if the child dies leaving issue, but not subject to divestment if the child dies without issue. [§246]
b.	**F AND G**	"To A's children *or* their issue" is an alternative limitation, not a divesting limitation as in the original question. A requirement that A's children must survive the life tenant is implied from the word "or" in an alternative limitation. [§247]
c.	**NO**	A requirement of survival is implied in a gift to "issue" (but not in a gift to "children"). "Issue" may include several generations. [§243]
56.	**YES**	A's gift is vested under *Clobberie's Case* because A is given the entire income; if not paid to her before she reaches 21 she receives the accumulated income at 21. A's administrator can demand the fund at A's death because, since A is dead, no purpose is served in withholding payment. [§§253, 254]

57.a. YES
Clobberie's Case says a gift "to be paid" at a designated age is vested. The supplanting limitation to C Charity is void; therefore, B's gift is indefeasibly vested. [§252]

b. YES
The divesting gift would be valid and there is no requirement that D survive. [§240]

58. SPLIT OF AUTHORITY
The majority holds that B does, applying a "successive" construction of "die without issue" here. A minority holds that the gift over is a provision for lapse ("substitutional" construction), and since A survived T, B is cut out. A's estate takes. [§266]

59. SPLIT OF AUTHORITY
Some cases apply the "successive" construction, thus giving C the property. Others apply the "substitutional" construction, thus giving the property to B absolutely when B survives A. In the latter case, it would go to B's estate. [§267]

60. SPLIT OF AUTHORITY
B shares. In almost all states today, C also shares. D may not share, though the trend is to include children born out of wedlock in the gift. [§§275, 278]

61.a.
A takes a life estate with remainder to A's children. Under the first resolution in *Wild's Case*, A takes a fee tail, which is converted into a fee simple or whatever estate a fee tail is converted into under local law. In most states, the first resolution in *Wild's Case* is not followed, and A takes a life estate with remainder to A's children. [§§292, 295]

b. SPLIT OF AUTHORITY
Under the second resolution in *Wild's Case*, A and B take as tenants in common; the class closes at T's death. But some courts give A a life estate, remainder to A's children. [§§293, 295]

62. B TAKES 1/2; C'S CHILDREN TAKE 1/2
Since B is of a closer generational relationship to T than are the children of C, presumably T wanted B to take one-half (as under intestacy). [§298]

63.a. C
Because of the incongruity in determining T's heirs at T's death (which would give A a fee simple when A was given only a life estate), T's heirs are ascertained at A's death. [§302]

b. PROBABLY B AND D
It is not entirely incongruous to give A a life estate and a one-half share in the remainder. Although the cases go both ways, the probable result (absent other factors) is that "heirs" would be given its technical meaning. [§302]

64.a. A AND B
B is included because he was conceived before T's death. C is excluded, because the class closes at T's death. [§313]

b. DEATH OF T'S CHILDREN
When there are no members of the class alive at T's death, the rule of convenience does not apply. [§314]

65. C, D, AND E
The class closes after A dies when any child of B reaches 21. F, conceived after this date, is excluded. [§323]

66.	**T'S DEATH**	With a gift of a specific sum to each member of the class, the class closes at the testator's death, unless the testator otherwise directs. No child of A takes anything. [§315]
67.	**C**	A gift to A's issue is usually implied in a limitation such as this. [§327]
68.	**B AND C**	The usual solution is to give the income to the surviving life tenants, either by implying cross remainders or treating them as joint tenants or members of a class. But other solutions are possible, including giving income to T's heirs or to A's estate or accumulating it for remaindermen. [§332]
69.a.	**NO**	The majority rule is that A's creditors may reach the trust fund only if the general power is exercised. This rule is changed by statute in some states. [§349]
b.	**YES**	For federal estate tax purposes, the donee of a general power is treated as owner of the trust fund. [§344]
c.	**B'S ISSUE**	For purposes of lapse, the donee of a general power is treated as the owner of property and the "testator" under the statute. [§400]
70.	**NEW YORK**	The law of the donor's domicile governs the exercise of the power. [§358]
71.a.	**YES**	[§360]
b.		B's interest becomes indefeasibly vested. [§360]
72.a.	**NO**	The donee of a testamentary power cannot contract to make an appointment. E is entitled neither to specific performance nor damages, but H might be able to get restitution of the consideration given for the promise. [§369]
b.	**B, C, D, AND E**	B, C, D, and E take in equal shares. The contract with B is a release of the power to the extent stated. A must allow three-quarters of the property to pass in default in order to satisfy her contract that B will take one-quarter. Thus, A has appointive power over only one-quarter of the property. [§372]
73.	**SPLIT OF AUTHORITY**	Under a strict approach, A has not exercised the power by a specific reference. But some courts admit extrinsic evidence to show the donee's intent to exercise, and it is possible that A may have exercised the power. [§377]
74.a.	**SPLIT OF AUTHORITY**	The majority rule is that a residuary clause does not operate as an exercise of a general power. The minority rule is that a residuary clause does operate as an appointment, and B would take under the minority rule. [§378]
b.	**DEPENDS**	If A's will, by blending his own property and the appointive assets, manifests an intent to capture the property, as it probably does, A's heirs take. If the court refuses to apply the capture doctrine, the property passes in default of appointment, or if no takers in default, to the donor's estate. [§406]
75.a.	**DEPENDS**	If A has an exclusive power, A can appoint all to one child. If A has a nonexclusive power, A must appoint some amount to each child. Most courts presume the power is exclusive, but "in such shares" might be construed as creating a nonexclusive power. [§388]

b. **YES**		Most cases hold that inasmuch as A could have appointed to C in fee, the appointment to C of a life estate coupled with a general power is tantamount to complete ownership. A few cases, however, hold that a special power cannot be exercised by creating a general power because it is a forbidden delegation of the power. [§385]
76.a. **NOTHING**		The condition conferring a benefit upon a non-object is void. [§393]
b. **DEPENDS**		The appointment is ineffective to the extent it was motivated by the purpose to benefit the non-object. Thus, depending upon extrinsic evidence, B could receive one-half or nothing. [§393]
77. **B AND C**		Either under the theory of an implied gift in default of appointment or an imperative power, the property passes to those persons to whom A could have appointed at his death, B and C. [§394]
78. **YES**		Under the doctrine of allocation, all the appointive property and $25,000 of A's own property is allocated to B. The balance of A's own property is allocated to C and C's children. With property so allocated, the entire disposition is valid. [§402]
79. **NO**		The first child of A to become a lawyer may be a child not now alive who becomes a lawyer more than 21 years after A dies. The bequest is void. [§415]
80.a. **YES**		The condition precedent (of B going to the moon) must happen within B's life. B is the validating life. [§415]
b. **NO**		B has a transmissible interest (can pass to his heirs or devisees), and the condition precedent may happen hundreds of years after T's death, at which time the then owner of B's interest claims the property. The vesting is too remote. [§415]
c. **YES**		All children of T are in being at T's death, and whichever child first goes to the moon, if any does, will necessarily happen within the lives of T's children (lives in being). [§415]
81.a. **FEE SIMPLE DETERMINABLE**		The executory interest in A violates the Rule Against Perpetuities, and is struck out. This leaves a possibility of reverter in O. The Board is left with the fee simple determinable given it by the grant. [§449]
b. **NO**		If we wait and see for the common law perpetuities period, A's interest is valid if it actually vests within A's life or within 21 years thereafter. [§531] If USRAP is adopted, A's interest is valid if it actually vests within 90 years. [§542]
82.a. **NO**		The class closes at A's death, but the executory interest may vest in possession hundreds of years from now. A's children have a transmissible interest that passes to their heirs or devisees, and onto subsequent successors in interest. [§451]
b. **NO**		Same reason as above. The class closes at T's death, but the problem is that the condition precedent will not necessarily be satisfied within lives in being plus 21 years. [§451]

c. **YES**   The class closes at *T's* death. The condition precedent must occur within the lives of the members of the class, who are limited to living persons, or the gift fails. [§472]

d. **NO**   The class closes at *A's* death, but the condition precedent may occur within the lives of members of the class not now in being. This is what might happen: One year after T dies, A has a child, B. Shortly thereafter, A and A's children alive at T's death all die, leaving B surviving. Eighty years later, the School Board ceases to use Whiteacre for school purposes. B claims possession of Whiteacre. The vesting of B's interest has not occurred within lives in being plus 21 years. [§472]

83.a. **YES**   B's remainder is vested upon creation. [§420]

b. **YES**   The class of B's children will close upon B's death, and the remainder will then vest (or fail if B has no children). [§432]

c. **NO**   The class of A's grandchildren will not close until the death of all A's children. One or more of these may be born after T's death, so the class may close at the death of an afterborn person. [§432]

d. **DEPENDS**   Under the technical meaning of "heirs," the heirs of A are determined at A's death. [§301] Given this meaning, the class of heirs will close at A's death and the gift is valid. There is, however, an incongruity in giving "heirs" its technical meaning. Since A's children will be A's heirs, and they are given a life estate, it appears that T wanted A's heirs to be determined when their remainder becomes possessory. [§302] If they are determined then (when A's children die), the gift to A's heirs is void. Also note that statutes in many states determine heirs when the remainder becomes possessory. [§303] Under these statutes, the gift to A's heirs is void.

84.a. **NO**   The class of grandchildren may close at the death of a child of B not now alive. [§426]

b. **PROBABLY**   The void gift to B's grandchildren will pass to T's heirs, A and B, in equal shares. This would mean that A's family ends up with 3/4 of T's property. The doctrine of infectious invalidity may apply on the ground that T was more interested in equal distribution between A and B than in putting B's one-half in trust. If T would prefer equal distribution, then the life estates in B and B's children must be struck down, as well as the gift to A, resulting in intestacy. In that manner, A and B share equally. [§447]

85.a. **YES**   The remainder to A's children vests at A's death because the class closes then. There is no condition precedent. [§§458, 471]

b. **NO**   The class of A's issue (which includes all A's descendants) may not close until the widow's death. We cannot determine who is in the class until then. As the widow may be an afterborn person, the class may vest too remotely. [§458]

c. **YES AND NO**   The gift is made on two separate contingencies: (i) the death of A; and (ii) the death of A's widow. The gift is valid if the first contingency happens, but void if A leaves a widow. [§465]

86.a. **YES**   The perpetuities period does not begin to run on interests in a revocable trust until the power to revoke ceases (O's death). At that time, all O's children will be in being, and the class of O's grandchildren will close physiologically at the death of persons in being. [§425]

b. **NO**   The class may not close until the death of all of O's children, all of whom are not necessarily now alive. [§473]

c. **YES**   The class will close under the rule of convenience at O's death. [§480]

87.a. **NO**   The remainder may not vest until 25 years after A's death because A may die leaving a child under the age of four. [§474]

b. **NO**   The same reasoning as above. The class closes at *A's* death, not T's death. Thus, the condition precedent of reaching 25 may not be satisfied for all members of the class within 21 years of A's death. [§474]

88.a. **NO**   The class of grandchildren may not close until the death of B's children, who may not all be in being at T's death. [§473]

b. **NO**   The class will not close at A's death under the rule of convenience because the devise says "whenever born," and the class may not close physiologically until the death of B's children. [§§316, 480]

89.a. **YES**   The doctrine of subclasses applies. The descendants of B can prove that their share will vest in possession, if at all, upon the death of B, a person in being at T's death. [§481]

b. **NO**   The descendants of C, born after T's death, cannot prove that their share will necessarily vest or fail at the death of any life in being at T's death. [§481]

c. **PROBABLY**   Under wait-and-see for the common law perpetuities period, the gift to C's issue will be valid if it vests within 21 years after the deaths of A and B. [§530] Under USRAP, it will be valid if it vests within 90 years after T dies. [§537]

90. **NO**   Each child of B will take $1,000. But no child of C can take because no child of C will necessarily take, or the gift fail, within lives in being. A gift to the children of an unborn person is void unless it is limited to vest or fail within the period. [§484]

91.a. **NO**   Although the class of grandchildren will close at the death of A's children, all grandchildren might not reach 25 within 21 years thereafter. One grandchild might be under the age of four at the death of the children. Here is what might happen: One of A's children could have a child after T's death. Before that grandchild attains age four, all of A's children and grandchildren alive at T's death might die. The afterborn grandchild might reach age 25 more than 21 years after any life in being. [§474]

b. **YES**   The class of grandchildren is closed physiologically at T's death. All of A's grandchildren are now in being; there cannot be any more born. The grandchildren are the validating lives. They will reach 25—or die under that age—in their own lifetimes. [§477]

c. **YES**		The class of grandchildren closes under the rule of convenience at T's death. Thus, the grandchildren are the validating lives. [§480]
d. **YES**		*See* above. [§480]
e. **NO**		The grandchild age four might not attain age 25 at all, but die under that age. Analysis is the same as in a. above. [§474]
92.	**YES**	Under *Clobberie's Case*, the gift of income to A's children makes their interest vested at A's death; only payment is postponed. Reaching age 25 is not a condition precedent. [§433]
93.a.	**NO**	The class of grandchildren might not close until the death of all B's children, some of whom may not be in being at T's death. [§472]
b. **NO**		The class of grandchildren might not close at the death of persons in being either physiologically (*see* above) or under the rule of convenience. [§476]
c. **YES**		The class will close under the rule of convenience, at the very latest, 15 years after A dies. The grandchild will then reach 25 and demand possession. If the grandchild dies under 25, his administrator has the right to possession (thus closing the class) whenever the grandchild could demand possession had he lived. Under *Clobberie's Case*, reaching 25 is not a condition precedent. All we are concerned with is when will the class close. [§486]
94.a.	**NO**	The testamentary power of appointment in any afterborn child of A is void ab initio, because it may be exercised at the death of a person not in being. Since C had no power, the appointment is a nullity. [§494]
b. **NO**		The appointment to D's children is void because it may not vest until the death of D, a person not in being at T's death. [§499]
c. **NO**		A general power presently exercisable is tantamount to ownership. C's power would become exercisable at A's death, and thus would be valid. At A's death C is treated, for perpetuities purposes, as the owner of one-half the property. Thus C's appointment is valid. [§490]
d. **NO**		Since B, as owner of a general power presently exercisable, is treated as owner, conveying B's own property, the appointment is wholly valid. It is just as if B made a conveyance of her own property to D for life, remainder to D's children. [§490]
95.	**NO**	A discretionary power in a trustee to pay income is like a special power of appointment. If it may be exercised beyond lives in being plus 21 years, it is void ab initio. This power is exercisable during the lives of A's unborn children and is void. [§496]
96.	**YES**	The second-look doctrine has been applied to gifts in default of appointment as well as to appointments. The validity should be judged at A's death. Since A left no children under the age of four, the remainder will vest within 21 years of A's death, if at all. [§500]

97. **YES** The option, which has no limitation in time and can continue for longer than the perpetuities period, is void. [§506]

98.a. **LIVES OF T'S ISSUE PLUS 21 YEARS** The trust may last for the lives of T's issue living at T's death plus 21 years. T's issue are beneficiaries and are therefore measuring lives. If this period ends before 90 years passes, the trust terminates. If the jurisdiction applies delayed cy pres, the trust principal passes to T's issue per stirpes on the termination of the trust. [§522]

b. **90 YEARS** The trust is entirely valid. [§537]

SAMPLE EXAM QUESTION I

In 1980, Oralee owns Whiteacre, a tract of 50 acres. In 1981, Oralee conveys one acre of Whiteacre "to the Booneville School Board so long as it is used for school purposes, and if it ceases to be used for school purposes, Oralee, her heirs, and assigns have a right to reenter." Subsequently, Oralee conveys to Annie the remaining 49 acres of Whiteacre "together with my interest in the one-acre I previously conveyed to the Booneville School Board." Oralee then dies, leaving a will devising "all my property" to Joe.

In 1996, the state, exercising its power of eminent domain, takes title to the one-acre tract still used for school purposes by the Booneville School Board. The state deposits in court $100,000, the value of a fee simple absolute in the one acre. Who is entitled to the $100,000?

SAMPLE EXAM QUESTION II

Some years ago, LaTonya died leaving the following will: "I devise Blackacre to my husband, Harry, and upon Harry's death, to my children in equal shares, the descendants of a deceased child to take the parent's share in equal proportions." LaTonya left surviving her husband, Harry, a son, Adam, and two daughters, Betty and Carol. Adam subsequently died intestate, survived by a widow, Dawn, but no children. Dawn was Adam's heir. Then Betty died, leaving a will devising all her property to her husband, Eric, and also leaving surviving an adopted son, Fritz.

Harry dies. Carol, Dawn, Eric, and Fritz survive. Who owns Blackacre?

SAMPLE EXAM QUESTION III

Ted bequeaths $400,000 to Security Bank in trust for "my brother Brian for life, with power to consume principal to maintain him in his accustomed style of living, and upon his death the principal shall go to my residuary estate." Ted bequeaths his residuary estate "to the children of Brian, the share of any child dying under 21 to go to the survivor, and in case all of Brian's children die before reaching 21, to my sister Sally." Ted is survived by Brian, by children of Brian, named Cindy (age five) and Dave (age three), and by Sally. Ten days after Ted's death, a third child, Eve, is born to Brian's wife. Five months after Ted's death, Brian disclaims any interest in Ted's estate.

Two months prior to Ted's death, Brian had a vasectomy. He and his wife then thought they had enough children. Before the operation, however, Brian deposited sperm in a sperm bank in case he and his wife decided to have a child after the vasectomy. One year after Ted died, Brian's wife, with Brian's consent, withdrew his sperm from the bank, impregnated herself therewith, and nine months later Faith was born to Brian's wife.

A statute in the jurisdiction provides: "An instrument disclaiming a present interest shall be filed not later than nine months after the death of the decedent. Unless the decedent has otherwise provided, the property or interest disclaimed devolves as though the person disclaiming had predeceased the decedent. A future interest that takes effect in possession or enjoyment after the termination of the estate or interest disclaimed takes effect as though the person disclaiming had predeceased the decedent. A disclaimer relates back for all purposes to the date of the death of the decedent."

Ted's executor is now ready to distribute the estate. Who is entitled to the $400,000 and the residue?

SAMPLE EXAM QUESTION IV

Testator's will left $100,000 in trust to pay the income to his widow, Wendy, for life, and then to pay the principal "to my daughter, Alicia, if she shall be living at the death of Wendy, but if Alicia shall predecease Wendy without issue surviving her, then to pay the principal to Beth." Testator left the residue of his estate to Cecil.

Wendy, Alicia, Darren (a child of Alicia), Beth, and Cecil all survived Testator. Then Alicia died, devising all her property to her husband, Ed. Darren died, devising all his property to his wife, Fran. Beth died, devising all her property to her husband, Harry. Wendy died.

Who will claim the fund and what arguments will they make?

SAMPLE EXAM QUESTION V

In 1980, Oscar, a bachelor, transferred $200,000 by deed to Maria in trust "to pay the income to Oscar for life, then to pay income and principal as Oscar shall by will appoint, and in default of appointment, to pay the principal to Oscar's heirs at law." In 1982, Oscar married, and in 1983 a son, Sam, was born to him. Sam was Oscar's only child. In 1996, Oscar died, survived by his wife, Betty, and his son, Sam. Oscar's will provided: "I hereby make my last will, intending to dispose of all property which I shall own at my death or over which I shall then have any power of appointment. I bequeath $300,000 to my wife, Betty. All other property I give to my son Sam for life, remainder in fee to my grandchildren."

Oscar's probate estate consists of $350,000. Debts and taxes are $40,000. Who takes the trust fund (still worth $200,000) at Oscar's death? How is Oscar's estate distributed? The jurisdiction follows the common law Rule Against Perpetuities, and has not adopted wait-and-see or cy pres.

ANSWER TO SAMPLE EXAM QUESTION I

First, who owns the future interest? The deed to the Booneville School Board is ambiguous. The words "so long as it is used for school purposes" indicate that the Board was given a fee simple determinable, in which case Oralee would retain a possibility of reverter. The words "and if it ceases to be used for school purposes, Oralee, her heirs, and assigns have a right to reenter," indicate that Oralee is retaining a right of entry, in which case the school board would take a fee simple subject to condition subsequent and not a determinable fee. It is impossible to have a determinable fee with right of entry, which is what this deed apparently intended. This answer will make alternative assumptions: (i) that Oralee retained a possibility of reverter, and (ii) that Oralee retained a right of entry. There is supposedly a preference for the right of entry rather than the possibility of reverter because the right of entry is optional rather than automatic. However, because this preference is not very strong, we must make both assumptions.

Annie's claim: Annie will claim that Oralee assigned her interest to Annie. Whether Oralee's interest in the one-acre property is assignable depends on whether it is a possibility of reverter, whether it is a right of entry, and the type of jurisdiction in which the property is located. Depending upon the jurisdiction, a possibility of reverter may be assignable, a right of entry may be assignable, either or both may not be assignable, and in some, an attempt to assign a right of entry may destroy it. Annie will argue that the interest is assignable, and if possibilities of reverter are assignable and rights of entry are not, Annie will argue this is a possibility of reverter. In a jurisdiction where attempted assignment of a right of entry destroys it, the Board will argue that the interest is a right of entry. In that case, the attempted assignment to Annie would destroy the right of entry, leaving the school board with a fee simple absolute. Joe will argue that the right of entry or possibility of reverter is not assignable, and is not destroyed by an attempted assignment. If a possibility of reverter is assignable but a right of entry is not, Joe will argue this is a right of entry. (Of course if the land is in a jurisdiction where the attempted transfer of a right of entry destroys it, it would not do Joe any good to argue this is a right of entry.) Joe will claim Oralee owned the reversionary interest at death.

Joe's claim: Joe will claim that Oralee held the possibility of reverter or right of entry at death, and that it was devised to him. These reversionary interests are devisable. If Oralee held the future interest at death, Joe holds it now by devise.

Division of the $100,000: School Board will argue that the entire $100,000 goes to the Board and nothing to the owner of the reversionary interest. This is the majority view. The reason is that a possibility of reverter or right of entry is impossible to value, for you cannot tell when the condition will be breached. This allows the owner of the fee to profit from the state's condemnation. The minority rule is that the $100,000 should be divided, the determinable fee owner being given that part of the $100,000 that equals the value of the one-acre for school purposes, and the owner of the reversionary interest being given the difference between that value and an unrestricted fee simple. This permits the owner of the reversionary interest to be paid something, even though there is no probability that school use would cease but for the condemnation. But this leaves the owner of a reversionary interest in a better position after condemnation than before. A third view is that the Board should be given the $100,000 to purchase a new school lot, and the reversionary interest should be transferred to the new lot. This last view seems fairest, because neither the owner of the fee nor the owner of the reversionary interest profits from the state's condemnation.

ANSWER TO SAMPLE EXAM QUESTION II

Blackacre is probably owned by Dawn, Fritz, and Carol, each holding one-third shares. This result is arrived at by looking at the share of each of LaTonya's children.

Adam's interest: LaTonya devised Blackacre "to my children in equal shares, the descendants of a deceased child to take the parent's share in equal proportions." Adam (LaTonya's child) did not survive Harry, but died childless and intestate. Under orthodox doctrine, there is no implied condition of survivorship in a class gift. Adam has a vested interest, which can be divested only by his descendants if he leaves descendants. Therefore Adam's interest passes by intestacy to Dawn.

Betty's interest: If Betty was not divested at her death by her descendants, her interest passed to Eric under her will. So the crucial question is whether Fritz, an adopted child, is considered a "descendant" of Betty for purposes of LaTonya's will. If so, Fritz divests Betty, and now holds Betty's share. The law of the particular state will have to be examined on this issue, for it varies considerably. The majority rule is that adopted children are considered "children" or "descendants" in a will, but this rule may have been adopted after LaTonya's death and may not apply retroactively. Or the jurisdiction may hold that Fritz is a "descendant" if adopted before LaTonya died, but not if adopted after.

Carol's interest: Carol survived Harry and owns a one-third interest in Blackacre.

ANSWER TO SAMPLE EXAM QUESTION III

Brian disclaimed his life estate and any interest in Ted's estate. Under the disclaimer statute, Brian is treated as having predeceased Ted. Therefore, the $400,000 in trust falls into the residuary estate and is to be distributed according to the residuary clause.

Cindy and Dave have vested interests in the residuary estate, subject to divestment if they die under age 21.

Eve has an interest in the residuary estate equal to that of Cindy and Dave. Though Eve was born after Ted's death, she was conceived before Ted's death, and therefore, is treated as in being at Ted's death. She is a child of Brian. The only argument for excluding Eve is that the gift over of the share of any child dying under 21 goes to the "survivor." It can be argued that the use of the singular word "survivor" indicated that Ted had in mind only the two children he knew, Cindy and Dave. But courts do not like to exclude children by a questionable construction such as this. Presumptively the word "children" includes all children of Brian, including Eve, and it requires stronger evidence than the use of the singular "survivor" to overcome this.

Faith's interest in the residue is questionable. The disclaimer statute provides that a disclaimant (here, Brian) is treated as having predeceased the decedent (here, Ted) *for all purposes.* If the statute is read literally, Faith was not conceived until after Brian was deemed to be dead under the statute, and thus, the issue is whether she may be considered to be Brian's child for purposes of taking the residue of Ted's estate. In the analogous situation of distributing a father's estate, only children born within 10 months of the father's death are considered his children. The facts of this case, however, present a new question, not yet settled by case authority. A persuasive argument could be made that it should be presumed that Ted intended to include anyone who is Brian's child, whenever conceived. Therefore, since Faith is

Brian's genetic child and would appear to be within any scientific or dictionary definition of "child," she should be included in the gift.

Assuming that Faith is considered to be Brian's child, the next hurdle she may encounter is whether the state considers her to be illegitimate, and if so, whether the state includes illegitimates in class gifts to someone's "children." If a literal reading of the disclaimer statute applies, even though Faith was born to Brian's wife, she would be presumed to have been conceived after Brian's death and, hence, after the end of his marriage. Thus, it could be argued that for this purpose Faith should be treated as though she were born out of wedlock. Under the old law, children born out of wedlock were not included in a gift to someone's "children," but many states now include nonmarital children in such gifts. The result will thus hinge on whether the state follows the old view or the new and better view, which would include Faith in the gift.

Assuming Faith overcomes the above two hurdles, the next issue is whether the disclaimer statute could exclude Faith from the class based on the timing of the sperm bank deposit. Again, the statute treats Brian as predeceasing Ted. The issue of timing is as follows: If Brian did not make the deposit before Ted's death, any child conceived with that sperm would not be within the class, because: (i) under the statute Brian was considered dead at the time he made the deposit, and (ii) it would be impossible for a dead person to make such a deposit. This leads to the following confounding result: Assuming that Faith is considered Brian's child and is not excluded on the basis of illegitimacy, she would be included in the gift to Brian's children if Brian deposited the sperm in the sperm bank prior to Ted's death. If Brian deposited the sperm or Faith were conceived by natural intercourse after Ted's death, Faith would be excluded because Brian would be "dead" when those events took place. Thus a child conceived from the sperm bank (assuming a timely deposit) would be included, but a child conceived naturally would be excluded. This conclusion may make a court reluctant to include in the gift any child conceived after the parent's death. Faith has a chance of sharing in the residue, but not a terribly good one.

Note that Faith is not excluded from the class by the rule of convenience, which closes the class when any member of the class can demand her share. No child of Brian can demand possession of his or her share until he or she reaches age 21, because the share is defeasible if the child dies under age 21. Cindy, Dave, and Eve are all minors—so the executor must hold the residue in trust until one child reaches 21, then give a fractional share of the principal to that child and close the class at that time.

ANSWER TO SAMPLE EXAM QUESTION IV

Cecil

Cecil, residuary devisee of Testator, will claim the fund. Cecil will argue that the words "if she shall be living at the death of Wendy" state a condition precedent of surviving Wendy. Since Alicia did not survive Wendy, Alicia's estate (devised to Ed) cannot take.

Then Cecil will argue—in order to eliminate the claimant of Beth's estate (devised to Harry)—that the word "her" in Testator's will means Alicia, not Wendy. The word "her" is ambiguous and could refer to either Alicia or Wendy. Since Alicia predeceased Wendy *with* issue (Darren) surviving Alicia, the condition precedent to Beth's gift (death of Alicia without issue surviving Alicia) has not occurred.

Fran

Fran will claim the fund. Fran will agree with Cecil's arguments, which eliminate Ed and Harry. To eliminate Cecil, Fran will argue that a gift to the issue of Alicia (Darren) should be implied. There is a gap in Testator's will: no disposition is made if Alicia predeceases Wendy with issue, which is what happened. Rather clearly, Testator would have wanted Alicia's issue to take, rather than Cecil; this can be inferred from the gift over if Alicia died without issue.

This would be a strong, and probably convincing, argument if Alicia had predeceased Wendy *with issue who survived Wendy* (had Darren survived Wendy). But the argument is weak in that this is Darren's wife who is arguing for an implied gift to issue, not Darren, a blood descendant of Alicia. Courts will often protect a blood descendant, but not an in-law. The fatal flaw, however, is that if a gift to Alicia's issue were implied, the word "issue" connotes a requirement of survivorship to the time of possession. If survivorship is required, Fran's argument would not prevail because Darren did not survive Wendy.

Harry

Harry, the successor to Beth's interest, will claim the fund. Harry will argue that "her" in Testator's will means Wendy, and that since Alicia predeceased Wendy without issue who survived Wendy, Beth (or Harry as Beth's successor) is entitled to the fund. On the grounds of Testator's intent, a strong argument can be made that Testator wanted to benefit Alicia, then Alicia's issue, but if, at Wendy's death, neither Alicia nor Alicia's issue were alive, Testator wanted to benefit Beth.

There is no condition precedent of survival on Beth's contingent remainder, and the vast majority of courts implies none.

Conclusion

Harry has the best argument based both on technical arguments and on Testator's presumed intent.

ANSWER TO SAMPLE EXAM QUESTION V

Validity of Appointment: Oscar indicated an intent to appoint the trust fund by the first clause in his will. He appointed to his son, Sam, who was not in being in 1980 when the power was created, with the remainder to Sam's children. If the trust is irrevocable, the appointment in remainder is void under the Rule Against Perpetuities since the appointment is read back into the original trust instrument and measuring "lives in being" for the appointment must be persons alive in 1980. The remainder will vest, if at all, at the death of Sam, a person not alive in 1980. This gift is too remote.

If this is a revocable trust, the gift to Sam's children is valid. Where a trust is revocable by one person, the property is not tied up and the perpetuities period does not begin to run until the power to revoke ceases (1996). Is the trust revocable or irrevocable? In almost all states, trusts are irrevocable unless an express power to revoke is retained. Thus, this trust is probably irrevocable and the remainder void.

Doctrine of Worthier Title: Although the trust may be presumed irrevocable, if the Doctrine of Worthier Title is applied to this trust, the settlor can revoke because the settlor will have the entire equitable interest in the trust. The Doctrine of Worthier Title provides that where a person makes a conveyance purporting to create a remainder in the person's heirs, the remainder is presumptively void and the grantor has a reversion. The Doctrine is a rule of construction and can be overcome by evidence of a contrary intent. The only evidence of contrary intent here is that Oscar retained a general testamentary power of appointment. The argument may go: Since Oscar retained a testamentary power, he intended to create a remainder in his heirs, which could be destroyed by his exercise of the power. If Oscar had intended a reversion, there would be no need to retain a power of appointment.

The Doctrine has been abolished in a number of states, but it is applied in some. It is hard to predict how a court will rule on whether the presumption of a reversion is overcome by a contrary intent. Extrinsic factors will likely influence the court. If the court applies the Doctrine, Oscar has the power to revoke the trust, since he has all interests in it. The settlor can revoke a trust when no one else has an equitable interest in it. If the Doctrine applies, the appointment by Oscar is valid, because the perpetuities period starts running in 1996, when the power to revoke ceases. If the appointment is valid, the trust fund and $10,000 of Oscar's own property will go to Sam for life, remainder to Sam's children; $300,000 goes to Betty.

In responding to the remainder of the question it is assumed that the Doctrine does not apply, and since Oscar had no power to revoke the trust, the appointment to Sam's children is void.

Allocation: If Oscar indicated an intent that the trust fund and his own assets be treated as "one pot" and allocated to the various dispositions in his will so as to give maximum effect to his intent, the trust fund and his assets will be so allocated. Here, Oscar exercised the power by the first clause treating the trust fund and assets as "one pot." He did not specifically appoint the trust assets to Sam and his children. The trust assets should be allocated to give effect to Oscar's whole will. Thus, the trust fund (worth $200,000) should be distributed to the trustee to hold for Sam for life, remainder to Sam's children. By this allocation (or "swap" of the trust assets for Oscar's own assets), Oscar's appointment is wholly valid.

GLOSSARY OF TERMS

acceleration—To put a beneficiary in possession prior to the time specified. Usually moving a remainder into possession when the life estate is disclaimed.

collaterals—Blood relations who are neither ancestors nor descendants.

condition precedent—A condition expressly attached to an interest that must occur before the interest can vest. A remainder subject to a condition precedent is contingent. (Since the word "precedent" is used here as an adjective, not a noun, it is pronounced condition pree-SEE-dent.)

condition subsequent—A condition providing for the divestment of a vested interest if a specified event occurs.

contingent remainder—A remainder created either (i) in an unascertained person or (ii) subject to a condition precedent.

cy pres—Law French for "as near as possible."

devise—A transfer by will.

devisee—A person devised an interest by will.

divestment—The cutting short or divestment of a vested interest upon the happening of a stated event.

executory interest—A future interest in a transferee that, in order to become possessory, must either (i) divest a vested interest in a grantee (shifting executory interest) or (ii) spring out from the grantor in the future (springing executory interest).

executory limitation—A limitation in a deed or will creating an executory interest.

fee simple—An estate without end, of infinite duration.

fee simple absolute—A fee simple that cannot be divested in any event.

fee simple defeasible—A fee simple that may or will end upon the happening of a stated event. This includes a fee simple determinable, a fee simple subject to condition subsequent (or right of entry), and a fee simple subject to executory limitation.

fee simple determinable—A fee simple that is to endure only until a stated event occurs (*e.g.*, "to School so long as used for a school"). It expires automatically when the event happens.

fee simple subject to condition subsequent—A fee simple that may be cut short by the grantor electing to exercise a right of entry.

fee simple subject to executory limitation—A fee simple that will be cut short automatically by an executory interest when a stated event happens.

general power of appointment—A power to appoint property to anyone, including the donee of the power or her estate.

grantee—A person given an interest by deed.

grantor—A person who conveys property.

heirs—Successors to a decedent's property when the decedent dies without a will. Heirs are ascertained at decedent's death, not before. No living person has heirs.

indefeasibly vested—A vested remainder certain to become possessory in the future.

intestate—*adj.* Having no valid will. *n.* A person who dies without a will.

issue—Descendants of any generation.

lapse—The failure of a gift because the beneficiary predeceases the testator.

limitation—Words that create an estate in possession or in remainder (*e.g.*, "to A *for life*").

per capita—Each person taking an equal share.

per stirpes—Taking an ancestor's share by right of representation (standing in her shoes).

possibility of reverter—The interest remaining in the grantor (or the heirs of a testator) who carves out of her estate a determinable estate of the same quantum. Almost always follows a fee simple determinable.

power of appointment—A power to appoint property held in trust. The power may be general or special.

remainder—A future interest in a grantee that can become possessory upon the expiration of the prior estate *and* cannot divest any interest in a grantee. It is to be distinguished from an executory interest, which cuts short the prior estate before the time fixed for its natural termination.

reversion—The interest remaining in the grantor (or her heirs) who transfers a vested estate of a lesser quantum than that of the vested estate she has.

right of entry—A power of termination retained by the grantor (or her heirs) that enables the holder to cut short the estate granted upon breach of a condition subsequent.

settlor—A person who creates a trust, either during life (inter vivos trust) or by will (testamentary trust).

special power of appointment—A power to appoint property to anyone other than the donee of the power, the creditors of the donee, the estate of the donee, or the creditors of the estate of the donee.

testator—A person who devises property at death.

transmissible—Transferable at death by will or by intestacy.

validating life (for the Rule Against Perpetuities)—Any person alive at the creation of an interest who enables one to prove that the contingency attached to the interest will necessarily be resolved during such person's life or within 21 years after such person's death.

vest—An interest not subject to a condition precedent or an interest that has satisfied the Rule Against Perpetuities.

vested remainder—A remainder created in an ascertained person and not subject to a condition precedent.

vested subject to open—A remainder created in a class of persons, of which at least one class member is qualified to take, and into which class more members can enter. Same as vested subject to partial divestment.

TABLE OF CASES

Abbiss v. Burney - §139
Aberg v. First National Bank - §191
Abo Petroleum Corp v. Amstutz - §143
Altman v. Rider - §243
American Security & Trust Co. v. Cramer - §481
Amerige v. Attorney General - §502
Anderson, *In re* Estate of - §528
Arnold v. Baker - §161
Atchison v. City of Englewood - §508

Bails v. Davis - §156
Bank of New York v. Black - §379
Bassett's Estate, *In re* - §455
Beals v. State Street Bank & Trust Co. - §§358, 363, 380
Belfield v. Booth - §462
Berry v. Union National Bank - §517
Bird's Estate, *In re* - §499
Blake, Estate of - §327
Bomberger's Estate - §240
Boone County National Bank v. Edson - §239
Braswell v. Braswell - §§176, 181
Bridgewater v. Turner - §§396, 397
Britton v. Miller - §318
Brown v. Independent Baptist Church of Woburn - §§44, 450
Brown, *In re* Estate of - §369
Brownell v. Edmunds - §464
Burchell, Matter of - §179

Cambridge Co. v. East Slope Investment Corp. - §510
Campbell's Estate, *In re* - §461
Capital Federal Savings & Loan Association v. Smith - §63
Carroll, *In re* - §393
Cattlin v. Brown - §481
Central Delaware County Authority v. Greyhound Corp. - §506
Charlotte Park & Recreation Commission v. Barringer - §63
City Bank & Trust Co. v. Morrissey - §167
City of Klamath Falls v. Bell - §62
Clapp v. Ingraham - §352
Clay v. Security Trust Co. - §253
Clobberie's Case - §§250, 255, 433, 485
Coddington v. Stone - §254
Coe, Estate of - §275
Colburn v. Burlingame - §224

Connecticut Bank & Trust Co. v. Brody - §§453, 473, 482
Continental Cablevision of New England, Inc. v. United Broadcasting Co. - §468
Cook v. Horn - §425
Crane, *In re* - §248
Curtis, *In re* Estate of - §336

Daniel v. Brown - §§396, 401
Dawson v. Yucus - §272
Dewire v. Haveles - §332
Dickerson v. Union National Bank of Little Rock - §458
District of Columbia v. Lloyd - §360
Doctor v. Hughes - §174
Dodge Testamentary Trust, Matter of - §301
Doe *dem.* Willis v. Martin - §238
Dollar Savings & Trust Co. v. First National Bank - §379
Donehue v. Nilges - §41
Dormer's Estate - §341
DuPont, Estate of - §391

Earle Estate - §316
Easter's Estate, *In re* - §302
Edgerly v. Barker - §517
Edwards v. Hammond - §235
Estate of—*see* name of party
Evans's Estate, *In re* - §321

Ferry, Estate of - §240
Festing v. Allen - §236
Fiduciary Trust Co. v. Mishou - §504
Finley v. Finley - §161
First National Bank v. Walker - §377
First National Bank of Bar Harbor v. Anthony - §239
First National Bank of Cincinnati v. Tenney - §§238, 240
First Portland National Bank v. Rodrique - §465
First Universalist Society of North Adams v. Boland - §§62, 450
Fleet National Bank v. Colt - §530
Forsgren v. Sollie - §52
Fox v. Snow - §218

Gaite's Will Trusts, *Re* - §457
Gautier's Will, *In re* - §245
Gertman v. Burdick - §§543, 554
Gilbert, *In re* Estate of - §192

Goldberger v. Goldberger - §266
Gustafson, Matter of - §273

Hargreaves, *In re* - §494
Harlan v. Citizens National Bank of Danville - §388
Harris Trust & Savings Bank v. Beach - §176
Harris Trust & Savings Bank v. Jackson - §300
Hatch v. Riggs National Bank - §182
Hayes v. Hammond - §263
Higbee Corp. v. Kennedy - §51
Hoblit v. Howser - §235
Hofing v. Willis - §240
Horne v. Title Insurance & Trust Co. - §393
Houston Estate - §246

In re—*see* name of party
Industrial National Bank of Rhode Island v. Barrett - §498
Ink v. City of Canton - §66
Institution for Savings v. Roxbury Home for Aged Women - §§62, 450
Irwin Union Bank & Trust Co. v. Long - §349

Jee v. Audley - §§436, 454
Johnson v. City of Wheat Ridge - §61

Kern, Esate of - §173
Kohler, Estate of - §388
Kost v. Foster - §§82, 91
Kroos, *In re* - §246

Landis, *In re* - §208
Latimer's Will, *In re* - §302
Lattouf's Will, *In re* - §455
Lawson v. Lawson - §241
Leake v. Robinson - §472
Leeco Gas & Oil Co. v. County of Nueces - §66
Lee's Estate, *In re* - §474
Loockerman v. McBlair - §313
Loring v. Marshall - §395
Lovering v. Worthington - §445
Lux v. Lux - §324
Lydick v. Tate - §151

Mahrenholz v. County Board - §41
Mansur's Will, *In re* - §252
Martin v. Knowles - §145
Martin v. Seattle - §61
Marx v. Rice - §499
Masson's Estate, *In re* - §352

Mayor & City Council of Ocean City v. Taber - §41
Metropolitan Transportation Authority v. Bruken Realty Corp. - §510
Minary v. Citizens Fidelity Bank - §276
Moore, *Re* - §525
Moss, *In re* - §297
Motes/Henes Trust v. Motes - §377

Nass' Estate - §245
New England Trust Co. v. Sanger - §§447, 453
North Bay Council, Inc., Boy Scouts of America v. Grinnell - §531
North Carolina National Bank v. Norris - §§453, 482
Northern Trust Co. v. Porter - §497

Old Colony Trust Co. v. Barker - §247
Old Colony Trust Co. v. Stephens - §302
Old Colony Trust Co. v. Tufts - §249
Oldfield v. Stoeco Homes, Inc. - §51
Osburn's Appeal - §298

Parant's Will, *In re* - §295
Parker, *In re* - §255
Pells v. Brown - §136
Perkins v. Igleheart - §458
Perrin v. Blake - §168
Petry v. Petry - §283
Peveto v. Starkey - §451
Picken v. Matthews - §480
Pound v. Shorter - §458
Proestler's Will, *In re* - §378
Proprietors of the Church in Brattle Square v. Grant - §§62, 451
Pruner's Estate, *In re* - §44
Purefoy v. Rogers - §137
Pyne v. Pyne - §267

Quilliams v. Koonsman - §92
Quinn v. Tuttle - §349

Ray v. Ray - §165
Re—*see* name of party
Reynolds, Estate of - §191
Rice v. Boston & Worcester Railroad - §55
Roberts v. Rhodes - §52
Robertson v. Robertson - §247
Rogers v. Mutch - §315
Rust v. Rust - §446
Ryan v. Beshk - §461
Ryan v. Ward - §425

Scott v. Scott - §223
Sears v. Coolidge - §500
Second Bank-State Street Trust Co. v. Second Bank-State Street Trust Co. - §483
Second National Bank of New Haven v. Harris Trust & Savings Bank - §497
Security Trust Co. v. Irvine - §246
Seidel v. Werner - §369
Sellick v. Sellick - §193
Seymour v. Heubaum - §167
Shelley's Case—*see* Rule in Shelley's Case in index
Smith, Estate of - §377
Smith, *In re* - §380
Society National Bank v. Jacobson - §148
Stanford's Estate, *In re* - §242
State Street Trust Co. v. Kissel - §354
Sterner v. Nelson - §218
Stoller v. Doyle - §136
Storke v. Penn Mutual Life Insurance Co. - §51
Storrs v. Benbow - §484
Sybert v. Sybert - §163

Talbot v. Riggs - §410
Tapley v. Dill - §240

Texaco Refining & Marketing Inc. v. Samowitz - §509
Thellusson v. Woodford - §§525, 554
Thomas v. Harrison - §444
Thall, *In re* - §326

Underwood v. Underwood - §215

Villar, *In re* - §§439, 524

Walker, *In re* Trust of - §242
Ward v. Van der Loeff - §§473, 480
Warner v. Warner - §246
Waterman v. New York Life Insurance & Trust Co. - §397
Weller v. Sokol - §243
Welles' Will, *In re* - §281
Wenmoth's Estate, *In re* - §325
Wild's Case - §291
Will of (*see* name of party)
Wong v. DiGrazia - §511
Wood, *In re* - §463
Wood v. Board of Commissioners - §52
Woodworth, Estate of - §301
Wright's Estate - §456

INDEX

A

ACCELERATION, §§97, 191-192
ACCUMULATIONS, RULE AGAINST, §554
ADOPTED CHILDREN, §§274-277
ADVERSE POSSESSION, §61
AGE CONTINGENCIES
    requiring survival to stated age, §§235, 250-255
    Rule Against Perpetuities, §§475, 480, 485-486
ALIENATION
    See Transferability
ALL-OR-NOTHING RULE, §§472-474
ALLOCATION, §§402-405, 505
ANIMALS
    measuring lives, §442
ASSIGNABILITY
    contingent remainders, §§197-203
    executory interests, §§197-203
    right of entry, §§55-58
    possibility of reverter, §47
    vested future interests, §196

B

BANKRUPTCY, §§208, 351
BLENDING CLAUSE, §§403-405, 409

C

CAPTURE, §§406-411
CHARITABLE GIFTS, §§421, 450
CHILDREN, §§273-280
    See also Class gifts
    adopted children, §§274-277
    grandchildren, §281
    nonmarital children, §278
    stepchildren, §279
CHOICE OF LAW, §§356-359
CLASS GIFTS, §§268-305
    children, meaning of, §§273-280. *See also* Children
    class closing rules, §§306-325
        Rule Against Perpetuities, §§478-480
    defined, §§268-272
    heirs, §§299-305
    issue, §§282-290
    per stirpes, §§284-290
    Rule Against Perpetuities, §§471-486
    Rule in Wild's Case, §§291-295
    rule of convenience, §§310-325
    survival requirement, §§240-241
CLASSIFICATION OF FUTURE INTERESTS,
        §§19-31, 116-120
    executory interest, §§101-113
    possibility of reverter, §§37-46
    remainder, §§77-100
    reversion, §§32-36
    right of entry, §§48-54

CONDEMNATION
    See Eminent domain
CONDITION PRECEDENT
    condition subsequent distinguished, §§92-93
    contingent remainders, §§90-91
    surplusage, §§234-235
CONDITION SUBSEQUENT
    condition precedent distinguished, §§92-93
    reversion with alternate contingent remainders, §94
    vested remainders, §84
CONFLICT OF LAWS
    powers of appointment, §§356-359
CONSTRUCTION RULES, §§225-333
    broad rules, preferences, §§225-232
        against partial intestacy, §§226-227
        blood relatives, §229
        general plan, §232
        heir protected, §227
        legislative scheme, §230
        maximum validity, §228
        technical meaning, §231
    class gifts, §§268-333. *See also* Class gifts
    gift over on death without issue, §§260-267. *See also*
            Death without issue
    implied gifts, §§326-333. *See also* Implication, gifts by
    survival requirement, §§239-259. *See also* Survival,
            requirement of
    vested interests preferred, §§100, 233-238
CONSUMABLES, §§215-217
CONTINGENT REMAINDERS, §§86-100
    See also Future interests; Remainders
    acceleration, §§97, 191
    age contingencies, §§250-255
    assignability, §§197-202
    condition precedent. *See* Condition precedent
    creditors' rights, §207
    defined, §86
    destructibility doctrine, §§98, 121-144
    gifts to issue or descendants. *See* Class gifts
    Rule Against Perpetuities, §419. *See also* Rule Against
            Perpetuities
    Rule in Shelley's Case, §§152-154, 158
    survival requirement. *See* Survival requirement
    vested remainders preferred, §100
CONVENIENCE, RULE OF, §§310-325, 478, 480
CREDITORS' RIGHTS, §§205-208
    bankruptcy, §208
    contingent remainders, §207
    Doctrine of Worthier Title, §180
    powers of appointment, §§349-355
    vested interests, §206
CROSS-REMAINDERS, §333
CY PRES DOCTRINE, §§514-519

D

DEATH WITHOUT ISSUE, §§260-267
    definite failure construction, §264

implied remainder to issue, §327
indefinite failure construction, §§261-263
substitutional construction, §§265-267
successive construction, §§265-267

DESCENDIBILITY, §§96, 204

DESTRUCTIBILITY OF CONTINGENT REMAIN-
DERS, §§121-144
abolition, §§143-144
avoidance, §§140-142
gap in seisin, §123
interests not affected, §§134-139
   executory interests, §136
   personal property, §138
   trusts, §139
   vested remainders, §135
statement of rule, §§122-124
termination of life estate, §§126-133
   artificial, §§128-133
      fee tail exception, §132
      forfeiture, §§129-130
      merger, §§131-133
      simultaneous creation exception, §132
   natural, §127

DETERMINABLE FEE, §§7, 23, 41, 449

DEVISABILITY, §§96, 204

DIE WITHOUT ISSUE
See Death without issue

DISCLAIMER, §§184-194
acceleration, §§191-192
relation back, §194
sequestration, §193

DISCRETIONARY TRUSTS, §§255, 341
Rule Against Perpetuities, §496

DIVIDE-AND-PAY-OVER RULE, §248

DOCTRINE OF WORTHIER TITLE, §§172-183
abolition, §§182-183
creditors' rights, §180
modern rule, §§174-175
New York law, §183
operation of, §§176-181
statement of, §§172-173
   inter vivos, §172
   testamentary, §173
trust revocation, §179

DYNASTY TRUSTS, §§539, 547

E

EDWARDS v. HAMMOND, RULE IN, §§235-237

EMINENT DOMAIN
possibility of reverter, §65
right of entry, §65

EXECUTORY INTERESTS, §§9, 28-30, 101-115
See also Future Interests
and remainders, §114
assignability, §§197-203
defined, §101
descendibility, §204
destructibility rule, §136
devisability, §204
English background, §§102-106

following defeasible fee, §§62, 451, 531, 542
following possessory fee simple, §§108-109
Rule Against Perpetuities, §§62, 451, 531
Rule in Shelley's Case, §160
shifting vs. springing, §§103-106
Statute of Uses, §107
statutory obliteration, §115
   New York law, §115
vesting, §§110-113

F

FEDERAL ESTATE TAX, §§209-213
powers of appointment, §§344-346
transmission of future interest, §§210-211
valuation of future interest, §§212-213

FEDERAL GIFT TAX, §214
powers of appointment, §§347-348

FEE SIMPLE, §§5-9
absolute, §6
determinable, §§7, 23, 41, 449
   executory interest following, §§62, 451
no remainder after, §§74, 109
subject to condition subsequent, §8
subject to executory limitation, §9

FEE TAIL, §10
in gift "to A and his children," §292
Rule in Wild's Case, §292

FEOFFMENT, TORTIOUS, §129

FERTILE OCTOGENARIAN, §§453-456

FRAUDULENT APPOINTMENT, §§392-393

FREEHOLD ESTATE, §4

FUTURE INTERESTS
acceleration, §§97, 191-192
alienability. *See* Transferability
class gifts. *See* Class gifts
classification, §§70-120. *See also* Classification of
   future interests
gifts by implication, §§326-333
in grantee, §§26-30
in grantor, §§21-25
summary, §§116-120
survival requirement, §§239-259
taxation. *See* Federal estate tax
types
   contingent remainder. *See* Contingent remainders
   executory interest. *See* Executory interests
   possibility of reverter. *See* Possibility of reverter
   remainder. *See* Remainders
   reversion. *See* Reversions
   right of entry. *See* Right of entry
   vested remainder. *See* Vested remainders

G

GIFT IN DEFAULT OF APPOINTMENT
capture, §§406-411
implication of, §395
second look doctrine, §500

GIFT TAX
See Federal gift tax
GIFTS BY IMPLICATION
See Implication, gifts by
GRANTEES, FUTURE INTERESTS IN, §§26-30
    executory interests, §28. *See also* Executory interests
        shifting, §29. *See also* Shifting interests
        springing, §30. *See also* Springing interests
    remainders, §§26, 133. *See also* Contingent remainders; Remainders; Vested remainders
GRANTOR, FUTURE INTERESTS IN, §§21-25
    correlative possessory estates, §25
    possibility of reverter, §23. *See also* Possibility of reverter
    reversions, §22. *See also* Reversions
    right of entry, §24. *See also* Right of entry

H

HEIRS
    defined, §301
    meaning of gift to, §§299-305
        spouse, §300
        time of ascertainment, §§301-303
    of grantee. *See* Rule in Shelley's Case
    of grantor. *See* Doctrine of Worthier Title
HIERARCHY OF ESTATES, §13
HONORARY TRUSTS, §442

IJK

ILLEGITIMATE CHILDREN, §278
ILLUSORY APPOINTMENT, §390
IMPLICATION, GIFTS BY, §§326-333
    cross-remainders, §333
    default of appointment, §§394-396
INDEFINITE FAILURE OF ISSUE, §§261-263
INFECTIOUS INVALIDITY, §447
ISSUE
    definite failure, §264
    die without, meaning, §§260-267. *See also* Death without issue
    gift to, §§282-290
        per stirpes or per capita, §§283-289
    indefinite failure, §§261-263

L

LAPSE
    life estate, §155
    powers of appointment, §§398-401
LIFE ESTATE, §§12-14
    disclaimer, §§186-187
    in consumable property, §§215-217
    merger, §131
    termination prior to death of life tenant, §§126-133

MN

MAGIC GRAVEL PIT, §463
MEASURING LIVES
See Rule Against Perpetuities
MERGER, DESTRUCTION BY, §§131-133
    and Rule in Shelley's Case, §146

O

OPTIONS, §§506-510, 544

P

PER CAPITA GIFTS
    class closing rules, §315
    Rule Against Perpetuities, §484
    to issue, §283
PER STIRPES
    gifts to issue, §§284-290
PERPETUITIES, RULE AGAINST
See Rule Against Perpetuities
PERSONAL PROPERTY
    consumables, §§215-219
    destructibility rule, §138
    right to security in, §§220-224
    Rule in Shelley's Case, §148
    Rule in Wild's Case, §174
POSSESSORY ESTATES, §§2-18
POSSIBILITY OF REVERTER, §§37-47, 59-67, 448-450
    adverse possession, §61
    automatically possessory, §45
    creation of, §§40-44
    defined, §§37-39
    eminent domain, §§65-67
    racial discrimination, §63
    retained in grantor, §37
        by will, §44
    reversion distinguished, §38
    right of entry distinguished, §§59-67
    Rule Against Perpetuities, §§62, 448-450
    transferability, §§47, 60
    vested, §46
POWER OF TERMINATION
See Right of entry
POWERS OF APPOINTMENT, §§334-411
    allocation, §§402-405, 505
    anti-lapse statutes, §§398-401
    capture, §§406-411
        Rule Against Perpetuities, §§502-504
    classification, §§334-341
    conflict of laws, §§356-359
    contract to appoint, §§367-371
        treated as release, §§372-373
    creditors of donee, §§349-355
    exercise, §§374-411
        by residuary clause, §§378-380
        contract for, §§367-373

general power, §§381-382
special power, §§383-397
specific reference, §376
federal estate tax, §§344-346
federal gift tax, §§347-348
general
    capture, §§406-411
    contract to appoint, §367
    creditors of donee, §§349-354
    exercise, §§381-382
    exercise by residuary clause, §§378-380
    release, §§362-363
    Rule Against Perpetuities, §§488-492
imperative, §395
implied gift in default of appointment, §394
inter vivos, §§337-338
marshaling. *See* Allocation
relation back, §§342-359
release, §§360-366
Rule Against Perpetuities, §§487-505
second look doctrine, §499
special powers
    contract to appoint, §368
    creditors' rights, §355
    defined, §340
    exclusive, §§387-388
    exercise, §§383-397
    fraud on, §§392-393
    nonexclusive, §§387-390
    release, §§364-365
    Rule Against Perpetuities, §§493-505
specific reference, §§375-377
taxation, §§344-348
testamentary, §336

PRECOCIOUS TODDLER, §457
***PUREFOY v. ROGERS,* RULE OF,** §137

Q

QUANTUM OF ESTATES, §18

R

RACIAL DISCRIMINATION, §63
RELATION BACK
disclaimer, §187
powers of appointment, §§342-359
    Rule Against Perpetuities, §§493, 497-498
REMAINDERS, §§27, 68-100
See also Contingent remainders; Vested remainders
acceleration, §§97, 191-192
alienability, §96
characteristics of, §§69-76
class closing rules. *See* Class gifts
classification, §§77-94
contingent. *See* Contingent remainders
cross-remainders, implied, §333
defined, §68
destructibility, §§98, 121-144. *See also* Destructibility
    of contingent remainders

indefeasibly vested, §81
transferability, §96
unascertained persons, §§87-89
valuation, §§212-213
vested subject to divestment, §84
vested subject to open, §§82-83
vested to open and complete defeasance, §85
RENUNCIATION
See Disclaimer
REPRESENTATION
meaning, §285
right of. *See* Per stirpes
REPUGNANCY, RULE OF, §§218-219
RESIDUARY CLAUSE
exercise of power of appointment by, §§378-380
REVERSIONS, §§22, 32-36
after alternative contingent remainders, §94
after contingent remainder in unascertained persons,
    §89
defined, §32
divestment by contingent remainder, §75
possibility of reverter distinguished, §38
retained by will, §34
rule of reversions, §33
transferability, §36
vested, §35
with alternative contingent remainders, §94
REVERSIONARY INTERESTS, §21
See also Possibility of reverter; Reversions; Right of
    entry
REVOCABLE TRUSTS
Rule Against Perpetuities, §425
RIGHT OF ENTRY, §§24, 48-67
adverse possession, §61
creation of, §§50-51
defined, §§48-49
eminent domain, §§65-67
possibility of reverter distinguished, §§49, 59-63
racial discrimination, §63
Rule Against Perpetuities, §62
termination, §64
transferability, §§52-58
vested, §54
ROYAL LIVES CLAUSES, §439
RULE AGAINST ACCUMULATIONS, §554
RULE AGAINST PERPETUITIES, §§412-547
abolition, §546
age contingencies reduced, §§517, 519, 529
alternative contingencies, §§465-468
class gifts. *See also* Class gifts
    all-or-nothing rule, §§472-474
    class closing rules, §§480, 484
    per capita gifts, §484
    rule of convenience, §480
    subclasses, §§481, 530
commercial transactions, §§506-511
    on-completion leases, §511
    options, §506
consequences of violation, §§445-447
cy pres doctrine, §§514-519

defeasible fees, interests following, §§446, 448-451, 531

discretionary trusts, §496

executory interest following defeasible fee, §§449-451

fertile octogenarian, §§453-456, 515, 527

Gray's statement of Rule, §412

honorary trusts, §442

infectious invalidity, §447

interests subject to, §§419-421

lives in being, §§413, 422-426, 434-443

magic gravel pit, §463

measuring lives. *See* Lives in being; Validating lives

    wait-and-see, §§520-531

New York law, §§548-553

options, §506

period of gestation, §443

possibility of reverter, §448

powers of appointment, §§487-505. *See also* Powers of appointment

    relation back, §§497-498

    second look doctrine, §499

precious toddler, §457

reforms, §§512-547

    cy pres, §§514-519

    specific remedies, §519

    wait-and-see, §§534, 537

relevant lives, §§435-436

revocable trusts, §425

right of entry, §448

royal lives clauses, §717

saving clause, §§469-470

separability of valid and invalid conditions, §§465-468

slothful executor, §§461-462, 528

suspension of power of alienation, §§548-553

twenty-one-year period, §444

unborn widow, §§458, 516

validating lives, §§434-442

vesting concept, §§427-433

    vested with possession postponed, §§485-486

wait-and-see doctrine, §§520-545

    common law period, §§520-534

        measuring lives, §§521-523

    pros and cons, §§533, 536

    Uniform Statutory Rule Against Perpetuities, §§535-545. *See also* Uniform Statutory Rule Against Perpetuities

wars that never end, §464

what-might-happen test, §§416, 452-464

RULE IN SHELLEY'S CASE, §§145-171

avoidance, §169

contingent remainder, §158

executory interest, §160

"heirs," §§161-166

joint life estate, §156

lapse of life estate, §155

life estate in remainder, §§152-154

merger, §146

modern status, §§170-171

operation of, §§149-167

personal property, §148

reasons for, §147

rule of law, §168

statement of Rule, §145

RULE IN WILD'S CASE, §§291-298

RULE OF CONVENIENCE, §§310-325, 480

RULE OF REPUGNANCY, §§218-219

RULE OF REVERSIONS, §33

See also Reversions

S

SECOND LOOK DOCTRINE, §§499-500

SECURITY FOR PERSONAL PROPERTY, §§220-224

SEQUESTRATION, §§193-194

SHELLEY'S CASE, RULE IN, §§145-171

See also Rule in Shelley's Case

SHIFTING INTERESTS

See also Executory interests

as future interest in grantee, §29

before Statute of Uses, §§103-104

divesting fee simple, §108

divesting remainder, §108

SLOTHFUL EXECUTOR, §§461-462

SPENDTHRIFT TRUSTS, §§552-553

SPRINGING INTERESTS

See also Executory interests

as future interest in grantee, §30

before Statute of Uses, §§105-106

STATE ACTION, §63

STATUTE OF USES, §107

STEPCHILDREN, §279

STRANGER-TO-THE-ADOPTION RULE, §274

SUBCLASSES, §§481-483

SUBSTITUTIONAL CONSTRUCTION, §§265-267

SUCCESSIVE CONSTRUCTION, §§265-267

SURVIVAL, REQUIREMENT OF, §§239-259

age contingencies, §§235, 250-255

alternative limitation, §247

class gifts, §§242-245

Clobberie's Case, §§250-255

divide-and-pay-over rule, §248

Edwards v. Hammond, §§235-236

SUSPENSION OF POWER OF ALIENATION, RULE AGAINST, §§548-553

T

TAXATION

See Federal estate tax; Federal gift tax

TERM OF YEARS, §§15, 112

defeasible, §16

used in avoiding

    destructibility doctrine, §141

    Rule in Shelley's Case, §169

TORTIOUS FEOFFMENT, §129

TRANSFERABILITY, §§195-204

assignability. *See* Assignability

creditors' rights, §§205-208

possibility of reverter, §47

reversion, §36

right of entry, §§55-58

TRUSTS
charitable. *See* Charitable gifts
destructibility rule, §§139, 142
discretionary
    Rule Against Perpetuities, §496
Doctrine of Worthier Title, §179
irrevocable
    Rule Against Perpetuities, §426
revocable
    Rule Against Perpetuities, §425
spendthrift, §§552-553
    New York statutory, §553

U

UNBORN WIDOW, §§458-460
**UNIFORM DISCLAIMER OF PROPERTY INTER-
    ESTS ACT, §186**
UNIFORM PROBATE CODE
adopted children, §§276, 280
choice of law, §359
Doctrine of Worthier Title abolished, §182
heirs determined, §303
nonmarital children, §280
power exercised by residuary clause, §§378-379
remainders made contingent, §§256-259
right of representation, §§285, 290
**UNIFORM STATUTORY RULE AGAINST PERPE-
    TUITIES, §§535-545**
commercial transactions, §544
dynasty trusts, §§539, 547
longer of two periods prohibited, §540
90-year period, §§537-539

noncharitable purpose trusts, §541
USES
See Statute of Uses

V

VEST
See Remainders; Rule Against Perpetuities; Vested
    remainders
VESTED REMAINDERS, §§77-85
See also Remainders
apparently contingent remainders construed as vested
    Clobberie's Case, §§250-255
    Edwards v. Hammond, §§235-237
conditions precedent, §79
constructional preference for vested, §§100, 233-238
defined, §§78-79
destructibility rule, §135
indefeasibly vested remainder, §81
Rule Against Perpetuities, §419
subject to divestment, §§84-85
subject to open, §§82-83
vested with possession postponed, §§250-255

WXYZ

WAIT-AND-SEE DOCTRINE, §§520-545
See also Rule Against Perpetuities
WARS THAT NEVER END, §464
WHAT-MIGHT-HAPPEN TEST, §416
WILD'S CASE, RULE IN, §§291-298
WORTHIER TITLE, DOCTRINE OF, §§172-183
See also Doctrine of Worthier Title

Notes

Notes

Notes

Notes

Notes

Notes

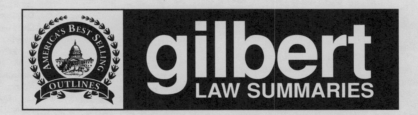

Income Tax II - Partnerships, Corporations, Trusts
By Professor Michael R. Asimow, U.C.L.A.
Taxation of Partnerships (including Current Partnership Income, Contributions of Property to Partnership, Sale of Partnership Interest, Distributions, Liquidations); Corporate Taxation (including Corporate Distributions, Sales of Stock and Assets, Reorganizations); S Corporations; Federal Income Taxation of Trusts.
ISBN: 0-15-900024-6   Pages: 237 $17.95

Labor Law
By Professor James C. Oldham, Georgetown University, and Robert J. Gelhaus
Statutory Foundations of Present Labor Law (including National Labor Relations Act, Taft-Hartley, Norris-LaGuardia Act, Landrum-Griffin Act); Organizing Campaigns, Selection of the Bargaining Representative; Collective Bargaining (including Negotiating the Agreement, Lockouts, Administering the Agreement, Arbitration); Strikes, Boycotts, and Picketing; Concerted Activity Protected Under the NLRA; Civil Rights Legislation; Grievance; Federal Regulation of Compulsory Union Membership Arrangements; State Regulation of Compulsory Membership Agreements; "Right to Work" Laws; Discipline of Union Members; Election of Union Officers; Corruption.
ISBN: 0-15-900340-7   Pages: 243 $17.95

Legal Ethics
By Professor Thomas D. Morgan, George Washington University
Regulating Admission to Practice Law; Preventing Unauthorized Practice of Law; Contract Between Client and Lawyer (including Lawyer's Duties Regarding Accepting Employment, Spheres of Authority of Lawyer and Client, Obligation of Client to Lawyer, Terminating the Lawyer-Client Relationship); Attorney-Client Privilege; Professional Duty of Confidentiality; Conflicts of Interest; Obligations to Third Persons and the Legal System (including Counseling Illegal or Fraudulent Conduct, Threats of Criminal Prosecution); Special Obligations in Litigation (including Limitations on Advancing Money to Client, Duty to Reject Certain Actions, Lawyer as Witness); Solicitation and Advertising; Specialization; Disciplinary Process; Malpractice; Special Responsibilities of Judges.
ISBN: 0-15-900026-2   Pages: 252 $18.95

Legal Research, Writing and Analysis
By Professor Peter J. Honigsberg, University of San Francisco
Court Systems; Precedent; Case Reporting System (including Regional and State Reporters, Headnotes and the West Key Number System, Citations and Case Finding); Statutes, Constitutions, and Legislative History; Secondary Sources (including Treatises, Law Reviews, Digests, Restatements); Administrative Agencies (including Regulations, Looseleaf Services); Shepard's Citations; Computers in Legal Research; Reading and Understanding a Case (including Briefing a Case); Using Legal Sourcebooks; Basic Guidelines for Legal Writing;

Organizing Your Research; Writing a Memorandum of Law; Writing a Brief; Writing an Opinion or Client Letter.
ISBN: 0-15-900305-9   Pages: 162 $16.95

Multistate Bar Examination
By Professor Richard J. Conviser, Chicago Kent
Structure of the Exam; Governing Law; Effective Use of Time; Scoring of the Exam; Jurisdictions Using the Exam; Subject Matter Outlines; Practice Tests, Answers, and Subject Matter Keys; Glossary of Legal Terms and Definitions; State Bar Examination Directory; Listing of Reference Materials for Multistate Subjects.
ISBN: 0-15-900030-0   Pages: 210 $17.95

Personal Property
Gilbert Staff
Acquisitions; Ownership Through Possession (including Wild Animals, Abandoned Chattels); Finders of Lost Property; Bailments; Possessory Liens; Pledges, Trover; Gift; Accession; Confusion (Commingling); Fixtures; Crops (Emblements); Adverse Possession; Prescriptive Rights (Acquiring Ownership of Easements or Profits by Adverse Use).
ISBN: 0-15-900031-9   Pages: 69 $12.95

Professional Responsibility
(see Legal Ethics)

Property
By Professor Jesse Dukeminier, U.C.L.A.
Possession (including Wild Animals, Bailments, Adverse Possession); Gifts and Sales of Personal Property; Freehold Possessory Estates; Future Interests (including Reversion, Possibility of Reverter, Right of Entry, Executory Interests, Rule Against Perpetuities); Tenancy in Common; Joint Tenancy; Tenancy by the Entirety; Condominiums; Cooperatives; Marital Property; Landlord and Tenant; Easements and Covenants; Nuisance; Rights in Airspace and Water; Right to Support; Zoning; Eminent Domain; Sale of Land (including Mortgage, Deed, Warranties of Title); Methods of Title Assurance (including Recording System, Title Registration, Title Insurance).
ISBN: 0-15-900032-7   Pages: 496 $21.95

Remedies
By Professor John A. Bauman, U.C.L.A., and Professor Kenneth H. York, Pepperdine University
Damages; Equitable Remedies (including Injunctions and Specific Performance); Restitution; Injuries to Tangible Property Interests; Injuries to Business and Commercial Interests (including Business Torts, Inducing Breach of Contract, Patent Infringement, Unfair Competition, Trade Defamation); Injuries to Personal Dignity and Related Interests (including Defamation, Privacy, Religious Status, Civil and Political Rights); Personal Injury and Death; Fraud; Duress, Undue Influence, and Unconscionable Conduct; Mistake; Breach of Contract; Unenforceable Contracts (including Statute of Frauds, Impossibility, Lack of Contractual Capacity, Illegality).
ISBN: 0-15-900325-3   Pages: 375 $20.95

Sales and Lease of Goods
By Professor Douglas J. Whaley, Ohio State University
UCC Article 2; Sales Contract (including Offer and Acceptance, Parol Evidence Rule, Statute of Frauds, Assignment and Delegation, Revision of Contract Terms); Types of Sales (including Cash Sale Transactions, Auctions, "Sale or Return" and "Sale on Approval" Transactions); Warranties (including Express and Implied Warranties, Privity, Disclaimer, Consumer Protection Statutes); Passage of Title; Performance of the Contract; Anticipatory Breach; Demand for Assurance of Performance; Unforeseen Circumstances; Risk of Loss; Remedies; Documents of Title; Lease of Goods; International Sale of Goods.
ISBN: 0-15-900034-3   Pages: 222 $17.95

Secured Transactions
By Professor Douglas J. Whaley, Ohio State University
Coverage of Article 9; Creation of a Security Interest (including Attachment, Security Agreement, Value, Debtor's Rights in the Collateral); Perfection; Filing; Priorities; Bankruptcy Proceedings and Article 9; Default Proceedings; Bulk Transfers.
ISBN: 0-15-900035-1   Pages: 213 $17.95

Securities Regulation
By Professor David H. Barber, and Professor Niels B. Schaumann, William Mitchell College of Law
Securities and Exchange Commission; Jurisdiction and Interstate Commerce; Securities Act of 1933 (including Persons and Property Interest Covered, Registration Statement, Exemptions From Registration Requirements, Liabilities); Securities Exchange Act of 1934 (including Rule 10b-5, Tender Offers and Repurchases of Stock, Regulation of Proxy Solicitations, Liability for Short-Swing Profits on Insider Transactions, S.E.C. Enforcement Actions); Regulation of the Securities Markets; Multi-national Transactions; State Regulation of Securities Transactions.
ISBN: 0-15-9000326-1   Pages: 415 $20.95

Torts
By Professor Marc A. Franklin, Stanford University
Intentional Torts; Negligence; Strict Liability; Products Liability; Nuisance; Survival of Tort Actions; Wrongful Death; Immunity; Release and Contribution; Indemnity; Workers' Compensation; No-Fault Auto Insurance; Defamation; Invasion of Privacy; Misrepresentation; Injurious Falsehood; Interference With Economic Relations; Unjustifiable Litigation.
ISBN: 0-15-900037-8   Pages: 439 $19.95

Trusts
By Professor Edward C. Halbach, Jr., U.C. Berkeley
Elements of a Trust; Trust Creation; Transfer of Beneficiary's Interest (including Spendthrift Trusts); Charitable Trusts (including Cy Pres Doctrine); Trustee's Responsibilities, Power, Duties, and Liabilities; Duties and Liabilities of

Beneficiaries; Accounting for Income and Principal; Power of Settlor to Modify or Revoke; Powers of Trustee Beneficiaries or Courts to Modify or Terminate; Termination of Trusts by Operation of Law; Resulting Trusts; Purchase Money Resulting Trusts; Constructive Trusts.
ISBN: 0-15-900039-4   Pages: 268 $18.95

Wills
By Professor Stanley M. Johanson, University of Texas
Intestate Succession; Simultaneous Death; Advancements; Disclaimer; Killer of Decedent; Elective Share Statutes; Pretermitted Child Statutes; Homestead; Formal Requisites of a Will; Revocation of Wills; Incorporation by Reference; Pour-Over Gift in Inter Vivos Trust; Joint Wills; Contracts Relating to Wills; Lapsed Gifts; Ademption; Exoneration of Liens; Will Contests; Probate and Estate Administration.
ISBN: 0-15-900040-8   Pages: 310 $19.95

All titles available at your law school bookstore or call to order: 1-800-787-8717

LAW SCHOOL LEGENDS SERIES

America's Greatest Law Professors on Audio Cassette

Wouldn't it be great if all of your law professors were law school legends? You know — the kind of professors whose classes everyone fights to get into. The professors whose classes you'd take, no matter what subject they're teaching. The kind of professors who make a subject sing. You may never get an opportunity to take a class with a truly brilliant professor, but with the Law School Legends Series, you can now get all the benefits of the country's greatest law professors…on audio cassette!

Administrative Law
Professor To Be Announced
Call For Release Date

TOPICS COVERED (Subject to Change): Classification Of Agencies; Adjudicative And Investigative Action; Rule Making Power; Delegation Doctrine; Control By Executive; Appointment And Removal; Freedom Of Information Act; Rule Making Procedure; Adjudicative Procedure; Trial Type Hearings; Administrative Law Judge; Power To Stay Proceedings; Subpoena Power; Physical Inspection; Self Incrimination; Judicial Review Issues; Declaratory Judgment; Sovereign Immunity; Eleventh Amendment; Statutory Limitations; Standing; Exhaustion Of Administrative Remedies; Scope Of Judicial Review.
3 Audio Cassettes
ISBN 0-15-900189-7 $39.95

Agency & Partnership
Professor Richard J. Conviser
Chicago Kent College of Law

TOPICS COVERED: Agency: Creation; Rights And Duties Of Principal And Agent; Sub-Agents; Contract Liability–Actual Authority: Express And Implied; Apparent Authority; Ratification; Liabilities Of Parties; Tort Liability–Respondeat Superior; Frolic And Detour; Intentional Torts. *Partnership:* Nature Of Partnership; Formation; Partnership By Estoppel; In Partnership Property; Relations Between Partners To Third Parties; Authority of Partners; Dissolution And Termination; Limited Partnerships.
3 Audio Cassettes
ISBN: 0-15-900351-2 $39.95

Antitrust Law
Professor To Be Announced
Call For Release Date

TOPICS COVERED (Subject to Change): How U.S. Antitrust Lawyers And Economists Think And Solve Problems: Antitrust Law's First Principle — Consumer Welfare Opposes Market Power; Methods Of Analysis — Rule Of Reason, Per Se, Quick Look; Sherman Act Section 1 — Civil And Criminal Conspiracies In Unreasonable Restraint Of Trade; Sherman Act Section 2 — Illegal Monopolization And Attempts To Monopolize; Robinson Patman Act Price Discrimination And Related Distribution Problems; Clayton Act Section Section 7 — Mergers And Joint

Ventures; Antitrust And Intellectual Property; U.S. Antitrust And International Competitive Relationships — Extraterritoriality, Comity, And Convergence; Exemptions And Regulated Industries; Enforcement By The Department Of Justice, Federal Trade Commission, National Association Of State Attorneys General, And By Private Litigation; Price And Non-Price Restraints.
2 Audio Cassettes
ISBN: 0-15-900341-5 $39.95

Bankruptcy
Professor Elizabeth Warren
Harvard Law School

TOPICS COVERED: The Debtor/Creditor Relationship; The Commencement, Conversion, Dismissal and Reopening Of Bankruptcy Proceedings; Property Included In The Bankruptcy Estate; Secured, Priority And Unsecured Claims; The Automatic Stay; Powers Of Avoidance; The Assumption And Rejection Of Executory Contracts; The Protection Of Exempt Property; The Bankruptcy Discharge; Chapter 13 Proceedings; Chapter 11 Proceedings; Bankruptcy Jurisdiction And Procedure.
4 Audio Cassettes
ISBN: 0-15-900273-7 $45.95

Civil Procedure
By Professor Richard D. Freer
Emory University Law School

TOPICS COVERED: Subject Matter Jurisdiction; Personal Jurisdiction; Long-Arm Statutes; Constitutional Limitations; In Rem And Quasi In Rem Jurisdiction; Service Of Process; Venue; Transfer; Forum Non Conveniens; Removal; Waiver; Governing Law; Pleadings; Joinder Of Claims; Permissive And Compulsory Joinder Of Parties; Counter-Claims And Cross-Claims; Ancillary Jurisdiction; Impleader; Class Actions; Discovery; Pretrial Adjudication; Summary Judgment; Trial; Post Trial Motions; Appeals; Res Judicata; Collateral Estoppel.
5 Audio Cassettes
ISBN: 0-15-900322-9 $59.95

Commercial Paper
By Professor Michael I. Spak
Chicago Kent College Of Law

TOPICS COVERED: Introduction; Types Of Negotiable Instruments; Elements Of Negotiability; Statute Of Limitations; Payment-In-

Full Checks; Negotiations Of The Instrument; Becoming A Holder-In-Due Course; Rights Of A Holder In Due Course; Real And Personal Defenses; Jus Teril; Effect Of Instrument On Underlying Obligations; Contracts Of Maker And Indorser; Suretyship; Liability Of Drawer And Drawee; Check Certification; Warranty Liability; Conversion Of Liability; Banks And Their Customers; Properly Payable Rule; Wrongful Dishonor; Stopping Payment; Death Of Customer; Bank Statement; Check Collection; Expedited Funds Availability; Forgery Of Drawer's Name; Alterations; Imposter Rule; Wire Transfers; Electronic Fund Transfers Act .
3 Audio Cassettes
ISBN: 0-15-900275-3 $39.95

Conflict Of Laws
Professor Richard J. Conviser
Chicago Kent College of Law

TOPICS COVERED: Domicile; Jurisdiction; In Personam, In Rem, Quasi In Rem; Court Competence; Forum Non Conveniens; Choice Of Law; Foreign Causes Of Action; Territorial Approach To Choice/Tort And Contract; "Escape Devices"; Most Significant Relationship; Governmental Interest Analysis; Recognition Of Judgments; Foreign Country Judgments; Domestic Judgments/Full Faith And Credit; Review Of Judgments; Modifiable Judgments; Defenses To Recognition And Enforcement; Federal/State (Erie) Problems; Constitutional Limits On Choice Of Law.
3 Audio Cassettes
ISBN: 0-15-900352-0 $39.95

Constitutional Law
By Professor John C. Jeffries, Jr.
University of Virginia School of Law

TOPICS COVERED: Introduction; Exam Tactics; Legislative Power; Supremacy; Commerce; State Regulation; Privileges And Immunities; Federal Court Jurisdiction; Separation Of Powers; Civil Liberties; Due Process; Equal Protection; Privacy; Race; Alienage; Gender; Speech And Association; Prior Restraints; Religion—Free Exercise; Establishment Clause.
5 Audio Cassettes
ISBN: 0-15-900319-9 $45.95

Contracts
By Professor Michael I. Spak
Chicago Kent College Of Law

TOPICS COVERED: Offer; Revocation; Acceptance; Consideration; Defenses To Formation; Third Party Beneficiaries; Assignment; Delegation; Conditions; Excuses; Anticipatory Repudiation; Discharge Of Duty; Modifications; Rescission; Accord & Satisfaction; Novation; Breach; Damages; Remedies; UCC Remedies; Parol Evidence Rule.
4 Audio Cassettes
ISBN: 0-15-900318-0 $45.95

Copyright Law
Professor Roger E. Schechter
George Washington University Law School

TOPICS COVERED: Constitution; Patents And Property Ownership Distinguished; Subject Matter Copyright; Duration And Renewal; Ownership And Transfer; Formalities; Introduction; Notice, Registration And Deposit; Infringement; Overview; Reproduction And Derivative Works; Public Distribution; Public Performance And Display; Exemptions; Fair Use; Photocopying; Remedies; Preemption Of State Law.
3 Audio Cassettes
ISBN: 0-15-900295-8 $39.95

Corporations
By Professor Therese H. Maynard
Loyola Marymount School of Law

TOPICS COVERED: Ultra Vires Act; Corporate Formation; Piercing The Corporate Veil; Corporate Financial Structure; Stocks; Bonds; Subscription Agreements; Watered Stock; Stock Transactions; Insider Trading; 16(b) & 10b-5 Violations; Promoters; Fiduciary Duties; Shareholder Rights; Meetings; Cumulative Voting; Voting Trusts; Close Corporations; Dividends; Preemptive Rights; Shareholder Derivative Suits; Directors; Duty Of Loyalty; Corporate Opportunity Doctrine; Officers; Amendments; Mergers; Dissolution.
4 Audio Cassettes
ISBN: 0-15-900320-2 $45.95

Criminal Law
By Professor Charles H. Whitebread
USC School of Law

TOPICS COVERED: Exam Tactics; Volitional Acts; Mental States; Specific Intent; Malice; General Intent; Strict Liability; Accomplice Liability; Inchoate Crimes; Impossibility; Defenses;

Insanity; Voluntary And Involuntary Intoxication; Infancy; Self-Defense; Defense Of A Dwelling; Duress; Necessity; Mistake Of Fact Or Law; Entrapment; Battery; Assault; Homicide; Common Law Murder; Voluntary And Involuntary Manslaughter; First Degree Murder; Felony Murder; Rape; Larceny; Embezzlement; False Pretenses; Robbery; Extortion; Burglary; Arson.
4 Audio Cassettes
ISBN: 0-15-900279-6 $39.95

Criminal Procedure
By Professor Charles H. Whitebread
USC School of Law
TOPICS COVERED: Incorporation Of The Bill Of Rights; Exclusionary Rule; Fruit Of The Poisonous Tree; Arrest; Search & Seizure; Exceptions To Warrant Requirement; Wire Tapping & Eavesdropping; Confessions (Miranda); Pretrial Identification; Bail; Preliminary Hearings; Grand Juries; Speedy Trial; Fair Trial; Jury Trials; Right To Counsel; Guilty Pleas; Sentencing; Death Penalty; Habeas Corpus; Double Jeopardy; Privilege Against Compelled Testimony.
3 Audio Cassettes
ISBN: 0-15-900281-8 $39.95

Evidence
By Professor Faust F. Rossi
Cornell Law School
TOPICS COVERED: Relevance; Insurance; Remedial Measures; Settlement Offers; Causation; State Of Mind; Rebuttal; Habit; Character Evidence; "MIMIC" Rule; Documentary Evidence; Authentication; Best Evidence Rule; Parol Evidence; Competency; Dead Man Statutes; Examination Of Witnesses; Present Recollection Revived; Past Recollection Recorded; Opinion Testimony; Lay And Expert Witness; Learned Treatises; Impeachment; Collateral Matters; Bias, Interest Or Motive; Rehabilitation; Privileges; Hearsay And Exceptions.
5 Audio Cassettes
ISBN: 0-15-900282-6 $45.95

Family Law
Professor To Be Announced
TOPICS COVERED (Subject to change): National Scope Of Family Law; Marital Relationship; Consequences Of Marriage; Formalities And Solemnization; Common Law Marriage; Impediments; Marriage And Conflict Of Laws; Non-Marital Relationship; Law Of Names; Void And Voidable Marriages; Marital Breakdown; Annulment And Defenses; Divorce — Fault And No-Fault; Separation; Jurisdiction For Divorce; Migratory Divorce; Full Faith And Credit; Temporary Orders; Economic Aspects Of Marital Breakdown; Property Division; Community Property Principles; Equitable Distribution; Marital And Separate Property; Types Of Property Interests; Equitable Reimbursement; Alimony; Modification And Termination Of Alimony; Child Support; Health Insurance; Enforcement Of Orders; Antenuptial And Postnuptial Agreements; Separation And Settlement Agreements; Custody Jurisdiction And Awards; Modification Of Custody; Visitation Rights; Termination Of Parental Rights; Adoption; Illegitimacy; Paternity Actions.
3 Audio Cassettes
ISBN: 0-15-900283-4 $39.95

Federal Courts
Professor To Be Announced
TOPICS COVERED (Subject to change): History Of The Federal Court System; "Court Or Controversy" And Justiciability; Congressional Power Over Federal Court Jurisdiction; Supreme Court Jurisdiction; District Court Subject Matter Jurisdiction—Federal Question Jurisdiction, Diversity Jurisdiction And Admiralty Jurisdiction; Pendent And Ancillary Jurisdiction; Removal Jurisdiction; Venue; Forum Non Conveniens; Law Applied In The Federal Courts; Federal Law In The State Courts; Collateral Relations Between Federal And State Courts; The Eleventh Amendment And State Sovereign Immunity.
3 Audio Cassettes
ISBN: 0-15-900296-6 $39.95

Federal Income Tax
By Professor Cheryl D. Block
George Washington University Law School
TOPICS COVERED: Administrative Reviews; Tax Formula; Gross Income; Exclusions For Gifts; Inheritances; Personal Injuries; Tax Basis Rules; Divorce Tax Rules; Assignment Of Income; Business Deductions; Investment Deductions; Passive Loss And Interest Limitation Rules; Capital Gains & Losses; Section 1031, 1034, and 121 Deferred/Non Taxable Transactions.
4 Audio Cassettes
ISBN: 0-15-900284-2 $45.95

Future Interests
By Dean Catherine L. Carpenter
Southwestern University Law School
TOPICS COVERED: Rule Against Perpetuities; Class Gifts; Estates In Land; Rule In Shelley's Case; Future Interests In Transferor and Transferee; Life Estates; Defeasible Fees; Doctrine Of Worthier Title; Doctrine Of Merger; Fee Simple Estates; Restraints On Alienation; Power Of Appointment; Rules Of Construction.
2 Audio Cassettes
ISBN: 0-15-900285-0 $24.95

Law School ABC's
By Professor Jennifer S. Kamita
Loyola Marymount Law School, and
Professor Rodney O. Fong
Golden Gate University School of Law
TOPICS COVERED: Introduction; Casebooks; Hornbooks; Selecting Commercial Materials; Briefing; Review; ABC's Of A Lecture; Taking Notes; Lectures & Notes Examples; Study Groups; ABC's Of Outlining; Rules; Outlining Hypothetical; Outlining Assignment And Review; Introduction To Essay Writing; "IRAC"; Call Of The Question Exercise; Issue Spotting Exercise; IRAC Defining & Writing Exercise; Form Tips; ABC's Of Exam Writing; Exam Writing Hypothetical; Practice Exam And Review; Preparation Hints; Exam Diagnostics & Writing Problems.
4 Audio Cassettes
ISBN: 0-15-900286-9 $45.95

Law School Exam Writing
By Professor Charles H. Whitebread
USC School of Law
TOPICS COVERED: With "Law School Exam Writing," you'll learn the secrets of law school test taking. In this fascinating lecture, Professor Whitebread leads you step-by-step through his innovative system, so that you know exactly how to tackle your essay exams without making point draining mistakes. You'll learn how to read questions so you don't miss important issues; how to organize your answer; how to use limited exam time to your maximum advantage; and even how to study for exams.
1 Audio Cassette
ISBN: 0-15-900287-7 $19.95

Professional Responsibility
By Professor Erwin Chemerinsky
USC School of Law
TOPICS COVERED: Regulation of Attorneys; Bar Admission; Unauthorized Practice; Competency; Discipline; Judgment; Lawyer-Client Relationship; Representation; Withdrawal; Conflicts; Disqualification; Clients; Client Interests; Successive And Effective Representation; Integrity; Candor; Confidences; Secrets; Past And Future Crimes; Perjury; Communications; Witnesses; Jurors; The Court; The Press; Trial Tactics; Prosecutors; Market; Solicitation; Advertising; Law Firms; Fees; Client Property; Conduct; Political Activity.
3 Audio Cassettes
ISBN: 0-15-900288-5 $39.95

Real Property
By Professor Paula A. Franzese
Seton Hall Law School
TOPICS COVERED: Estates—Fee Simple; Fee Tail; Life Estate; Co-Tenancy—Joint Tenancy; Tenancy In Common; Tenancy By The Entirety; Landlord-Tenant Relationship; Liability For Condition Of Premises; Assignment & Sublease; Easements; Restrictive Covenants; Adverse Possession; Recording Acts; Conveyancing; Personal Property—Finders; Bailments; Gifts; Future Interests.
4 Audio Cassettes
ISBN: 0-15-900289-3 $45.95

Remedies
By Professor William A. Fletcher
University of California at Berkeley, Boalt Hall School of Law
TOPICS COVERED: Damages; Restitution; Equitable Remedies (including Constructive Trust, Equitable Lien, Injunction, and Specific Performance); Tracing; Rescission and Reformation; Specific topics include Injury and Destruction of Personal Property; Conversion; Injury to Real Property; Trespass; Ouster; Nuisance; Defamation; Trade Libel; Inducing Breach of Contract; Contracts to Purchase Personal Property; Contracts to Purchase Real Property (including Equitable Conversion); Construction Contracts; and Personal Service Contracts.
3 Audio Cassettes
ISBN: 0-15-900353-9 $45.95

Sales & Lease of Goods
By Professor Michael I. Spak
Chicago Kent College of Law
TOPICS COVERED: Goods; Contract Formation; Firm Offers; Statute Of Frauds; Modification; Parol Evidence; Code Methodology; Tender; Payment; Identification; Risk Of Loss; Warranties; Merchantability; Fitness; Disclaimers; Consumer Protection; Remedies; Anticipatory Repudiation; Third Party Rights.
3 Audio Cassettes
ISBN: 0-15-900291-5 $39.95

Secured Transactions
By Professor Michael I. Spak
Chicago Kent College of Law
TOPICS COVERED: Collateral; Inventory; Intangibles; Proceeds; Security Agreements; Attachment; After-Acquired Property; Perfection; Filing; Priorities; Purchase Money Security Interests; Fixtures; Rights Upon Default; Self-Help; Sale; Constitutional Issues.
3 Audio Cassettes
ISBN: 0-15-900292-3 $39.95

Torts
By Professor Richard J. Conviser
Chicago Kent College of Law
TOPICS COVERED: Essay Exam Techniques; Intentional Torts—Assault; Battery; False Imprisonment; Intentional Infliction Of Emotional Distress; Trespass To Land; Trespass To Chattels; Conversion; Defenses: Defamation—Libel; Slander; Defenses; First Amendment Concerns; Invasion Of Right Of Privacy; Misrepresentation; Negligence—Duty; Breach; Actual And Proximate Causation; Damages; Defenses; Strict Liability; Products Liability; Nuisance; General Tort Considerations.
4 Audio Cassettes
ISBN: 0-15-900185-4 $45.95

Wills & Trusts
By Professor Stanley M. Johanson
University of Texas School of Law
TOPICS COVERED: Attested Wills; Holographic Wills; Negligence; Revocation; Changes On Face Of Will; Lapsed Gifts; Negative Bequest Rule; Nonprobate Assets; Intestate Succession; Advancements; Elective Share; Will Contests; Capacity; Undue Influence; Creditors' Rights; Creation Of Trust; Revocable Trusts; Pourover Gifts; Charitable Trusts; Resulting Trusts; Constructive Trusts; Spendthrift Trusts; Self-Dealing; Prudent Investments; Trust Accounting; Termination; Powers Of Appointment.
4 Audio Cassettes
ISBN: 0-15-900294-X $45.95

**All titles available at your law school bookstore
or call to order: 1-800-787-8717**

Legalines

Legalines gives you authoritative, detailed case briefs of every major case in your casebook. You get a clear explanation of the facts, the issues, the court's holding and reasoning, and any significant concurrences or dissents. Even more importantly, you get an authoritative explanation of the significance of each case, and how it relates to other cases in your casebook. And with Legalines' detailed table of contents and table of cases, you can quickly find any case or concept you're looking for. But your professor expects you to know more than just the cases. That's why Legalines gives you more than just case briefs. You get summaries of the black letter law, as well. That's crucial, because some of the most important information in your casebooks isn't in the cases at all...it's the black letter principles you're expected to glean from those cases. Legalines is the only series that gives you both case briefs and black letter review. With Legalines, you get everything you need to know—whether it's in a case or not!

Administrative Law
Keyed to the Breyer Casebook
ISBN: 0-15-900042-4   206 pages $17.95

Administrative Law
Keyed to the Gellhorn Casebook
ISBN: 0-15-900043-2   268 pages $19.95

Administrative Law
Keyed to the Schwartz Casebook
ISBN: 0-15-900044-0   155 pages $17.95

Antitrust
Keyed to the Areeda Casebook
ISBN: 0-15-900046-7   209 pages $17.95

Antitrust
Keyed to the Handler Casebook
ISBN: 0-15-900045-9   174 pages $17.95

Civil Procedure
Keyed to the Cound Casebook
ISBN: 0-15-900314-8   316 pages $19.95

Civil Procedure
Keyed to the Field Casebook
ISBN: 0-15-900048-3   388 pages $21.95

Civil Procedure
Keyed to the Hazard Casebook
ISBN: 0-15-900324-5   253 pages $18.95

Civil Procedure
Keyed to the Rosenberg Casebook
ISBN: 0-15-900052-1   312 pages $19.95

Civil Procedure
Keyed to the Yeazell Casebook
ISBN: 0-15-900053-X   240 pages $18.95

Commercial Law
Keyed to the Farnsworth Casebook
ISBN: 0-15-900054-8   170 pages $17.95

Conflict of Laws
Keyed to the Cramton Casebook
ISBN: 0-15-900056-4   144 pages $16.95

Conflict of Laws
Keyed to the Reese Casebook
ISBN: 0-15-900057-2   279 pages $19.95

Constitutional Law
Keyed to the Brest Casebook
ISBN: 0-15-900059-9   235 pages $18.95

Constitutional Law
Keyed to the Cohen Casebook
ISBN: 0-15-900261-3   235 pages $18.95

Constitutional Law
Keyed to the Gunther Casebook
ISBN: 0-15-900060-2   395 pages $21.95

Constitutional Law
Keyed to the Lockhart Casebook
ISBN: 0-15-900062-9   348 pages $20.95

Constitutional Law
Keyed to the Rotunda Casebook
ISBN: 0-15-900315-6   281 pages $19.95

Constitutional Law
Keyed to the Stone Casebook
ISBN: 0-15-900064-5   296 pages $19.95

Contracts
Keyed to the Calamari Casebook
ISBN: 0-15-900065-3   256 pages $19.95

Contracts
Keyed to the Dawson Casebook
ISBN: 0-15-900268-0   188 pages $19.95

Contracts
Keyed to the Farnsworth Casebook
ISBN: 0-15-900067-X   219 pages $18.95

Contracts
Keyed to the Fuller Casebook
ISBN: 0-15-900069-6   206 pages $17.95

Contracts
Keyed to the Kessler Casebook
ISBN: 0-15-900070-X   340 pages $20.95

Contracts
Keyed to the Murphy Casebook
ISBN: 0-15-900072-6   272 pages $19.95

Corporations
Keyed to the Cary Casebook
ISBN: 0-15-900073-4   407 pages $21.95

Corporations
Keyed to the Choper Casebook
ISBN: 0-15-900074-2   270 pages $19.95

Corporations
Keyed to the Hamilton Casebook
ISBN: 0-15-900313-X   248 pages $19.95

Corporations
Keyed to the Vagts Casebook
ISBN: 0-15-900078-5   213 pages $17.95

Criminal Law
Keyed to the Boyce Casebook
ISBN: 0-15-900080-7   318 pages $19.95

Criminal Law
Keyed to the Dix Casebook
ISBN: 0-15-900081-5   113 pages $15.95

Criminal Law
Keyed to the Johnson Casebook
ISBN: 0-15-900082-3   169 pages $17.95

Criminal Law
Keyed to the Kadish Casebook
ISBN: 0-15-900083-1   209 pages $17.95

Criminal Law
Keyed to the La Fave Casebook
ISBN: 0-15-900084-X   202 pages $17.95

Criminal Procedure
Keyed to the Kamisar Casebook
ISBN: 0-15-900088-2   310 pages $19.95

Decedents' Estates & Trusts
Keyed to the Ritchie Casebook
ISBN: 0-15-900089-0   277 pages $19.95

Domestic Relations
Keyed to the Clark Casebook
ISBN: 0-15-900090-4   128 pages $16.95

Domestic Relations
Keyed to the Wadlington Casebook
ISBN: 0-15-900091-2   215 pages $18.95

Enterprise Organization
Keyed to the Conard Casebook
ISBN: 0-15-900092-0   316 pages $19.95

Estate & Gift Taxation
Keyed to the Surrey Casebook
ISBN: 0-15-900093-9   100 pages $15.95

Evidence
Keyed to the McCormick Casebook
ISBN: 0-15-900095-5   310 pages $19.95

Evidence
Keyed to the Sutton Casebook
ISBN: 0-15-900096-3   310 pages $19.95

Evidence
Keyed to the Waltz Casebook
ISBN: 0-15-900334-2   224 pages $17.95

Evidence
Keyed to the Weinstein Casebook
ISBN: 0-15-900097-1   241 pages $18.95

Family Law
Keyed to the Areen Casebook
ISBN: 0-15-900263-X   262 pages $19.95

Federal Courts
Keyed to the McCormick Casebook
ISBN: 0-15-900101-3   213 pages $17.95

Income Tax
Keyed to the Andrews Casebook
ISBN: 0-15-900102-1   239 pages $18.95

Income Tax
Keyed to the Freeland Casebook
ISBN: 0-15-900304-0   154 pages $17.95

Income Tax
Keyed to the Klein Casebook
ISBN: 0-15-900302-4   174 pages $17.95

Labor Law
Keyed to the Cox Casebook
ISBN: 0-15-900107-2   211 pages $17.95

Labor Law
Keyed to the Merrifield Casebook
ISBN: 0-15-900108-0   202 pages $17.95

Partnership & Corporate Taxation
Keyed to the Surrey Casebook
ISBN: 0-15-900109-9   118 pages $15.95

Property
Keyed to the Browder Casebook
ISBN: 0-15-900110-2   315 pages $19.95

Property
Keyed to the Casner Casebook
ISBN: 0-15-900111-0   291 pages $19.95

Property
Keyed to the Cribbet Casebook
ISBN: 0-15-900112-9   328 pages $20.95

Property
Keyed to the Dukeminier Casebook
ISBN: 0-15-900264-8   186 pages $17.95

Real Property
Keyed to the Rabin Casebook
ISBN: 0-15-900114-5   208 pages $17.95

Remedies
Keyed to the Re Casebook
ISBN: 0-15-900115-3   333 pages $20.95

Remedies
Keyed to the York Casebook
ISBN: 0-15-900118-8   289 pages $19.95

Sales & Secured Transactions
Keyed to the Speidel Casebook
ISBN: 0-15-900166-8   320 pages $19.95

Securities Regulation
Keyed to the Jennings Casebook
ISBN: 0-15-900253-2   368 pages $20.95

Torts
Keyed to the Epstein Casebook
ISBN: 0-15-900120-X   245 pages $18.95

Torts
Keyed to the Franklin Casebook
ISBN: 0-15-900122-6   166 pages $17.95

Torts
Keyed to the Henderson Casebook
ISBN: 0-15-900123-4   209 pages $17.95

Torts
Keyed to the Keeton Casebook
ISBN: 0-15-900124-2   278 pages $19.95

Torts
Keyed to the Prosser Casebook
ISBN: 0-15-900301-6   365 pages $20.95

For more information visit our World Wide Web site at http://www.gilbertlaw.com or write for a free 32 page catalog:
Harcourt Brace Legal and Professional Publications, 176 West Adams, Ste. 2100, Chicago, Illinois 60603

Wills, Trusts & Estates
Keyed to the Dukeminier Casebook
ISBN: 0-15-900127-7   192 pages $ 17.95

Also Available:

Accounting For Lawyers
ISBN: 0-15-900041-6   75 pages $ 12.95

Criminal Law Questions & Answers
ISBN: 0-15-900087-4   179 pages $ 12.95

Excelling on Exams/How to Study
ISBN: 0-15-900098-X   101 pages $ 12.95

Torts Questions & Answers
ISBN: 0-15-900126-9   174 pages $ 12.95

Legalines

Summary of Subjects Available

- Administrative Law
- Antitrust
- Civil Procedure
- Commercial Law
- Conflict of Laws
- Constitutional Law
- Contracts
- Corporations
- Criminal Law
- Criminal Procedure
- Decedents' Estates & Trusts
- Domestic Relations
- Enterprise Organization
- Estate & Gift Taxation
- Evidence
- Family Law
- Federal Courts
- Income Tax
- Labor Law
- Partnership & Corporate Taxation
- Property
- Real Property
- Remedies
- Sales & Secured Transactions
- Securities Regulation
- Torts
- Wills, Trusts & Estates

Current & Upcoming Software Titles

Gilbert Law Summaries
Interactive Software For Windows
Gilbert's Interactive Software features the full text of a Gilbert Law Summaries outline. Each title is easy to customize, print, and take to class. You can access the Lexis and Westlaw systems through an icon on the tool bar (with a valid student I.D.), as well as CaseBriefs Interactive Software, and Gilbert's On-Screen Dictionary Of Legal Terms (sold separately).

Administrative Law 0-15-900205-2	Asimow $27.95
Civil Procedure 0-15-900206-0	Marcus, Rowe $27.95
Constitutional Law 0-15-900207-9	Choper $27.95

Contracts 0-15-900208-7	Eisenberg $27.95
Corporations 0-15-900209-5	Choper, Eisenberg $27.95
Criminal Law 0-15-900210-9	Dix $27.95
Criminal Procedure 0-15-900211-7	Marcus, Whitebread $27.95
Evidence 0-15-900212-5	Kaplan, Waltz $27.95
Income Tax 1 0-15-900213-3	Asimow $27.95
Property 0-15-900214-1	Dukeminier $27.95
Secured Transactions 0-15-900215-X	Whaley $27.95
Torts 0-15-900216-8	Franklin $27.95

CaseBriefs
Interactive Software For Windows
Each title is adaptable to *all* casebooks in a subject area. For example, the Civil Procedure CaseBriefs title is adaptable to Civil Procedure by Cound, Hazard, Yeazell, etc... Simply select the casebook you're using when installing the software, and the program will do the rest! CaseBriefs is easy to customize, print, and take to class. You can access the Lexis and Westlaw systems through an icon on the tool bar (with a valid student I.D.), as well as Gilbert Law Summaries Interactive Software, and Gilbert's On-Screen Dictionary Of Legal Terms (sold separately).

Administrative Law 0-15-900190-0	Adaptable To All Casebooks $27.95
Civil Procedure 0-15-900191-9	Adaptable To All Casebooks $27.95
Conflict Of Laws 0-15-900192-7	Adaptable To All Casebooks $27.95
Constitutional Law 0-15-900193-5	Adaptable To All Casebooks $27.95

Contracts 0-15-900194-3	Adaptable To All Casebooks $27.95
Corporations 0-15-900195-1	Adaptable To All Casebooks $27.95
Criminal Law 0-15-900196-X	Adaptable To All Casebooks $27.95
Criminal Procedure 0-15-900197-8	Adaptable To All Casebooks $27.95
Evidence 0-15-900198-6	Adaptable To All Casebooks $27.95
Family Law 0-15-900199-4	Adaptable To All Casebooks $27.95
Income Tax 0-15-900200-1	Adaptable To All Casebooks $27.95
Property 0-15-900201-X	Adaptable To All Casebooks $27.95
Remedies 0-15-900202-8	Adaptable To All Casebooks $27.95
Torts 0-15-900203-6	Adaptable To All Casebooks $27.95
Wills, Trusts & Estates 0-15-900204-4	Adaptable To All Casebooks $27.95

Gilbert's On Screen Dictionary Of Legal Terms:
Features over 3,500 legal terms and phrases, law school shorthand, common abbreviations, Latin and French legal terms, periodical abbreviations, and governmental abbreviations.

ISBN: 0-15-900-311-3   Macintosh $24.95
ISBN: 0-15-900-308-3   Windows $24.95

All titles available at your law school bookstore
or call to order: 1-800-787-8717

Current & Upcoming Titles

 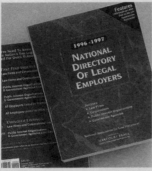  

Gilbert's Pocket Size Law Dictionary
Gilbert

A dictionary is useless if you don't have it when you need it. If the only law dictionary you own is a thick, bulky one, you'll probably leave it at home most of the time — and if you need to know a definition while you're at school, you're out of luck!

With Gilbert's Pocket Size Law Dictionary, you'll have any definition you need, when you need it. Just pop Gilbert's dictionary into your pocket or purse, and you'll have over 3,500 legal terms and phrases at your fingertips. Gilbert's dictionary also includes a section on law school shorthand, common abbreviations, Latin and French legal terms, periodical abbreviations, and governmental abbreviations.

With Gilbert's Pocket Size Law Dictionary, you'll never be caught at a loss for words!

Available in your choice of 4 colors, $7.95 each:
- ■ Black   ISBN: 0-15-900255-9
- ■ Blue   ISBN: 0-15-900257-5
- ■ Burgundy   ISBN: 0-15-900256-7
- ■ Green   ISBN: 0-15-900258-3

Limited Edition: Simulated Alligator Skin Cover
- ■ Black   ISBN: 0-15-900316-4 $7.95

What Lawyers Earn: Getting Paid What You're Worth
NALP

"What Lawyers Earn" provides up-to-date salary information from lawyers in many different positions, all over the country. Whether you're negotiating your own salary — or you're just curious! — "What Lawyers Earn" tells you how much lawyers really make.
ISBN: 0-15-900183-8 $17.95

The 100 Best Law Firms To Work For In America
Kimm Alayne Walton, J.D.

An insider's guide to the 100 best places to practice law, with anecdotes and a wealth of useful hiring information. Also included are special sections on the top law firms for women and the best public interest legal employers.
ISBN: 0-15-900180-3 $19.95

The 1996-1997 National Directory Of Legal Employers
NALP

The National Association for Law Placement has joined forces with Harcourt Brace to bring you everything you need to know about 1,000 of the nation's top legal employers, fully indexed for quick reference.

It includes:
- Over 22,000 job openings.
- The names, addresses and phone numbers of hiring partners.
- Listings of firms by state, size, kind and practice area.
- What starting salaries are for full time, part time, and summer associates, plus a detailed description of firm benefits.
- The number of employees by gender and race, as well as the number of employees with disabilities.
- A detailed narrative of each firm, plus much more!

The National Directory Of Legal Employers has been published for the past twenty years, but until now has only been available to law school career services directors, and hiring partners at large law firms. Through a joint venture between NALP (The National Association For Law Placement) and Harcourt Brace, this highly regarded, exciting title is now available for students.
ISBN: 0-15-900179-X $49.95

Proceed With Caution: A Diary Of The First Year At One Of America's Largest, Most Prestigious Law Firms
William Formon

In "Proceed With Caution" the author chronicles the trials and tribulations of being a new associate in a widely coveted dream job. He offers insights that only someone who has lived through the experience can offer. The unique diary format makes Proceed With Caution a highly readable and enjoyable journey.
ISBN: 0-15-900181-1 $17.95

The Eight Secrets Of Top Exam Performance In Law School
Charles Whitebread

Wouldn't it be great to know exactly what your professor's looking for on your exam? To find out everything that's expected of you, so that you don't waste your time doing anything other than maximizing your grades?

In his easy-to-read, refreshing style, nationally-recognized exam expert Professor Charles Whitebread will teach you the eight secrets that will add precious points to every exam answer you write. You'll learn the three keys to handling any essay exam question, and how to add points to your score by making time work for you, not against you. You'll learn flawless issue spotting, and discover how to organize your answer for maximum possible points. You'll find out how the hidden traps in "IRAC" trip up most students… but not you! You'll learn the techniques for digging up the exam questions your professor will ask, before your exam. You'll put your newly-learned skills to the test with sample exam questions, and you can measure your performance against model answers. And there's even a special section that helps you master the skills necessary to crush any exam, not just a typical essay exam — unusual exams like open book, take home, multiple choice, short answer, and policy questions.

"The Eight Secrets of Top Exam Performance in Law School" gives you all the tools you need to maximize your grades — quickly and easily!
ISBN: 0-15-900323-7 $9.95

Guerrilla Tactics for Getting the Legal Job of Your Dreams
Kimm Alayne Walton, J.D.

Whether you're looking for a summer clerkship or your first permanent job after school, this revolutionary new book is the key to getting the job of your dreams!

"Guerrilla Tactics for Getting the Legal Job of Your Dreams" leads you step-by-step through everything you need to do to nail down that perfect job! You'll learn hundreds of simple-to-use strategies that will get you exactly where you want to go.

"Guerrilla Tactics" features the best strategies from the country's most innovative law school career advisors. The strategies in "Guerrilla Tactics" are so powerful that it even comes with a guarantee: Follow the advice in the book, and within one year of graduation you'll have the job of your dreams… or your money back!

Pick up a copy of "Guerrilla Tactics" today…and you'll be on your way to the job of your dreams!
ISBN: 0-15-900317-2 $24.95

Checkerboard Careers: How Surprisingly Successful Attorneys Got To The Top, And How You Can Too!
NALP

Fast paced and easy to read, "Checkerboard Careers" is an inspirational guide, packed with profiles and monologues of how successful attorneys got to the top and how you can, too.
ISBN: 0-15-900182-X $17.95